Meat Market

MEAT MARKET
Animals, Ethics, and Money

ERIK MARCUS

Brio Press • Ithaca, New York

Brio Press, Ithaca, New York.

Printed in the United States of America.

This book was printed on acid-free paper using soy-based ink.

Excerpt on pages 41–42 reprinted with permission of Simon & Schuster Adult Publishing Group from *Farm: A Year in the Life of an American Farmer* by Richard Rhodes. © 1989 by Richard Rhodes.

Cover design by Theresa Lee. Some books from this printing may ship with full-color dust jackets bearing a bar code — these covers were designed by Free Range Graphics.

Typeset and indexed by the author.

10 9 8 7 6 5 4 3 2 1 0

Limited Advance Printing First Edition

Library of Congress Cataloging-in-Publication Data

Marcus, Erik, 1966–
   Meat market : animals, ethics, and money / Erik Marcus.– 1st ed.
      p. cm.
   Includes bibliographical references and index.
   ISBN 0-9758679-0-3 (hardcover : alk. paper) – ISBN 0-9758679-1-1 (pbk. : alk. paper)
1. Animal industry–United States–Moral and ethical aspects. 2. Livestock factories–Moral and ethical aspects. 3. Animal welfare–United States. I. Title.

HV4764.M22 2005
179'.3–dc22

2004016174

For my parents,
Sonja and David Marcus,
who put up with a lot.

Contents

Introduction

In 1966, the year I was born, my family lived across the street from an egg farm. The couple who owned the farm lived in a simple white farmhouse that was surrounded by dozens of chicken coops. In addition to caring for the chickens and gathering their eggs, the couple operated a small farm stand that stood alongside their house.

My mother used to walk across the street several times each month to buy fresh eggs. She loved being able to purchase them so conveniently. It made up for hearing the rooster crows that rang out from the farm each morning at sunrise.

One day, heavy machinery appeared on the property. As my mother watched from her living room window, a backhoe dug out an enormous trench near the farmhouse. After the trench was dug, a bulldozer swept the land clear of its chicken coops and pushed the broken mass of plywood, metal roofing, and chicken wire into the trench. By sunset, the land was totally bare, save for the farmhouse, the farm stand, and the half-filled trench.

The next morning, more workers arrived. The crew made short work of gutting the farmhouse and farm stand, which by mid-afternoon had been toppled and swept by the bulldozer into the trench. With that accomplished, the workers poured kerosene into the trench and set the whole thing ablaze.

To my parents, what happened to the egg farm was an isolated incident. They had no idea that during the 1960s, more than 75 percent of America's egg farms went out of business.[1] Nor could they have known that what happened to the farm across the street was a microcosm for changes occurring throughout animal agriculture. Fifty years ago, small family-owned farms supplied the overwhelming majority of the nation's meat, eggs, and dairy products. Today, nearly all of these farms have been driven out of business—replaced by large-scale operations that raise animals in a profoundly different manner.

This book looks at the transformation of animal agriculture since 1950. Most of the changes have been driven by money, particularly the incessant drive to cut costs. But this book is about more than dollars and cents—it is also about the lives of animals raised to produce food. I therefore give considerable attention to how competitive pressures and persistent cost-cutting within animal agriculture have continually lowered the welfare standards accorded to farmed animals.

By looking closely at the evolution of animal agriculture, this book provides a different perspective on the ethics of farming than what is generally offered by the vegetarian and animal rights movements. I don't expect all readers to arrive at one particular judgment regarding diet. I anticipate that some readers will remain comfortable with eating animal-based foods, but will nevertheless recognize that welfare reforms for farmed animals are urgently needed. I expect that other readers will decide that any form of animal agriculture is exploitive, and that the most reasonable response is to work toward weakening and, ultimately, overturning the industry.

No matter where you fall within this spectrum, this book will provide ideas for action. Most farmed animal suffering is rooted in the fact that the general public remains uninformed about how modern animal agriculture operates. This book was written to provide reliable information about the ethical problems associated with animal agriculture, and to guide people to whatever level of action they find appropriate.

Part I

Animal Agriculture

"And it shook me, and I'm still shaking now."
—Graham Parker

Chapter 1

The Economics of Animal Agriculture

In 2003, the United States became the first nation to raise more than ten billion farmed animals in a single year.[1] That's over twice the animals that America's farmers raised in 1980, and ten times the animals they raised in 1940.[2]

Immense profits are being wrung from all this killing, making the barons of animal agriculture wealthier than kings. Wendell Murphy, who built his family's company into America's second-largest pig operation, became a billionaire in 1997.[3] That same year, Don Tyson, senior chairman of Tyson Foods, also had his net worth surpass one billion dollars.[4] Early investors in America's top meat companies have likewise made out spectacularly. A $10,000 purchase of Tyson stock in 1973 would have grown to a $1.76 million stake in the company by 2003.[5]

Enormous fortunes are being made in animal agriculture, and the top companies regularly deliver sensational returns to their investors. But what about the ten billion farmed animals raised each year? How much do they suffer in order to produce all this cash? It depends on who you ask. Peter Singer, who is regarded as the father of the modern animal rights movement, says, "Agribusiness isn't interested in animal welfare, it is only interested in profitability. If that means crowding six hens into a cage so small that one of them couldn't stretch her wings even if she had the entire cage to herself, that's what they'll do. If it means confining a calf or a pig so that they can't walk a single step, or even turn around, for months at a time, they'll do that too."[6]

The meat industry sees things differently. According to Tyson Foods, conditions for their chickens are quite comfortable: "Tyson chickens are grown on farms located in areas ideal for poultry raising, with clean air and water and moderate temperatures. All grow-out houses are single level and the birds are allowed to roam free on the floor of these houses."[7]

As pleasant as it sounds to be a Tyson chicken, it might be even nicer to be a beef industry calf. The National Cattlemen's Beef Association asserts that: "Cattlemen are committed to providing the utmost in humane care for their livestock. They view this responsibility as both a moral obligation to the animals and an economic necessity, since animals who are cared for properly perform more effectively as meat-producing animals."[8]

It's impossible to reconcile Singer's claims with those of Tyson Foods and the Cattlemen. So, which point of view is more valid? Are animal protection advocates like Singer correct in asserting that virtually all farmed animals suffer profoundly? Or is the industry right in its contention that these animals overwhelmingly receive a decent level of care? These questions demand reliable answers since the quality of life for more than ten billion animals killed each year is at stake. Fortunately, it's not too difficult to get to the bottom of this.

The best way to assess the welfare of America's farmed animals is to first learn a bit about the poultry and livestock business. Farmed animals are, after all, the product of a massive and highly organized industry. By understanding the essentials of how this industry operates, the factors that govern how farmed animals are raised and slaughtered will become apparent.

Get Big or Get Out

It's well known that, nearly every year, the dollar declines in purchasing power. Between 1950 and 2003, the Consumer Price Index rose by about 770 percent.[9] Part of the Index is related to the thousand little things that Americans purchase, from chewing gum to movie tickets. But the Index is primarily driven by what people spend the bulk of their money on: housing, food, transportation, and clothing.

A look at the cost of housing and automobiles explains the massive increase in the Consumer Price Index since 1950. Between 1950 and 2001, the cost of the average new house surged from $11,000 to $175,000—an increase of nearly 1500 percent.[10] Over the same period, new car prices climbed more than 1400 percent.[11] While the prices of many goods and services have risen rapidly over the years, the price of animal products has lagged far behind the overall inflation rate. The price of milk is up only about 350 percent between 1950 and 2003.[12] And, during that time, the prices of eggs and chicken meat haven't even doubled.[13] These comparatively small price increases mean that, when inflation is taken into account, animal products cost less today than ever before.

Why has the cost of animal products resisted inflationary pressures? The primary reason is that animal agriculture operates more efficiently than in the past. Fewer workers tend more animals, and the animals themselves are vastly more productive than their predecessors. The big changes in animal agriculture began fairly recently. Prior to 1950, small family farms produced the majority of America's meat, milk, and eggs. These farms were rooted in tradition, and animal farms of the 1950s looked scarcely different from how they looked during the 1800s. Farmers relied on longstanding methods regarding animal care, which entailed providing substantial amounts of space and human attention. Given the amount of care that each animal required, most farmers personally knew each of the pigs and cows they raised.

Visiting a typical animal farm in 1950 was like stepping back a century in time. To many farmers, it must have seemed as though their livelihoods were immune to the wrenching effects of industrialization. Yet time was running out for small family farms, especially those that concentrated on raising poultry and livestock. At agriculture colleges across the country, animal scientists were developing ways to raise more animals in less space than ever before. Battery cages were introduced for layer hens, while farrowing crates made their way into the pig industry. Automatic feeding and watering systems were invented. These and other advances made the concept of individualized care obsolete. As confinement methods came into widespread use, the economics of chicken and pig farming shifted to favor ever-larger producers.

The squeeze tightened in 1971, when President Nixon appointed Earl Butz as the Secretary of Agriculture. Like his boss, Butz had a penchant for making offensive jokes, one of which (about why blacks tend not to join the Republican party), forced his resignation in 1976. But there's no doubt that, during his five years as Agriculture Secretary, Butz was enormously influential. Butz had no patience for people who romanticized the family farm. His vision of agriculture was that bigger is better: America will feed the world, and large-scale farming conglomerates will make it all possible. Butz relentlessly sought to accelerate the trend toward large-scale corporate farming. He is best remembered today for repeatedly telling farmers to "get big or get out."

The trouble was that few farmers heeded this advice—most thought they could hang on, regardless of what Earl Butz had to say. But the trends in agriculture were all moving against the little guy. Every aspect of agriculture was becoming industrialized, and the changes were most profound when it came to the raising of animals.

The first giant animal farms were built for egg production. In the early 1970s, a Los Angeles farm began keeping three million layer hens on a single property. The hazards of keeping so many animals in one place quickly became apparent when the entire flock had to be slaughtered and incinerated due to disease.[14]

But egg producers have been undeterred by setbacks like this, and have raced each other to build enormous facilities within the United States. By 2003, 62 giant companies each owned a million or more hens.[15] The largest of these companies, Cal-Maine Foods, has an inventory of more than 20 million hens.[16]

Other segments of animal agriculture followed the egg industry's lead. In the 1980s and 1990s, Wendell Murphy almost single-handedly restructured North Carolina's pig industry. Prior to Murphy, the industry was controlled by family farmers, who generally raised fewer than twenty pigs at a time. Murphy's company contracted with these farmers and arranged to build massive pig sheds on their properties. The farmers essentially became modern-day sharecroppers, raising more pigs than ever before, but now receiving only a small payment for each pig. Murphy, however, made out spectacularly. He became a North Carolina State Senator, drafted laws that were favorable to large pig farmers, and rapidly became the pork industry's dominant figure.

For every animal farming tycoon like Wendell Murphy, Don Tyson, or Frank Perdue, hundreds of thousands of farmers were driven into bankruptcy. Between 1950 and 1980, the number of U.S. farms with dairy cows fell 92 percent, from 3.65 million to 278,000.[17] And by 2001, fewer than 92,000 such farms remained in the United States.[18] Most small pig farms have also been driven out of business. Between 1992 and 2002, the number of farms raising pigs fell by more than two-thirds.[19] These bankruptcies have led to enormous anguish in farming families across the United States. According to recent studies, American farmers are four times more likely than the general population to commit suicide.[20]

Meat Packing

While one side of animal agriculture involves raising animals to slaughter weight, the other side is devoted to killing these animals and cutting them up. And just as farmers have had their livelihoods stripped away as the meat industry has consolidated, meat-cutters and packinghouse towns have also paid dearly.

Since the 1960s, industry has made great strides in reducing the costs related to meat processing. They've accomplished this mainly by driving small butcher shops out of business and by transferring every step of meat-cutting back to the slaughterhouse. Large slaughterhouses are typically sited in rural towns that are desperate for jobs, where the companies can wrangle steep tax concessions in exchange for building a plant.

The work at these facilities is highly efficient, owing to worker specialization and rapid line speeds. But the jobs are grueling, and the pay is low. Industry wages have been driven down for decades, and today's slaughterhouses are staffed mainly by illegal aliens or first generation Latino immigrants. Hazards abound, and health care services and insurance coverage for workers are lacking. In short, many of the injustices depicted in Upton Sinclair's 1906 classic *The Jungle* are still with us a century after the book's publication.*

Advances in Breeding

For fifty years, the costs of raising and butchering animals have been constantly pushed down. Meanwhile, the animals themselves have become vastly more efficient. Starting around 1950, animal scientists have continually increased the productivity of every kind of farmed animal. Today's meat animals grow bigger and faster than ever before, while dairy cows produce vastly more milk, and hens lay substantially more eggs.

A few examples will show why animal scientists take pride in their profession. In 1950, the average dairy cow in America produced 665 gallons of milk per year. By 1975, yields per cow jumped to 1295 gallons. And by 2002, the typical cow produced

---

*Appendix H covers the deteriorating circumstances confronting slaughterhouse workers and packinghouse towns.

2320 gallons of milk per year—a staggering 340 percent increase over a dairy cow from 1950.[21]

Pigs grow bigger and faster than they did a few decades ago. Born weighing just 2 pounds, today's animals reach 260 pounds in just under six months.[22] That's at least 40 pounds more than six-month old pigs weighed in the 1950s, and today's pigs also have a much higher ratio of muscle to fat.[23]

The advances made by chicken breeders are even more impressive. In 1950, chickens required 70 days to reach slaughter weight. By 2000, the necessary time had been reduced to 47 days. And that 47-day-old chicken, at five pounds, is two-thirds bigger than a 70-day-old chicken from 1950.[24]

The rapid growth and increased yields achieved by today's farmed animals have continually driven down the cost of animal products. Because of what has been accomplished through selective breeding, American consumers can buy more meat, milk, and eggs for less money than ever before.[25]

Modern Breeding Techniques and Animal Suffering

While there's no doubt that breeding programs have helped America's food dollar go further, the animals pay a terrible price for these advances. Because of undesired traits that emerge through selective breeding efforts, farmed animals suffer from a range of health problems that were practically unheard-of before the 1960s.

Of all the breeding efforts conducted on farmed animals, the greatest productivity gains have occurred with chickens raised for meat—birds the industry terms "broilers." The metabolism of these chickens is so revved up that today's birds commonly suffer heart or lung failure. In fact, a primary reason why they are slaughtered at just seven weeks of age—which is well before they have finished growing—is that many of these birds would die of heart attacks if allowed to live another week or two.[26] These heart attacks usually come in the late stages of the animals' growth, and they are linked to modern chickens' extreme metabolic needs—the heart cannot keep pace with the body's demand for blood.

Like chickens, pigs suffer from a variety of health problems attributable to decades of selective breeding. Although growth rates have been pushed to undreamed-of levels, no progress has been made in breeding pigs with sturdier feet and limbs to accommodate this extra weight. Foot and joint problems are therefore commonplace, and the hard flooring that is standard in modern pig farms aggravates these ailments. Pigs are generally slaughtered at about 260 pounds, but they can ultimately attain weights of 600 to 800 pounds. In consequence, nearly all pigs who are rescued and given lifetime shelter develop crippling leg problems as they age.

Today's dairy cows also experience numerous infirmities due to their enormous milk yields. Each year, about 20 percent of dairy cows develop either clinical mastitis or milk fever, and both conditions have grown increasingly common as cows are bred to produce ever-greater amounts of milk.[27] Untreatable mastitis infections or other udder problems have become so pervasive that they are responsible for sending about 27 percent of dairy cows to slaughter.[28] Every year, more than 100,000 dairy cows suffer from health problems that leave them unable to stand up.[29] Much of the time, the illness is traceable to excessive milk production or to complications resulting from pregnancy. In 2004, after the discovery of the first mad cow in the United States, it became illegal to drag downed cattle into a slaughterhouse, a practice that had formerly been widespread. The remains of downed cattle can no longer be sold for human consumption, but are still used for dog and cat food, and are also rendered into feed for poultry and pigs.

There are dozens of maladies related to the selective breeding of farmed animals, so there's no way this brief discussion can do justice to the problem. My main point is that diseases arising from selective breeding programs have become widespread throughout the poultry and livestock industries. These diseases are widely covered in industry journals, and often involve unpleasant treatments. For example, a common topic of study in poultry science journals involves deliberately withholding feed from young chickens, in the hope that doing so will reduce premature deaths.[30]

The meat industry often claims that animals must be healthy in order to be productive. But the truth is that today's animals are bred to be so productive that it's become increasingly unlikely that they will ever experience health. Given the precarious genetic profile that today's farmed animals inherit, most of these animals would have tough lives even if raised in ideal surroundings. Pigs and chickens rescued from modern-day agriculture operations could receive unlimited pasture, fresh mountain air, nutritious and natural food, and individualized veterinary care. Yet even when all these things are provided, many of these animals still develop crippling conditions and die prematurely as a result of their genetic background. The conditions on large-scale animal farms—wherein virtually all of America's farmed animals are raised—are devoid of any of these advantages. Most farmed animals today suffer intensive confinement, routine mutilation, detestable and unnatural food, and dangerous transport to stockyards and slaughterhouses. These factors combine with the animals' selective breeding heritage to vastly increase the degree to which they suffer.

Now that we've looked at the evolution of animal agriculture, the next chapter will relate the conditions under which today's animals are raised.

Chapter 2

Farmed Animal Lives

There are profound differences between the family-owned farms that existed before the 1950s and the large-scale operations that dominate animal agriculture today. Activists call today's large-scale operations "factory farms"—a term the industry hates, since it evokes vivid and unpleasant images. The industry prefers to call these facilities "CAFOs," which stands for Concentrated Animal Feeding Operations. I think the CAFOs term is clumsy and deliberately non-descriptive. So, throughout this book, I will refer to industrialized animal agriculture operations as factory farms. As we'll see, this term is an accurate representation of the conditions that exist within animal agriculture.

Although factory farms share a number of basic characteristics, standards vary considerably depending on the type of animal being raised. This chapter looks at what chickens, pigs, and cattle experience on factory farms. We'll see that these facilities have developed a variety of procedures that deliberately frustrate each species' instinctive needs. And, while chickens arguably suffer the worst conditions of any farmed animal, in many cases pigs and cattle are not far behind.

Layer Hens

The chicken industry breeds two kinds of birds: chickens raised for meat, who grow unbelievably fast, and layer hens, who are specifically bred to produce large numbers of eggs.

Within 24 hours of hatching, layer chicks are put into trays, and the males are separated out. These males grow too slowly to be worth raising for meat, so they are immediately put to death. Although some hatcheries gas these chicks, many use cheaper and less humane methods. Probably the most common way to kill male chicks is by putting them—while fully conscious—into a grinder. On some occasions, these grinders fail to instantly chew up the chicks,[1] so the resultant deaths are surely agonizing. There are also some hatcheries that don't even bother to kill their unwanted males—the chicks are discarded alive into trash bags, where they die from smothering.

These killing methods have been practiced for decades. The number of male chicks put to death each year is staggering—America's hatcheries killed more than 272 million male chicks in 2002.[2] Yet the egg industry's trade associations have never required that hatcheries adopt humane methods for killing these unwanted males.

Beak Searing and Confinement

After the male chicks have been discarded, attention turns to the females. Animal rights activists call what happens next "debeaking," while the industry prefers to call it "beak trimming." Both terms are misleading and ought to be replaced. The practice cannot rightfully be called debeaking, since about two-thirds of the beak is normally left intact. Nor should the practice be called beak trimming, since the term equates this painful and dangerous procedure to something as trivial as a manicure. I therefore propose the term "beak searing," which, as we'll see, is a fair description of what actually occurs.

During beak searing, a worker picks up an unanesthetized chick and inserts the bird's beak into a clipping device. A hot blade snips off the end of the beak, and simultaneously cauterizes the exposed blood vessels to minimize bleeding.

To understand why beak searing is a standard industry practice, you need to know a bit about chicken behavior. No matter how chickens are kept, they will occasionally peck at each other. In natural settings, this pecking is usually harmless, because the birds have plenty of room to back away from conflicts. But when chickens are kept in cages, they have no ability to escape from being pecked. By searing off the ends of their hens' beaks, egg producers are able to stock the birds at densities at which they would otherwise kill each other. With mutilated and blunted beaks, the hens cannot peck each other apart, no matter how severe the stresses of overcrowding.

Beak searing will likely fall out of practice in the years ahead. Chicken breeders are working to raise less aggressive birds who will refrain from pecking no matter how tightly they are confined. Already, a small percentage of egg farms are using these calmer birds and doing away with the practice of beak searing. A far more humane way to address the problem would be to give the birds sufficient space to move freely and spread their wings. Among hens kept in humane conditions, pecking rarely becomes a problem.

For now, however, beak searing is carried out on nearly all layer hens in America. While beak searing lets egg farmers pack their chickens more tightly, the procedure is probably incredibly painful, since it involves cutting out part of the chicks' mouths. For several days thereafter, the birds eat less food, no doubt because of the pain arising from this partial amputation. Research indicates that chicks suffer chronic pain for five to six weeks after beak searing.[3] And, because the procedure is done hurriedly by workers without veterinary education, there's little to prevent accidents from occurring.[4] The typical hatchery worker makes close to minimum wage, and will sear hundreds of chicks' beaks every hour. Chicks sometimes die of hunger or thirst following beak searings that are too severe.

When the birds reach seventeen weeks of age, they are transported to a commercial egg farm. Upon arriving, they are loaded into battery cages, where they will spend the rest of their lives. Battery cages are small wire-mesh units about the size of a filing cabinet drawer. Egg farms are notorious for packing eight or more hens into each cage.[5] The outcry over this overcrowding has forced McDonald's, Burger King, and Wendy's to require their egg suppliers to give the birds more room. Hens raised for these fast-food giants get at least 72 square inches of floor-space, compared to the industry average of 59 square inches, which is scheduled to gradually increase to 67 square inches by 2008.[6] There's no doubt that extra space reduces suffering, but even birds raised under the 72-inch standards lack sufficient room to spread their wings.

I have visited a number of egg farms, and the hens invariably appear wretched. As you walk through the various sheds at these facilities, you can tell right away which sheds house young birds, and which sheds house older hens. The younger hens are always in far better condition. The older birds commonly have large patches of bare and bruised skin. It's impossible to offer comfort to any of these birds because they panic upon being approached. Regular visitors to these farms report frequently discovering hens whose limbs have become caught in the cage wire.[7] Once trapped, these birds are likely to die of suffocation or dehydration.

When I walk into these places, I invariably feel engulfed by the pain and fear of the surrounding birds. The first time I visited an egg farm, I recognized at once that the conditions were just as deplorable as the pictures on any animal rights flier. Shortly after I returned home, I sat down to work at my computer, and I caught a strong whiff of chicken urine. When I sniffed my shirt, I realized that the mist of urine saturating the air at the egg farm had soaked into my clothes. I had only been there a half hour.

Within the harsh and industrialized setting of egg farms, there is one area where gentleness prevails. Because of their fragility, eggs receive a level of babying found nowhere else in animal agriculture. Upon being laid, eggs roll from their cages, which are slightly angled, onto "soft-ride" conveyor belts.[8] Later, the eggs are gently plucked from the conveyor and packaged in foam for shipping.

The hens who lay these eggs get none of this coddling. Their cages have wire bottoms, which permit feces and urine to drop through. This uncomfortable and unnatural flooring causes foot and leg problems. As the hens age, their bones become thin and brittle—largely because of the calcium depletion that results from laying eggs. The egg industry has made no concerted effort to determine the percentage of layer hens who suffer broken bones, but the problem appears to be severe.[9] In 1993, at a poultry industry symposium, a British professor of veterinary medicine gave a lecture about layer hen welfare. He told his audience, "Of live birds arriving at the slaughterhouse, 30 percent have been found to have one or more freshly broken bones."[10]

It's under these painful conditions that chickens must live for two years, until they are slaughtered.[11] When awake, they stand on wire that damages their feet. And when the birds sleep, the wire rubs away their feathers and bruises their skin. The smallest factory egg farms hold thousands of birds per barn. The largest operations confine more than a million hens on a single piece of property. Periodically throughout the day, layer houses erupt in a cacophony, as the panic of one highly-strung bird spreads like a wave throughout the entire building. From these anguished animals, kept under such deplorable conditions, come the nation's supermarket and restaurant eggs. Each of these eggs comes at a cost of substantial suffering. The average hen endures more than 24 hours in a battery cage in order to lay just one egg.[12]

Layer Hen Mortality

Layer hens are worth so little that it is never financially viable to give them individualized veterinary care. Yet egg laying, like childbirth, presents a number of perils. Probably the worst thing that can happen is what's called a prolapse. As the egg is ready to pass, it can stick onto the walls of the uterus. If this happens, when the egg is passed during laying, the uterus can be pushed out along with the egg.[13]

Since 1950, the yield of a layer hen has about doubled. And the more eggs a hen lays, the greater the chances of a prolapsed uterus. In the event of a severe prolapse, the hen will die unless somebody trained in veterinary care gingerly guides out the egg and then carefully stuffs the uterus back through her vent. I've witnessed this procedure at a rescue shelter for farmed animals. It's time consuming, taking at least an hour, but the hen will die without this human intervention.

Large-scale egg farms never do things like treat hens who suffer prolapses. There's no financial payback to taking all that time and trouble to save a prolapsed hen, when healthy seventeen-week-old hens can be purchased from a grower at less than three dollars apiece.[14] Besides, given the extreme crowding of layer houses, it's exceedingly unlikely that a hen suffering a prolapse would even be noticed. The only way to discover prolapsing hens is to hear the soft, cooing distress call these birds typically make. Inside the din of a commercial egg farm, there's no way this call could be heard, even if there were employees trained and motivated to listen for it.

In the absence of human intervention, a prolapsed hen is certain to die an agonizing death. In most cases, other hens will peck at her uterus, and the hen will die in her cage from blood loss or infection. Each year in the United States, more than two million layer hens die from prolapses left untreated.[15] It takes at least two days for a prolapsed hen to die, so at any given moment, eleven thousand hens are dying from prolapses in America.[16]

Untreated prolapses are just one of many factors behind the high mortality rates of layer hens. United States Department of Agriculture (USDA) surveys of commercial egg farms show that fifteen percent of hens die of illness or injury.[17] That comes to more than twenty million hens who die in their cages each year, each of them pressed against wire by their cage-mates while they suffer a slow and agonizing death.

Forced Molting

Egg production peaks when hens are about seven months old, and thereafter begins a gradual decline.[18] At fifteen months of age, the drop in egg yield steepens dramatically, and one of two fates awaits the birds. If the layer house sells eggs to the top three burger chains, the hens are sent to slaughter. But if the layer house is supplying supermarkets and restaurants that lack meaningful animal welfare policies, the hens are usually subjected to "forced molting." This procedure wrings another six months of egg production from the birds.[19]

During forced molting, the hens have their food taken away for seven to fourteen days.[20] Lighting is dimmed, with the intention to mimic winter conditions, stressing the body in anticipation of spring. Several weeks after the forced molt ends, egg production recovers to profitable levels. But forced molting bears a heavy cost. It kills the weaker birds, and doubtless causes all birds to suffer—while molting, hens may lose up to 30 percent of their body weight.[21]

Through forced molting, it can be economical to keep hens in battery cages for well over two years.[22] The extra production brought about by forced molting comes out of animals who could not be more wretched in appearance. In fact, slaughtered layer hens are never sold as regular chicken meat—the flesh is too stringy and low quality to be sold as whole carcasses. Instead, the meat finds its way into pet food and the lowest-grade processed consumer products, such as soups and pot pies.

Now that several leading fast-food chains refuse to buy eggs from farms that utilize forced molting, the practice may soon be stamped out. In the meantime, however, most hens are still subjected to forced molting. The most recent figures available, from

1999, indicate that 82 percent of U.S. egg farms practice forced molting.[23]

It's generally thought, by both the public and many animal rights activists, that veal calves are the most unfortunate and badly treated of all farmed animals. Having visited both egg farms and veal farms, I personally believe that the average battery hen has it worse than the average veal calf. I think it's probable that a forkful of egg comes at a cost of greater suffering than a forkful of veal. And there is no doubt in my mind that a bite of egg involves more animal suffering than a bite of hamburger or bacon. For people making a gradual switch to vegetarianism out of concern for animals, I therefore believe that the first food to give up should be, not meat, but eggs.

Meat Chickens

Layer hens and meat chickens are raised with opposite intentions. Layer hens are kept as long as possible—generally until their egg production drops to unprofitable levels. Meat chickens, by contrast, are rushed to slaughter the moment the flock reaches market weight. At a slaughter age of just seven weeks, no other farmed animals (besides male layer chicks) die so young. Even veal calves live longer.

Since meat chickens never reach adulthood, they are less likely to experience the painful and debilitating conditions that plague other types of farmed animals. Additionally, because they are not raised in cages, meat chickens suffer far less than layer hens. In the sheds that are used for raising meat chickens, the flooring is usually concrete topped with a layer of wood shavings or discarded paper. While such flooring isn't ideal, it is far less likely to produce injuries than the wire-bottomed cages found at egg farms.

If you use the conditions of layer hens as a basis to measure quality of life, you might decide that meat chickens don't have it too badly. But that's mainly because layer hens are subjected to conditions that are so atrocious that practically anything else looks good by comparison. To determine the welfare of today's meat chickens, it's more useful to compare these animals to the barnyard chickens that were widely raised up through the 1950s. Back then, meat chickens were kept in coops, with no more than sixty birds sharing a given space. Such conditions resembled the flock sizes that wild chickens once maintained. Each chicken was able to know and recognize every other bird in the flock.

Today's broiler houses are a world apart from the environments in which chickens were traditionally raised. A modern broiler house holds upwards of 20,000 chickens, with each bird getting less than a square foot of space.[24] It's hard to credibly claim that, under this kind of crowding, the chickens have any opportunity for a decent life. In most of these facilities, by the time the chickens reach slaughter weight, crowding is so severe that you can hardly see any open floor space.

So while meat chickens don't suffer to the same degree as layer hens, they are nevertheless kept under crowded and profoundly unnatural conditions. These birds endure constant sensory overload involving the noise of other birds and the stench of urine and manure. Like layer hens, meat chickens never see the sun nor breathe fresh air until they are loaded onto trucks bound for the slaughterhouse.

Slaughter

At seven weeks of age, meat chickens are gathered up for slaughter. Workers descend upon the flock and carry the birds, upside down by their legs, three or four at a time, to small cages. Once the cages are loaded onto a truck, the ride to the slaughterhouse may take minutes or hours. However long it takes, there's no food available, because the chickens would not have enough time to convert the food to meat.

Weather conditions during transport commonly produce suffering or death. Large chicken operations are located throughout the United States, from frigid Michigan to sweltering Arkansas.

The trucks used for transporting chickens offer no protection from extreme temperatures. Given their genetic predisposition to heart failure, it's common for some birds to die during transport, particularly during hot and humid weather.

At a chicken slaughterhouse, two things are plainly apparent. The first is the degree of fear shown by the birds. You can see panic in their movements, and hear it in their vocalizations. If you can pull your attention away from the chickens, the second thing you will notice is how quickly these plants run. So many animals are killed so rapidly that it's hard to focus attention on any one animal.

All modern slaughterhouses are blurs of motion, and chicken slaughterhouses run the fastest of all. The newest chicken slaughterhouses kill 8400 birds per hour.[25] This is about twenty times faster than the fastest cattle slaughterhouse.[26] One reason poultry slaughterhouses can run so quickly is that chickens are much smaller than cattle or pigs, so there is less work to be done on each animal. Another reason for the high slaughter rate is that chicken slaughterhouses automate the killing process to a greater degree than cattle or pig slaughterhouses. The stunning, throat cutting, and even the plucking are all done mechanically.

The killing begins with a team of about six people, who grab the birds from a conveyor belt. The workers clamp the chickens' feet into shackles, and the birds, dangling upside down, are whisked away. As the birds leave the shackling area and head down the line, they flap their wings and jerk their bodies in a futile effort to free themselves.

Seconds after starting down the line, each bird descends toward a bath of electrified water. Most chicken slaughterhouses in the United States are set up so that the chicken's head momentarily dips into the water, resulting in a brief stun. Numerous poultry industry articles assert that water baths exist for humane purposes—for rendering birds unconscious prior to throat cutting. After extensively reviewing this literature, I've reached the opinion that the primary purpose of stunning is *not* to make slaughter more humane. Rather, I believe the whole point of stunning is merely to immobilize the bird—unless the bird's head droops like a wet rag, the mechanical blade is likely to miss his throat.

There are substantial differences in poultry stunning methods between the United States and Europe. As in America, all poultry slaughterhouses in the European Union electrically shock their birds prior to slaughter. But Europe's water baths are charged with a much stronger electrical current than in the United States. And many European slaughterhouses pull the entire body through the bath, rather than just the head. As a result of this powerful shock, European chickens often suffer cardiac arrest. In consequence, they are always either unconscious or dead when their throats are cut.

By contrast, America's chickens commonly experience a double horror. The stun renders their bodies momentarily limp, and their throats are then immediately cut. But the voltage used during the stun is usually not sufficient to induce lasting unconsciousness.[27] These birds can rapidly regain awareness, bleeding to death from a gashed throat.

It unfortunately makes good economic sense to keep stunning amperage to minimal levels. Stunning a bird with sufficient current to cause cardiac arrest often causes convulsions strong enough to break bones.[28] These broken bones will downgrade carcasses, resulting in the slaughterhouse receiving less money per bird.[29] Additionally, if the bird's heart is still beating after the throat is cut, he will "bleed out" more thoroughly. European governments have clearly decided that the importance of a lasting stun outweighs losses to carcass quality. But American poultry slaughterhouses, lacking government regulations on the matter, put their financial interests ahead of ensuring the birds remain unconscious during slaughter.

Although poultry slaughter is demonstrably inhumane, there appears little prospect of fixing the worst abuses. The poultry industry seems disinclined to research issues related to pain and suffering—at any agricultural library, you can page through a hefty stack of poultry science journals without finding a single article that investigates slaughterhouse welfare concerns. Additionally, animal protection advocates often resist seeking slaughter improvements. Some activists worry that if the worst cruelties are eradicated, the public might look more favorably on chicken production. Other activists believe that seeking incremental welfare reform gives legitimacy to exploiting animals.

Despite the efforts of several animal protection groups, there have not yet been any meaningful welfare improvements concerning chicken slaughter. This is not to say that the situation at pig and cattle slaughterhouses is always better. But, unlike poultry slaughterhouses, pig and cattle slaughterhouses possess equipment that can dramatically reduce suffering—as long as it is properly maintained and operated.

The Numbers

Even if stunning methods for chickens were perfected, there is something uniquely troubling about chicken slaughter that separates this product from beef or pork. As the late Jay Dinshah, the founder of the American Vegan Society, memorably put it: "When people say they just eat a little chicken, I have to agree with them. They just eat *a* little chicken."

Dinshah was so keen to focus attention on chicken meat because he understood the consequences of its growing popularity. Starting around 1970, American demand for red meat fell into a long and steep decline, while consumption of chickens soared ever upward.[30] This trend has undoubtedly spared millions of pigs and cattle from being born into factory farm environments, but it has necessitated the raising and slaughter of billions of chickens. Chickens are tiny animals, and you've got to kill more than 220 of them in order to get the same amount of meat available from just one steer.[31] The number of meat chickens slaughtered annually in the United States jumped from three billion in 1970 to more than eight billion in 2000.[32]

With minuscule resources, the animal protection movement has done a remarkable job of publicizing how farmed animals are treated. But the movement has rarely gone out of its way to show the public that, in terms of numbers of animals killed, chickens deserve special attention. Activists need to publicize the fact that, compared to chicken, no other food choice demands so much suffering and killing per pound of meat. As it stands today, many people think they are taking steps toward vegetarianism by eating chicken instead of beef or pork. For people moving away from meat due to ethical considerations, chickens ought to be the first animal spared rather than the last.

Pigs

The conditions under which factory farmed pigs live may not be quite as bad as what layer hens endure. But there are nonetheless several aspects of pig production that are deeply troubling.

To properly understand a modern pig's environment, you must first know a bit about how pigs care for their young. Mother pigs have strong maternal instincts, and wild pigs nurse their litters for more than three months. One oddity concerning pregnancy in pigs is the enormous difference between the weights of mother and newborn. Today's breeder sows can weigh well over six hundred pounds, whereas each of their newborn piglets typically weighs about two pounds—a three hundred to one ratio![33] Pigs have evolved an effective method of preventing accidental crushing deaths during nursing. A day or so before giving birth, a mother pig combs the forest for grasses and leaves. She assembles these materials into a huge nest, which rises to nearly waist-height of an adult human. After completing her nest, she goes into labor and gives birth to between five and twelve piglets. The nest provides ample room for mother and piglets to lie together. The piglets have their own cushioned space, set apart from their mother, where they can nurse without danger of being crushed.

When pigs were first domesticated, farmers quickly discovered the importance of providing plenty of straw. Pregnant pigs, be-having as though they were still in the wild, built nests from the straw prior to giving birth. And it wasn't just pregnant pigs who made use of straw. The other pigs in the barn would continually play with the straw and move it about in order to create bedding. This task kept them busy by day and comfortable by night.

Apart from enhancing welfare, straw significantly improves overall health. Pigs who are denied straw suffer higher rates of foot injuries and joint swelling.[34] They also take longer to heal from injuries and show decreased immune response.[35] Unfortu-nately, as ever-larger producers have taken control of the pork industry, it has become standard to raise pigs without straw. In facilities that hold thousands of pigs, keeping all these animals supplied with straw would demand substantial expense.[36] What's more, the use of straw makes the task of cleaning pig barns vastly more time consuming.

But what about pregnant sows, who instinctively build nests from straw in order to protect their newborns? The industry long ago recognized that bare concrete floors result in too many piglets crushed during nursing. In response, new confinement methods were developed specifically for breeder sows.

Gestation and Farrowing Crates

In commercial pig operations, about 2 percent of female piglets are taken away upon weaning in order to become breeder sows. These animals are allowed to live much longer than pigs who are raised for meat, but their lengthy lives are filled with both emotional and physical duress.

At eight months of age, breeder sows are impregnated for the first time. A sow spends her entire pregnancy in what the industry calls a "gestation crate." A great deal of publicity has gone into exposing the atrocities of veal crates, whereas hardly anyone has heard of gestation crates. Yet gestation crates are every bit as confining for a sow as veal crates are for a calf. They offer no space for a sow to walk, or even to turn around. Nearly every large American pig operation uses gestation crates. The crates' small size maximizes the number of sows who can be kept in a building, while giving workers the ability to immediately locate any particular animal. Since management knows exactly when each sow has been impregnated, the animals are moved out of gestation crates and into "farrowing crates" a couple days before they are ready to give birth.

Farrowing crates are nearly as cramped as gestation crates. The primary difference between the two units is that farrowing crates have recessed pockets on either side, in which newborn piglets can lie during nursing. Since farrowing crates are specifically designed to prevent piglets from being crushed, it would be logical to suppose that, whatever psychological torments the mother pig may suffer in these devices, piglet mortality rates should at least be low. Yet more than 5 percent of piglets are crushed to death while nursing.[37] The piglets, instinctively craving the warmth and comfort of their mothers, manage to edge themselves upward onto the exposed flooring inside the farrowing crate. Once a piglet wiggles onto this flooring, he is likely to be accidentally crushed or smothered by his mother.[38] Crushing isn't the only hazard confronting piglets: about 3 percent die of diarrhea or starvation.[39]

It's no wonder that piglet mortality rates are so high, given the scarcity of staff employed by most breeders. At Murphy Family Farms, a standardized breeding facility packs in 3600 sows and employs just 15 people.[40] Assuming a forty-hour workweek, that means that each sow and her piglets receive barely one minute of human attention per day. That's only enough time to spot the most obvious of problems.

Unlike wild pigs, who give birth once a year, breeder sows are impregnated every five to six months. After finishing puberty, these sows spend almost their entire lives either pregnant or nursing. If the stresses of continual pregnancies do not wear them down, the effects of being continually crated often prove their undoing. Each year, about 35 percent of breeder sows are sent to slaughter, either because of health problems or because they are getting too old to breed efficiently.[41] An additional 6 percent are found dead in their farrowing or gestation crates—the USDA makes no attempt to identify or report the reason for all these deaths.[42]

Perhaps more troubling than the health problems suffered by breeder sows is the emotional toll connected to confinement. The boredom resulting from isolation can give rise to an abnormal psychological state called stereotypy, in which sows do the same senseless repetitive motion thousands of times each day. Sows have also been witnessed trying to attack the crates that keep them so tightly confined.

Piglets

In the wild, a sow will nurse her piglets for upwards of three months. But in large breeding facilities, piglets are taken from their mothers after about seventeen days.[43] Early weaning shortens the time the farmer must wait before the sow can be re-impregnated. Also, the sooner piglets are forced onto solid food, the faster they will grow. To speed weight gain, some pig producers rely on dried blood plasma, which is collected from slaughterhouses. The trouble is that this feed ingredient can undermine the piglets' health. One study published in 2002 by the *Journal of Animal Science* found that feeding dried blood plasma to piglets, "causes major damage to the mucosa of the gastrointestinal tract."[44]

Around the time of weaning, piglets suffer several mutilations, all of which are inflicted without anesthetic. The males are nearly always castrated, since meat from noncastrated males has a pungent odor. For identification purposes, most piglets have deep notches cut into their ears. There are gentler methods for marking pigs, but ear-notching is the fastest and cheapest available method. And since it's legal, the practice is widespread.

Just as egg producers minimize confinement-related injuries by resorting to beak searing, a comparable practice occurs in the pig industry. When pigs are overcrowded, they tend to bite each other's tails. Tail-biting occurs occasionally among pigs raised under any conditions, but it can get out of control in overcrowded factory farm settings. Rather than solve the problem by giving the animals sufficient room, pig producers resort to tail docking. The little nub of tail that is left in place after tail docking is extraordinarily sensitive, and even the most depressed and sickly pig will act vigorously to protect it from being bitten.

I believe that at least some farmers would prefer to raise their pigs without resorting to tail docking. But any farmer who refused to amputate tails would face a ruinous competitive disadvantage.[45] It's far cheaper to dock pigs' tails than it is to solve the tail-biting problem by giving the animals adequate space.

Nurseries and Finishing

Since commercial pigs are weaned prematurely, they weigh barely ten pounds at the time they are separated from their mothers. At this size, they could be trampled to death if mixed with pigs who are approaching slaughter weight. Newly weaned piglets are therefore sent to a holding area, where they share a crowded floor with numerous other young pigs. The pig industry calls these places "nurseries"—a deceptively pleasant word for what are often cramped windowless sheds with concrete or wooden flooring. During the five to seven weeks that piglets spend in nurseries, 2.4 percent of the animals die.[46]

After the piglets reach about forty pounds, they are transferred to "finishing sheds," where they remain the final four months of their lives. During that time, the pigs grow to almost 260 pounds. The largest finishing sheds contain more than a hundred pens, together housing well over a thousand pigs. Each pen is about the size of a mid-sized bedroom, and holds ten to twenty pigs.

There are several welfare problems associated with finishing sheds. Almost 90 percent of pigs kept in these sheds are never allowed outdoors.[47] The flooring is usually bare concrete, wood, or hard-packed dirt. Since farmers don't provide straw, the pigs have no opportunity to construct bedding. They therefore spend the remainder of their lives standing and sleeping on a hard filthy surface.

During the four months they stay in finishing sheds, 3.7 percent of pigs die of disease or injury.[48] Some of these deaths occur because nobody is on hand to notice a sick animal. In my experience, I've found finishing sheds to be practically unmonitored, and I've seldom seen a worker inside one of these buildings. On the rare occasions when workers are present, it's often to repair feeding machinery or to clean up between batches of pigs. Even if a sick pig is lucky enough to be detected, life-saving treatment may be deliberately withheld—veterinary care is expensive, and the costs may exceed the pig's market value.

Of pigs who die before reaching slaughter weight, respiratory disease is by far the leading killer, and is responsible for 39 percent of deaths.[49] It's easy to see why respiratory disease kills so many pigs. All factory farms have terrible air quality, but the air inside pig sheds is especially bad. Pig excrement produces harsh fumes that create a substantial health hazard. Even though pigs only stay in finishing sheds for four months, that's still enough time for the ammonia-filled air to eat into lung tissue. Studies of lungs taken from slaughtered pigs indicate that between 30 and 70 percent of pigs have developed chronic respiratory disease.[50] Predictably, workers in pig confinement facilities are also at high risk of lung trouble. Researchers have found that at least 25 percent of these workers have respiratory ailments.[51]

Transport and Slaughter

After four months in the finishing sheds, workers load the pigs onto trucks bound for the slaughterhouse. The drive is often lengthy, since the slaughterhouse is usually at least fifty miles away.[52] About one-third of the time, the pigs are driven between one hundred and five hundred miles.[53]

Conditions during transport are jarring and unsafe, due in large part to a glaring omission in the federal Animal Welfare Act.

According to the Act, pigs are entitled to a number of protections when transported by train or airplane, yet these protections don't apply when pigs are transported by truck. Since nearly all pigs are trucked to slaughter, the protections afforded by the Animal Welfare Act are largely meaningless. Pig producers frequently overcrowd their trucks in order to reduce their expenses. These savings come at the cost of enormous suffering. Pork industry journals commonly cite the statistic that 80,000 pigs die each year during the trip to the slaughterhouse.[54]

Some of these deaths could be avoided if government inspectors did their jobs properly. During a heat wave in the summer of 2003, hundreds of pigs died every day from heatstroke after being sent to one Illinois slaughterhouse. The USDA inspector assigned to the facility apparently knew of the problem but waited several days before ordering the plant shut down. By then, heatstroke had killed nearly 1600 pigs.[55]

This lapse in responsibility was so severe that it prompted the head of the USDA's Food Safety and Inspection Service to remark: "Is it such a stretch of the imagination...(w)hen animals are dying in large numbers in transporters awaiting slaughter—day after day—that there may be something inhumane about these losses and it is our responsibility to intervene?"[56]

More than 120 million pigs are slaughtered each year in the United States.[57] Their final moments are brutal. They are prodded out of their holding pens and onto a narrow walkway. As they approach the front of the line, they often see the squealing animals ahead of them being stunned, cut in the throat, and hung upside down. In many pig slaughterhouses, stunning is done with electricity. This equipment is often unreliable. Records taken from one U.S. slaughterhouse during the late 1990s indicate that, despite stunning pigs up to four different times before slaughter, some of the pigs nonetheless remained conscious.[58] Yet even if the stun appears successful, and the pig collapses, research done on sheep suggests that mammals often remain at least partially conscious following an electric stun.[59]

After the stunning, the next step on the line is throat-cutting. A few minutes after the pig's throat is cut, his body is dropped into a scald tank. Most pigs have already bled to death by the time they hit the water. But there is evidence that at least some pigs are still alive when they enter the scald tank. These animals undoubtedly face an agonizing death—the water is 140° Fahrenheit. A USDA Swine Inspection Module published in 2000 says: "A hog that is scalded alive dies from asphyxia and will frequently have a scarlet red appearance and have organs that are engorged with blood."[60]

As we're about to see, a case can be made that there are flashes of contentment in the lives of many dairy cows and beef cattle. But the lives of pigs are undoubtedly filled with nonstop anguish. I don't think it's possible to argue that pigs have any opportunity, at any time of their lives, to feel joy or comfort. Their most basic needs are continually frustrated from birth to slaughter.

Dairy Cows

At traditional dairies, cows are let out each morning to graze on grassy hillsides. Despite the spread of confinement systems throughout animal agriculture, there are still tens of thousands of American dairies that allow cows to graze outdoors. But these dairies are rapidly giving way to operations that have adopted factory farm techniques. This trend has been partly driven by the upsurge in dairy production in America's southwestern states.

Between 1970 and 2001, Nevada more than tripled its milk production, while Arizona's milk output increased nearly five-fold.[61] Factory farming methods have made this explosive growth possible. Prior to confinement-oriented dairies, milk producers could never get a foothold in the Southwest. These states have hot, dry climates, which are bad for dairy cows and inhospitable for the grasses upon which they feed.

Dairies that don't allow their cows to graze pasture are called "dry-lot" facilities. There are two kinds of dry-lot dairies, and it's hard to say which offers worse conditions. In one type, cows are kept in metal-roofed sheds. Feed is delivered to the animals by conveyor belt, which decreases labor costs but also reduces the opportunity for workers to interact with animals and to notice health problems. Dairy sheds are invariably crowded, since the cost of these buildings creates financial pressure to pack in as many cows as possible. The cows are usually chained by the neck, and each cow is confined to a cramped stall.

The other kind of dry-lot dairy dispenses with sheds and is instead modeled after beef feedlots, with the animals crowded into fenced outdoor areas.[62] The ground the cows walk upon is a soot-like black. Cattle manure turns this color when it is incessantly trampled into soil and saturated with urine. The cows spend their days standing and lying atop this foul surface, and eating feed from the troughs that line the fences.

As southern U.S. dairies have gained market share, northern dairies have fought back by embracing dry-lot techniques. Back in the 1970s, virtually every cow raised in the Northeast and Upper Midwest got to graze pasture, at least for part of the year. But today, dry-lot dairies are common in every region of the United States.

Cows, Pregnancies, and Milk Cycles

A typical dairy cow is kept pregnant nine months out of each year. On top of this, she annually produces more than 2000 gallons of milk.[63] The stresses of repeated pregnancies and the metabolic demands of milk production frequently lead to lameness or disease. Every year, more than one million dairy cows are slaughtered early because of health problems that arise from pregnancy or milking.[64]

Given the fragile health of today's dairy cows, it's hardly surprising that their calves are often born sickly. Almost 9 percent of dairy calves die before weaning.[65] This mortality figure is especially troubling in light of the fact that dairy calves are usually weaned within just two days of birth. In fact, the main reason these calves get any milk at all is because—for about 48 hours after giving birth—cows produce colostrum, which has a distinctive flavor and cannot be sold as regular milk. Since colostrum has limited resale value, and because it confers immunity to various bovine diseases, it's usually fed to newborn calves. After the colostrum changes over to regular milk, dairy workers take the calf away so that all of the cow's milk can be processed for sale. The calf is usually fed formula, which consists largely of animal fat and blood products gathered from slaughterhouses.

I suppose that there's no psychologically gentle way to take away the calf, but the method for doing this deserves telling. For the past fifty years, cows have been bred for ever-increasing milk yields. It's gotten so that no calf could possibly drink all the milk his or her mother produces. Within two days of giving birth, the mother's udder is swollen with milk, and she is led to the milking parlor. While the milking is taking place, the calf is hustled off to another part of the dairy. When the cow returns from the milking parlor, she discovers her calf is missing. This has to be the most traumatic experience imaginable for a mother cow, and it shows. The cow will often bellow nonstop for a day or two, frantically looking about for her calf.

The cow's experience is not a one-time ordeal. Dairy cows usually give birth about three times in their lives, and every one of their calves is taken away within 48 hours of birth. I think the trauma caused by these separations is one reason why some cows are sent to slaughter early. In most cases, cows go to slaughter either because they have fallen ill, or because their milk yields have declined to unprofitable levels. But in about 1 percent of cases, a cow goes to slaughter because her disposition has turned nasty.[66] When brought into milking parlors, some cows will kick at workers who operate the milking machines. Dairy cows can weigh upwards of a thousand pounds, and a well-aimed kick can be murderous. Cows who repeatedly attempt to kick workers are sent to slaughter, since they are too dangerous to keep around, regardless of how much milk they produce.

Having spent a great deal of time around cattle, I know that dairy cows are some of the sweetest animals you could ever meet. Not all breeds of cattle have such a gentle temperament—Brahma bulls and Texas Longhorns, for example, can be unpredictable and violent—but most breeds of dairy cattle are incredibly gentle. While I can't offer documentation on this point, I believe that it's the forcible separation of mother and newborn that causes a substantial number of dairy cows to attack their handlers.

After being taken away from their mothers, the fate of the calves is determined primarily by their gender. The females are usually raised to become dairy cows. By contrast, the dairy industry has little use for its male calves, and many of these animals are sold to the veal industry.

Veal Operations

When animal rights started to attract national attention in the mid-1970s, veal became the fledgling movement's primary target. This was a wise choice. A new movement with scarce resources needed to select an egregious and indefensible cruelty as a starting point toward informing the public about factory farms. The animal rights movement has kept a spotlight on veal ever since. As a result, most Americans today know about the unconscionable degree of confinement that veal crates impose. Some Americans also know that veal calves are deliberately fed a diet with insufficient iron.[67] The lack of iron and exercise creates a soft grayish pink flesh that fetches a premium price, and, to this day, veal still appears in many upscale American restaurants.[68]

Despite the substantial negative publicity surrounding veal, the dairy industry's role in supplying veal farmers goes largely unpublicized. Because most cows give birth at least two or three times during their lives, the dairy industry is awash with calves. In 2002, America's dairy cows gave birth to just over eight million calves.[69] Female calves who have good potential for being milk cows can command significant money at auction. Males are less desired, and they are frequently sold to veal farmers, often at surprisingly low prices.

Veal farms can sometimes purchase newborn calves for $50 or less, which has to be considered an incredibly low price for a healthy hundred-pound animal.[70] The reason such low prices are possible is because the dairy industry keeps the market for calves continuously glutted. Dairy cows are not impregnated in order to produce yet more unwanted calves—they are made pregnant to generate another year's milk production. The male calves are therefore byproducts of the dairy industry, and the low prices these animals fetch reduce the veal industry's costs and fatten its profit margins.

Veal calf auctions are among the saddest things I've ever witnessed. The calves usually enter the auction ring with a few inches of umbilical cord still hanging from their bellies. Their hides are often still slick from the womb. Yet the calves are as alert as can be. I've watched these animals look me in the eye while they nuzzle my finger. Their nervous manner suggests that they know they are in a bad place, and I suspect they are still looking for their mothers.

Fortunately, American publicity campaigns against veal have had a powerful effect. This once-popular meat now has a stigma that rivals fur coats, and demand has consequently collapsed. In 2001, the average American ate just a half-pound of veal, down from 4.2 pounds per person in 1960.[71]

Despite the decline in veal consumption, more than one million calves are slaughtered each year in the United States.[72] Every single one of these calves comes from dairy farms. Yet, somehow, the dairy industry avoids any significant publicity regarding how it keeps veal producers afloat. Activists often say that each glass of milk contains a bit of veal, and in a sense, this is true.

Beef Cattle

Beef cattle are not subjected to the same degree of confinement as pigs, poultry, or most dairy cows. Young beef calves experience better surroundings than other farmed animals, and better health as well.

In fact, beef calves are born with the healthiest bodies of any farmed animal. This is mainly because cattle breeding programs have lagged behind similar efforts made by poultry and pig breeders.* Since cattle grow comparatively slowly, they are spared the growth-related diseases that plague pigs, chickens, and turkeys. Beef cattle rarely suffer from the crippling arthritis and leg conditions so common in pigs, nor do they succumb to the heart problems that afflict poultry.

No farmed animal has a better overall quality of life than a young beef calf. The ranching industry is rooted in tradition, and little has changed in the way that cattle are raised. Just like 150 years ago, most of today's beef calves are still born on the open range. The calves grow up alongside their mothers, and rarely encounter people during the months that they graze. Although beef cattle go to slaughter at a much younger age than in the past, their lives are fairly good while they graze the range.

Anybody who compares the treatment of beef calves to other farmed animals will likely come away puzzled. How come beef calves get to graze in nature for more than six months—and spend all this time growing up with their mothers—while chicken and pigs spend their entire lives confined indoors?

Federal subsidies are the primary force that makes it economically attractive for large numbers of cattle to freely graze. These subsidies are also the main reason why the cattle industry is still viable, in terms of being able to produce large amounts of beef at prices that stay competitive with chicken and pork.

The U.S. government rents grazing land at fantastically low rates. Despite the fact that beef consumption has clear ties to heart disease, cancer, and obesity, the government subsidizes cattle ranchers as though they produce a socially desirable food. For decades, environmentalists have sought to end "welfare ranching"

---

*In Appendix F, I explain why the cattle industry faces overwhelming inefficiencies when it comes to breeding more productive farmed animals.

by urging the government to strip away grazing fee subsidies. But ranchers carry enormous clout in Congress, and efforts to reform grazing policies have gotten nowhere. In 2002, it cost just $1.43 per month to graze a steer on federal land.[73] That's less than the monthly cost of feeding a house cat—an absurd situation considering that beef calves grow to more than six hundred pounds while grazing federal land.[74] For further perspective, consider that when ranchers lease privately owned land for grazing, they usually pay more than ten times what the government charges.[75]

Subsidized grazing fees enrich ranchers at the expense of taxpayers. On the other hand, these subsidies probably prevent a great deal of chicken slaughter, since lower beef prices encourage people to eat beef instead of chicken.

Separation

During their months grazing, beef calves see the rancher at least twice. The first time is when the calf is about three months old. On this occasion, the rancher comes not for the calf, but for the mother. The rancher and his assistants ride up on horseback, lasso the mother, and hold her stationary. To inseminate her, the rancher uses a device that looks like a turkey baster. With that accomplished, the men ride off.

Three to five months later, the rancher returns, this time for the calf. Taking the calf from the mother is difficult and dangerous. Beef cows are much less docile than dairy cows, and they are likely to become violent if they see their offspring being taken away. And cowboys can't use the trick that's done with dairy cows—the one that involves leading the mother to a milking parlor, then hiding her calf before she returns. Given the chance, a beef cow will fight furiously to prevent her calf from being taken. To reduce their risk of injury, many ranchers throw a hood over the mother's head. The calf is then led aboard a pickup truck or escorted far away by cowboys on horseback. The hood is not removed from the mother until her calf is far out of sight.

For the mother, this ordeal occurs every year. Beef cows have up to ten pregnancies before they are taken to slaughter.

A New Life

The calf's life starts anew the moment he is taken from his mother. It begins with his being led into a corral, which usually holds a number of other calves bound for the feedlot. Before they are transported, the calves are branded and dehorned. The males are also castrated.[76]

It's difficult to determine how much pain branding inflicts; it could be a great deal or it could be fairly trivial. Calves invariably bellow as the red-hot iron is pressed against hide. However, the branding of cattle does not cause the degree of pain that it would cause to humans, since cattle skin is thick and lacks nerve endings near the surface.

Dehorning is probably much more painful than branding—the horns are either sawed off or dissolved with a caustic paste. Unlike branding, the degree of pain felt during dehorning is not subject to much debate. Although horns are as dead as a fingernail on the outside, inside they have plenty of nerve endings. I doubt a credible case can be made that the pain of dehorning is anything but severe.

Castration, as it is often practiced, seems gratuitously cruel. In 1989, Pulitzer prizewinning author Richard Rhodes came out with a remarkable nonfiction book titled: *Farm—A Year in the Life of an American Farmer,* which focused on a moderately successful grain and pig farmer. The book is overwhelmingly supportive of farmers in general, and it's clear that Rhodes carries little in the way of animal rights sentiment. Yet I found Rhodes' passage about castrating bulls, which he tells in a matter-of-fact style, to be among the most disturbing things I've ever read:

> The young vet moved the calf's tail aside, took firm hold of its bag and deftly slit it open. The bull jumped at the cut and tried to look around to see what was

happening, its eyeballs straining from its head. Quickly Doc popped out a testicle—egg shaped, blue veined, white, big as a man's fist—and began pulling it firmly and decisively down, the muscles standing out on his forearms, the strain showing in his neck. The pulling stretched blood vessels and muscles until they tore free. Tearing rather than cutting them made them less likely to bleed. With the tearing, the bull raised its rump, going swayback, fighting the painful, relentless pull. Its neck curved down, its muzzle went up into the air, its eyeballs rolled up into its head until the whites were showing and then with the worst of the tearing its tongue came out, blue-gray and twisted, and flailed in a long, terrible bellow. When Doc had the white tube of the vas stretched to its full extent he quickly cut it through. With a flip of the wrist he tossed the testicle into the bucket. He pulled the other testicle, the bull writhing again in pain, cut the vas, sprayed the incision with antiseptic, let himself out of the chute, released the choke and slapped the bull on the rump. It bolted from the chute, ran off a few yards and stopped to shake its head, foam flying from its mouth. Then, seeming to forget its ordeal, it wandered over to join the heifer.[77]

Rhodes' last sentence strikes me as wildly improbable. Yet even if Rhodes is correct that the newly minted steer immediately forgot his agonies, that doesn't make his experience any less traumatic. I think if you put Rhodes' passage alongside one of Amnesty International's accounts of torture, it would be obvious that both acts are cut from the same cloth, even though the steer's castration was done for financial rather than sadistic or political ends.

To me, the most disturbing aspect of cattle castration is that much of this agony could easily be prevented. Rhodes acknowledges this and concludes his castration account by writing, "The fact was, anesthesia would have been a blessing before castration, but it cost too much."[78]

In his otherwise meticulously researched book, Rhodes neglects to mention the cost of anesthesia. Lidocaine is an inexpensive local anesthetic that works admirably in reducing pain in cattle during castration. A dose of lidocaine costs about twenty-five cents, and it takes less than a minute to load a syringe and inject a calf.[79] Yet ranchers have collectively decided that even this tiny expense is prohibitive, so anesthetic is virtually never applied. About 19 million beef cattle are castrated in the United States each year, practically all without anesthetic.[80] Many of these animals suffer ordeals comparable to what Rhodes has described. And twenty-five cents per animal would be all it would take to diminish this vast and pointless amount of suffering.

The Feedlot

After the last steer has been castrated, the animals travel by truck or train to a feedlot. In many cases, cattle are transported hundreds of miles. Despite their long journeys, the animals usually arrive in good health—they have, after all, spent six to eight months grazing the open range. But once they arrive at the feedlot, matters go steadily downhill. Essentially, the business of a feedlot is to trade health for size.

We've already seen that beef producers suffer a serious competitive disadvantage, since pigs and chickens grow much faster than cattle. To get past this handicap, the beef industry devised feedlots, which serve as a brute-force method of overcoming genetics. During the time that cattle stay at feedlots, the animals gain almost a hundred pounds each month.[81]

Nearly all feedlot cattle in America receive hormone implants, which speed growth and increase muscle mass. Each dollar spent on implants delivers about fifteen dollars in added profits.[82] But the main engine for fattening cattle is not hormones, but corn. Because corn is far richer than grass in calories, cattle gain hundreds of extra pounds when switched to feedlot rations.

It's a remarkable system, really—except for one complication. Because cattle evolved on a diet of grass and brush, corn-based feed damages their livers and causes other health problems. Researchers analyzing organ samples taken from slaughterhouses have found that 13 percent of cattle have liver abscesses—an ailment conclusively tied to feedlot rations.[83] Corn-based feed also drives digestive tract pH down to abnormally acidic levels, which allow a variety of harmful bacteria to populate the digestive system. To deal with these bacteria, most large feedlots lace their feeds with antibiotics.[84]

Cattle suffer from more than an inappropriate diet. Conditions at feedlots are bleak, crowded, and filthy. Just like cows at outdoor dry-lot dairies, feedlot cattle walk and sleep atop a blackened layer of dirt and manure. A single large feedlot may contain several thousand cattle, and the stench is unbelievable. There have been a number of occasions when I have smelled a feedlot from several miles away.

The Last Ride

After four to five months at the feedlot, the cattle are sent to slaughter. Transport is especially dangerous. If these bloated animals slip and fall, they can be fatally trampled by other cattle. Unfortunately, neither the government nor the beef industry publishes records of how many cattle die during transport.[85]

The likelihood of animals being trampled increases with the length of the journey to slaughter. Transportation times have grown longer in recent years, with the consolidation of America's meatpacking plants. Between 1980 and 2000, more than two-thirds of America's cattle slaughterhouses went out of business.[86] As slaughterhouses all across the United States have closed, cattle must be trucked longer distances. Many of these animals face journeys lasting sixteen or even twenty-four hours.[87] When they finally reach the slaughterhouse, they are offloaded into a corral. There they remain until the gate opens to the chute that leads to the kill floor.

Cattle Slaughter in the Post-McDonald's Era

Cattle slaughter has changed enormously over the past fifty years. And in several respects, these changes have been for the better.

Up through the 1970s, nearly all American cattle were knifed in the throat while fully conscious. In 1978, this barbarism was halted when the Senate revised the Humane Slaughter Act, which applies to all federally inspected slaughterhouses. For the first time, America's largest slaughterhouses were required to stun cattle and pigs prior to throat-cutting.[88] Further welfare improvements came in the 1990s, when animal rights activists forced the beef industry to abandon an exceptionally cruel method of slaughter known as shackle-and-hoist.[89] With this victory achieved, activists stepped up pressure on the fast-food industry to assume some responsibility for animal welfare. In September 2000, McDonald's agreed to regularly conduct unannounced welfare inspections at its beef suppliers. McDonald's decision forced its competitors to follow suit, and in less than two years both Burger King and Wendy's enacted similar policies.

Humane slaughter expert Temple Grandin believes that the McDonald's initiative has brought far-reaching improvements to America's slaughterhouses. She says that, in terms of what cattle experience during slaughter, "There is the pre-McDonald's era and the post-McDonald's era—it's night and day."

Grandin is correct in her assertion that cattle slaughter has improved significantly in recent years. But her praise for McDonald's accomplishments is a tacit acknowledgment of the USDA's failure to enforce the Humane Slaughter Act. If the USDA had been adequately enforcing the law in America's slaughterhouses, McDonald's would never have needed to start policing its suppliers.

The welfare inspections carried out by the burger giants have no doubt prevented enormous amounts of suffering. But there are numerous large and small slaughterhouses that never supply the fast-food industry. At many of these slaughterhouses, business continues as usual. In consequence, even in the post-McDonald's era, there is still substantial evidence of horrendous abuses occurring at cattle slaughterhouses. Proof that system-wide reform is still urgently needed came in April of 2001—more than six months after the post-McDonald's era began—when *The Washington Post* published a front-page story titled, "They Die Piece by Piece." The article presented evidence of rampant cruelties occurring at some of America's biggest cattle slaughterhouses.[90]

Many of the abuses cited by the *Post* arise from a common point of failure. Ever since the Humane Slaughter Act's 1978 passage, nearly all cattle slaughterhouses have used what's called a captive bolt pistol. On the kill floor, the pistol is shot point-blank, right between a steer's eyes. When fired, a thick steel rod smashes through the steer's skull, causing severe brain damage and instantly inducing a coma. While this is undoubtedly a violent way to treat an animal, it's undoubtedly far less gruesome and troubling than what went on before the Humane Slaughter Act was passed.

But the *Post* uncovered evidence that captive bolt guns are prone to failure. When this happens, fully conscious animals have been sent down the line. The most disturbing part of the *Post's* revelations pertained to the cattle who remained conscious even as they were being butchered. One slaughterhouse worker interviewed by the *Post* said he saw conscious cattle make it all the way to the disemboweling machine.[91]

These abuses occur because workers in some slaughterhouses are expected to keep the line moving at all costs. When visibly conscious animals are sent down the line, the workers continue cutting, afraid that signaling for the line to stop will cost them their jobs. Workers sometimes commit horrifying cruelties for the sake of keeping the line moving. For instance, at one slaughterhouse in Colorado, a cow got her leg caught in some machinery. Workers responded by cutting off her leg—while she was fully conscious.[92]

Slaughterhouses commonly get away with abusing animals because many USDA staffers are loath to get tough with the plants they supervise. On this matter, the *Post* article reported the story of Tim Walker, who was employed by the USDA as an animal health technician. While on assignment to monitor a Florida beef-packer, Walker frequently witnessed cattle being butchered while still alive. According to Walker, his superiors at the USDA didn't want to hear about it. Walker says, "I complained to everyone—I said, 'Lookit, they're skinning live cows in there.' Always it was the same answer: 'We know it's true. But there's nothing we can do about it.' "[93]

Walker filed several complaints about the situation, and his efforts to expose the facility cost him his job. His dismissal letter claimed that his actions had "irreparably damaged" the USDA's relationship with the slaughterhouse.[94]

Slaughter Speeds in America

Every slaughterhouse is capable of properly stunning 100 percent of the cattle it handles. A proper stun can be guaranteed if slaughterhouses operate at reasonable speeds and feature appropriate kill floor design, equipment, training, and supervision. Moreover, botched stuns cannot happen without everybody on the kill floor knowing exactly what's going on. So there is no reason, and no excuse, for a conscious steer to be sent down the meat-cutting line.

Yet reports continue of live cattle being cut apart. The underlying problem is that slaughter rates on kill floors have relentlessly increased over the past century. In the early 1970s, the largest slaughterhouses killed about 170 cattle an hour.[95] Today, the fastest American slaughterhouses kill 400 cattle per hour on each line they operate.[96] That means that every nine seconds, the pistol crew must shoot another animal between the eyes. At these speeds, mistakes are bound to occur. Compare the American situation to that of Europe, where cattle slaughterhouses run at only about sixty animals per hour.[97]

Given the speeds at which American slaughterhouses operate, there are only two ways that proper stunning practices can be assured: either slow the lines, or add multiple stunning stations to each line. The cost of proper stunning is trivial—it would cost no more than fifty cents per animal to guarantee that every steer receives an appropriate stun.[98]

The beef industry continually claims that it cares about animal welfare, but its leadership has not acted accordingly. The National Cattlemen's Beef Association has not yet demanded rigorous enforcement of the Humane Slaughter Act and harsh penalties for violations. The Cattlemen's refusal to show leadership on this matter is bound to become increasingly costly as time goes by. Until the day comes when strict industry-wide measures are in place to ensure that all cattle receive proper stuns, the beef industry will have a shameful secret that activists must expose at every opportunity.

Chapter 3

Possibilities for Reform in Animal Agriculture

Nothing would spare so many animals from harm as a spirited national debate about whether people have the moral right to raise and slaughter animals for food. If this question could attract even half the attention that the media constantly heaps upon meaningless stories about celebrities, a substantial portion of the public would quickly embrace veganism. I truly believe that one day the cruelties associated with animal agriculture will win intense and sustained national exposure, and that America's eating habits will thereafter change rapidly. But at the moment, it's still foolishly optimistic to believe that such a change will occur in the immediate future. So what can be done in the meantime, to protect as many animals as possible?

One effective way to reduce farmed animal suffering is to publicize the most egregious and widespread cruelties and to call for rapid reform. The general public may not yet be ready to rise up against animal agriculture, but even the most enthusiastic meat eater would surely agree that many of the abuses pointed out in the previous chapter need to be halted.

This chapter will look at the possibilities for welfare reform. We'll see what reforms are capable of accomplishing. And, just as importantly, we'll identify specific injustices that are inherent

49

in animal agriculture, which no amount of reform can remove. A good starting point for analyzing the potential of reforms is to investigate how much killing could be removed from animal agriculture. For instance, would it be possible to restructure the egg and dairy industries so that the animals are raised in comfortable conditions and are never sent to slaughter?

We'll see in this chapter that slaughter-free egg and dairy industries are indeed possible, but they would be tremendously wasteful of resources, and therefore outrageously expensive to run. It's nevertheless enlightening to examine how and where this waste would occur. As we look at the inefficiencies that would emerge, we will gain a basis for understanding why current alternatives to factory farms, such as free-range chicken farms and organic dairies, leave much to be desired when it comes to animal welfare.

Later in this book, we'll look at how activists can pressure industry to enact the most urgently needed welfare reforms. But before we do that, let's look at how slaughter is intertwined not just with meat production, but also with dairy products and eggs.

Slaughter-Free Eggs

The egg industry could operate without killing birds, but the costs would be immense. Remember that half of all layer chicks are males. Each of these males could typically live five to eight years, requiring care and taking up space, but providing nothing in return. During this time, each rooster would eat more than a thousand pounds of grain.[1] That's not exactly chickenfeed.

Additionally, refusing to kill aging layer hens would impose even more waste. Most commercial hens are slaughtered at just under two years of age because their egg production is by then in steep decline.[2] Hens do lay some eggs after the age of two, but without forced molting, the output is tiny. And even with forced molting, egg yields decline with each new laying cycle.[3]

Beyond the increased feed and housing costs we've just looked at, there would be other expenses necessary to achieve a cruelty-free egg industry. Battery cages would have to be eliminated, with the birds receiving both indoor and outdoor space to perch, forage, and nest. There would also be problems stemming from genetics to overcome. Modern layers are fantastically productive, but they suffer numerous health problems that rarely afflicted traditional breeds of hens. It would therefore be desirable to switch away from modern high-yield varieties and toward less-productive but healthier breeds. Finally, we should also assume that there would be some degree of individualized veterinary care introduced, particularly for older hens.

While it is indeed possible to concoct a cruelty-free, slaughter-free egg industry, doing so would be terribly wasteful of natural resources, while also demanding substantially more human labor. The resultant eggs would carry outrageous price tags—probably more than a dollar per egg.[4]

In light of the massive expenses that a slaughter-free egg farm would generate, it's worth looking at the "free-range" egg industry that exists today. Free-range eggs are relatively inexpensive, selling for about twenty-five cents each.[5] The main reason why these eggs are affordable is that free-range egg farmers make no attempt to eradicate slaughter from their business model. In fact, free-range egg farms typically buy their layer chicks from the same hatcheries that supply large commercial egg farms. These hatcheries sell only female layer chicks, killing the males. So right from the start, we see that free-range egg farms are as culpable as factory farms when it comes to the slaughter of male chicks. Additionally, just like conventional egg farms, virtually all free-range egg farms send their hens to slaughter at an early age. Since free-range farms have higher shelter costs, they are under greater financial pressure to keep only the most productive hens.

Making matters worse, there are no meaningful U.S. government standards that define what can be considered free-range.[6] So long as the chickens are permitted outdoors, they can be called free-range, no matter how intolerable their conditions may be.

While most free-range hens live in markedly better environments than their factory farm counterparts, there are still many free-range facilities that have substandard conditions. The only way to determine how the hens at a given facility are treated is to pay the farm a visit. Even for farms that offer good conditions, it's important to remember that every single free-range egg comes from a chicken who is destined for the slaughterhouse.

Slaughter-Free Dairies

If the cost of producing eggs without resorting to slaughter seems exorbitant, it nevertheless pales beside the expense of producing slaughter-free milk. Let's now turn to the grim economic realities a dairy would face if it refused to send cows to the slaughterhouse. By briefly discussing why slaughter-free dairies are economically infeasible, I hope to shed additional light on the overall welfare problems confronting both organic and conventional dairies.

Most dairy cows today are slaughtered by their sixth birthday. But at a dairy that refused to send its animals to slaughter, most cows would live about twenty years.[7] To minimize the enormous resources that a slaughter-free dairy system would require, you would need to keep the number of calves being born to a minimum, while getting as much milk as possible from each cow. But that's the catch, since to maximize a cow's milk production, you've got to put her through as many pregnancies as possible.

The only sensible response, therefore, would be to impose a breeding limit of two calves per cow. Since the cow's milk yield reaches its peak during her first two lactations, this two-calf strategy would ensure the greatest possible milk yield per pregnancy. The females born under this system would ultimately grow into mature dairy cows. The males, however, would be dead weight— each male calf imposing a continual and massive drain on resources for twenty years or more.[8]

You can see why a slaughter-free dairy system is ludicrous in terms of economics. For every two years that a cow produces milk, you would have to support her in retirement, as well as her prodigal son, each taking up valuable grazing land for more than twenty years while providing nothing in return. With this resource wastage taken into consideration, a slaughter-free dairy industry would require roughly *twenty times* more land and resources in order to produce the same amount of milk as a traditional dairy.[9]

In any natural foods store, you can buy organic milk for less than twice the price of conventional milk.[10] The good thing about organic milk is that the cows receive better feed, and perhaps better care, than cows at conventional dairies. Most organic milk comes from cows who are allowed to graze for at least half the year. But there's no guarantee that organic milk is the product of higher welfare standards. In fact, it's possible to operate an organic dairy in which the cows are never let outdoors. And even the best organic milk cannot be considered cruelty-free. Every drop of organic milk comes from a cow who is destined for the slaughterhouse. Finally, just as with regular dairies, the male offspring of organic dairy cows are routinely sold to veal farms.

The Ethical Shortcomings of Free-Range Eggs and Organic Milk

Free-range eggs and organic milk can offer significant advantages in terms of animal welfare. But, as we've just seen, there is no cost-effective method for producing eggs and dairy products without slaughtering the animals involved. In fact, animal slaughter is the primary reason that eggs and dairy products remain competitively priced with vegan foods. The slaughter of unproductive animals dramatically reduces expenses while simultaneously generating additional revenue from the meat that is produced.

Organic dairies and free-range egg farms never seem to volunteer the fact that they rely on killing every bit as much as their factory farm counterparts. Consumers who avoid conventional dairy products in favor of organic are nonetheless still subsidizing somebody else's veal and hamburger. And for every 350 free-range eggs purchased, a male layer chick and a "spent" layer hen go to slaughter.[11]

For anyone opposed to the slaughter of healthy animals, free-range eggs and organic milk will never be acceptable food choices. That said, many people aren't troubled by animal slaughter, but passionately object to cruelty. For people who feel this way, patronizing free-range egg farms and organic dairies can make a difference on at least two levels. Purchase of these foods supports forms of animal agriculture that are less exploitive, and customers of these industries can be especially influential in urging the enactment of meaningful welfare standards.

Industry Reactions to Welfare Reform Proposals

Although welfare reforms can never take the killing out of animal agriculture, there are many possible reforms that could ease suffering in important ways. Some reforms would demand significant expense, which industry would understandably resist. For example, there's no way we can expect the egg industry to cooperate in getting rid of battery cages.

But not all potential welfare improvements are costly, and it's disturbing to see how vigorously the industry fights off reforms regardless of their expense. Over the past few decades, industry has consistently fought tooth-and-nail against even the cheapest and most urgently needed initiatives. Perhaps industry fears a slippery slope—that by implementing inexpensive reforms they will hasten the day when the public will demand comprehensive improvements in farmed animal welfare.

While suffering will always be part of animal agriculture, some of the worst cruelties can be removed at little cost. The industry could, if it chose, quickly enact the following five steps:

- Provide either prompt veterinary care or euthanasia to all downer cows and pigs.

- Kill all male layer chicks using a gas other than carbon dioxide.

- Rigorously improve standards for stunning poultry and livestock at slaughterhouses.

- Ban farrowing and gestation crates for breeder sows.

- Provide local anesthetic to calves and piglets prior to castration.

These reforms would not come close to wiping out all abuses occurring in animal agriculture, but they would be an inexpensive way to eliminate several of the most widespread cruelties. Yet even basic reforms like these are scorned by the industry. To get a sense of how hostile animal agriculture is to welfare reform efforts, let's look at how the industry has responded to the first reform on my list, which would mandate veterinary care or euthanasia for downed farm mammals.

Downed Animal Reform Efforts

For almost twenty years, Gene Bauston of Farm Sanctuary has witnessed industry's hostility toward reform. Since the late 1980s, he has worked full-time to diminish cruelty in animal agriculture. He has participated in dozens of campaigns pertaining to the treatment of farmed animals. And the centerpiece of his work is the struggle to outlaw the abandonment of downer animals.

Downer animals are the cattle, sheep, and pigs who collapse from poor health and are too weak to get back on their feet. Despite their inability to stand, many of these animals are not as desperately ill as they appear. A high percentage of these animals could recover if given appropriate veterinary care. And for some of these animals, all that's needed for recovery is rest, shade, and water. But, all too often, these basic needs are withheld, and the animal is abandoned to suffer a lingering death.

Bauston learned of the downer problem during a 1986 visit to the East Coast's largest stockyard.[12] On a pile of carcasses made up of animals who died during transport to the auction, he and his wife Lorri discovered a lamb who had been left overnight but was nevertheless still alive. They pulled her off the pile and drove her to the local veterinarian's office. She was back on her feet fifteen minutes later, and all it took to accomplish this was a vitamin shot and some water. Gene and Lorri named this animal Hilda, and they cared for her for twelve years, until she died of old age.

Bauston's experience with Hilda inspired him to look more closely at downed animal abandonment. He began visiting factory farms and stockyards several times each month, and quickly caught onto the magnitude of the problem. He told me, "Visit any stockyard, any dairy, or any pig farm, and you're likely to encounter at least one downer animal on the premises. Many times, these animals are dragged off to a corner and left to die, and are not even provided with water. On a number of occasions, I've even seen conscious animals shackled by one leg and dragged into dumpsters."

Many thousands of cattle become downers every year—the only credible estimate I've found puts the number at 195,000.[13] And while that's a huge number, it's still only about 1 percent of all the cattle slaughtered annually in America. If livestock producers were serious about rooting out needless cruelty, downed animal reform would be an obvious place to start. The cost of promptly euthanizing downer animals is negligible, and doing so would save vast numbers of animals from protracted agony.

Unfortunately, every attempt to address the downed animal problem has been derailed by factory farming interests. Meat industry lobbying of Congress has created an imposing barrier to anti-downer legislation. The House Agriculture Committee is made up of Congresspeople from the country's top agriculture states. Before an agriculture-related bill can make it to the House Floor for a vote, the Agriculture Committee must first approve it.

Invariably, Committee members receive substantial campaign contributions from the top meat and poultry companies. In consequence, there is no place on this Committee for acts of conscience.

The Committee consistently does the bidding of factory farming interests, and shoots down any bills intended to promote animal welfare. Despite the Agriculture Committee's power, Bauston has refused to give up on seeking anti-downer legislation. New York Congressman Gary Ackerman has championed Bauston's efforts. On seven different occasions between 1991 and 2003, Congressman Ackerman authored downed animal reform bills for consideration by the House of Representatives. But each time these bills were submitted, they were quashed by the Agriculture Committee.

Bauston's take on the matter is that, "Animal protection efforts are being stonewalled by the meat industry. If something as cheap and urgently needed as downer reform is being kept from becoming law, you can imagine the dim prospects that exist for remedying other abuses inflicted upon farmed animals."

Common Farming Exemptions

Although poultry and livestock interests wield enormous influence in Congress, their clout on the state level is even more striking. Attorney David J. Wolfson has become an authority on how state laws have shifted to exempt factory farms from being held accountable for animal cruelty.[14] Wolfson has uncovered a specific type of legislation that has been cropping up across the country. He calls this legislation Common Farming Exemptions (CFEs).

The majority of states have put CFE laws on their books. Fourteen of these states enacted CFEs since 1990, all of which carry similar language. Using words like "common," "customary," "accepted," and "established," CFE laws allow any method of raising farmed animals to continue, no matter how cruel, so long as it is commonly practiced within the industry.

Nevada's law is representative of how CFE legislation is written. Under the Nevada CFE, the state's welfare laws cannot be enforced to "...prohibit or interfere with established methods of animal husbandry including the raising, handling, feeding, housing, and transporting, of livestock or farm animals."[15]

Prior to the introduction of CFEs, it was primarily up to state courts to decide what kinds of farmed animal treatment deserved to be outlawed. CFEs have stripped state courts of this responsibility, making the industry's most inhumane practices exempt from state cruelty laws. According to David Wolfson:

> CFEs give complete power to the farming community to decide what is cruelty to a farmed animal. If the industry adopts a practice it automatically becomes legal, and farmers cannot be prosecuted for cruelty, no matter how horrific the practice.[16]

By lobbying on both the federal and state levels, factory farm interests deliver a devastating one-two punch against welfare reform. The industry uses its influence to thwart passage of even the most basic federal protections for animals, as evidenced by the repeated torpedoing of Gary Ackerman's downed animal protection bills. Meanwhile, industry lobbyists have been systematically working on a state-by-state basis to enact CFEs—and, by doing so, they are rolling back the already meager protections that exist for farmed animals.

Reform and Beyond

There will always be violence inherent in factory farming that reform cannot address. Many cruel farming practices deliver such great efficiencies that calling for their reform is tantamount to demanding the annihilation of factory farming. And, if factory farming is eliminated, the price of animal products will rise markedly.

Activists need to embrace reform even though it is limited in what it can accomplish. As this chapter has shown, many of animal agriculture's most widespread cruelties lack any reasonable justification. Specifically, this chapter presented five reforms that would—at small expense—ease the suffering of billions of farmed animals. Poultry and livestock producers have always fought furiously against all such reforms. The good news is that, to the degree that animal agriculture publicly opposes the most cheap and reasonable welfare reforms, the industry will inflict long-lasting damage to its reputation.[17] As time goes by, the industry's efforts to block reform are likely to inspire increasing numbers of consumers to reduce or eliminate their consumption of animal products.

Welfare reform is only the start of what is possible in terms of protecting farmed animals. Part Two of this book looks at current activist efforts, and identifies areas be that can be expanded or improved. As bad as things are for farmed animals today, there is good reason for hope and optimism.

Part II

Dismantlement

"When the time comes for the world to be helped, some people are given the will, the wisdom, and the power to make great changes."— Sri Nisargadatta Maharaj

Chapter 4

The Movement's Scorecard

Part One of this book looked at the desperately unhappy situation confronting today's farmed animals. The question now turns to what can be done on their behalf.

There is great reason to be excited about recent advances made for farmed animals, and the accompanying shift in public opinion about how animals deserve to be treated. A Gallup Poll released in May 2003 found that 96 percent of Americans believe that animals deserve some protection from harm and exploitation.[1] And 62 percent of Americans favor the passage of strict laws protecting the welfare of animals raised on farms.[2]

Improved attitudes toward animals have led to progress on many fronts. The fur industry has been severely weakened by the work of animal activists.[3] Seventeen cities, out of concerns over cruelty, have banned circuses that feature animals. And between 1990 and 2003, voters passed seventeen of the twenty-three animal welfare initiatives that were put on state ballots. These ballot initiatives have delivered some of the most strategically significant victories yet won by animal protectionists. Meanwhile, penalties for animal cruelty are becoming more widely enforced. The year 1999 marked the first time that factory farm workers received felony-level indictments for animal cruelty.[4] And in 2002, three men pleaded guilty to felony animal abuse charges for torturing a calf to death.[5] This case set another encouraging legal precedent:

in addition to the felonies, the men were also convicted of misdemeanor offenses for tormenting the calf in front of his mother,
thereby inflicting psychological distress on the cow.

As efforts intensify to protect animals through legislation, activists will be in a position to win substantial gains. One of the
most hopeful developments on this front is that animal protection
is becoming a popular field of study for future lawyers. In 1990,
animal law was taught at just two schools in America. By 2004,
at least twenty U.S. law schools were offering classes related to
animal protection. With increasing numbers of young lawyers deciding to specialize in animal law, the future for farmed animals
is bound to grow brighter.

Organizations like People for the Ethical Treatment of Animals
(PETA) and Farm Sanctuary, neither of which existed before the
1980s, now have tens of thousands of active members and assets
in the millions. Meanwhile, traditional animal protection groups
like HSUS and the ASPCA* have begun addressing farmed animal
issues—an area they once largely ignored. And the financial resources of these groups have grown significantly. Assets of HSUS
and the ASPCA grew about tenfold between 1982 and 2002.[6]

While animal protection groups are growing in size and influence, the natural foods industry is knocking down the barriers
that keep people from becoming vegan. It's constantly getting easier to eat a cruelty-free diet. Prior to the 1990s, becoming vegan
required a great deal of effort, since there were few vegan cookbooks and only a slim assortment of vegan convenience foods. But
today, there are well over a hundred exclusively vegan cookbooks,
and the market for vegan convenience foods has become crowded
with fantastic products. The natural foods industry in the United
States is witnessing incredible gains. Sales have jumped almost
fivefold between 1996 and 2002, and growth shows no signs of
slowing.[7] One reason for this rapid growth is the spread of natural foods stores nationwide. The largest U.S. retailer of natural

---

*The Humane Society of the United States and the American Society for the
Prevention of Cruelty to Animals.

foods, Whole Foods Market, started with one store in 1980 and grew to 147 stores by 2004.[8]

The burgeoning market for vegetarian foods has prompted the food industry's largest companies to invest heavily. In 1999, Kraft Foods purchased Boca Burger, and Kellogg's bought analog meat producer Worthington Foods. Soymilk has become so popular that it is now carried in just about every supermarket in America, and it's also available at Starbucks coffeehouses. Perhaps the biggest coup for convenient meatless eating came in 2002, when Burger King began selling the BK Veggie sandwich in all eight thousand of its U.S. restaurants.

The word "vegan," which was recently as obscure as any word in the dictionary, has come into widespread use. Celebrities like Kim Basinger and Alicia Silverstone have talked about their vegan diets on The Late Show and The Tonight Show. In the music world, platinum-selling musicians such as Prince and Moby have come forward as outspoken vegans. Congressman Dennis Kucinich, a Democratic candidate during the 2004 presidential primaries, is a longtime vegan who has drawn fresh attention to the diet.

Trends in U.S. Meat Consumption

Considering the developments that have occurred in recent years, it might seem as though farmed animal protection efforts are on an unstoppable roll. But the only way to maintain such optimism is to ignore the one statistic that matters most: the amount of meat eaten per person in the United States. That quantity has been steadily on the rise, despite the best efforts of the animal protection movement. In 2002, America's meat and poultry consumption hit an all-time high of 219 pounds per person.[9] American slaughterhouses killed 9.15 billion animals in 2003, up from 3.36 billion animals in 1975.[10]

But aren't there at least a higher percentage of vegetarians and vegans in America today than ever before? This would seem a reasonable expectation, given the increasing visibility of vegetarian options in America. Unfortunately, surveys don't indicate that any substantial progress has been made in convincing Americans to stop eating animal products. The most reliable figures show that, since the 1980s, there has been hardly any increase in the percentage of Americans who are vegetarian or vegan.[11]

It's an incredibly discouraging situation. Every year, the animal protection movement grows larger and richer. Meanwhile, increasing numbers of delicious vegan foods continually come to market, obliterating any excuses that a vegan diet is hard to follow. Yet each year, the number of animals slaughtered sets a new record. Even in regard to welfare issues, the situation has deteriorated in several respects. Since the start of the modern animal protection movement in the mid-1970s, factory farming's grip on animal agriculture has tightened with each passing year.

None of this analysis is intended to belittle the efforts of people who work to keep animals from harm. If the modern animal protection movement had not come into existence, conditions for farmed animals would doubtless be even worse than they are today. But we owe it to the animals to continually assess the work done on their behalf, and to come up with ever-improving ways to make a difference. The sad but painfully obvious truth is that the modern animal protection movement has, so far, utterly failed in its three most important tasks:

- Increasing the percentage of Americans who are vegetarian or vegan.

- Encouraging nonvegetarians to reduce their consumption of meat, dairy products, and eggs.

- Diminishing the suffering of farmed animals.

I am convinced that these failures can be halted. By looking at how the animal protection movement has evolved since the 1970s, it's possible to determine where the movement has gone off course. We need to understand where mistakes were made and take corrective action where appropriate. The remainder of this book will analyze what has gone wrong with the animal protection movement, and how we can remedy the situation. We'll see how the movement could restructure itself to maximize its ability to protect farmed animals and to inspire rapid social change.

Chapter 5

The Three Existing Movements for Animal Protection

Animal agriculture can be likened to a giant. It is simply too big and strong for any one approach to defeat. Fortunately, there are three different movements—vegetarian, animal rights, and animal welfare—that work to protect farmed animals. Together, these three movements work like tag-team wrestlers. Each of these movements undermines animal agriculture in a unique way, and specializes in exploiting a different vulnerability.

The Vegetarian Movement

The first wrestler animal agriculture must confront is the vegetarian movement. One of the meat industry's greatest strengths is that most Americans have no idea how easy it is to switch to a vegetarian or vegan diet. Animal products are heavily embedded in our culture, from television commercials to restaurant meals to cookbooks. To most Americans, veganism seems as though it would require tremendous amounts of will and self-denial.

Into this gulch of misperception steps the vegetarian movement, which organizes dinners, distributes advocacy materials, and lines up presentations by public speakers. The vegetarian movement breaks through the isolation and worries that a person can experience when contemplating a change of diet. Vegetarian societies publicize the numerous advantages of becoming vegetarian, and bring people together to socialize and to encourage each other. Many long-time vegans owe their first exposure to the diet to their local vegetarian societies. These organizations help to make vegetarianism fun, accessible, and easy.

The Animal Rights Movement

Our next wrestler in this tag-team match is equally formidable. Animal agriculture owes its continued existence to the widespread belief that it is morally acceptable to raise animals for human food. The animal rights movement counters this belief with an extraordinarily persuasive set of philosophical arguments. The modern animal rights movement is heavily indebted to Peter Singer's book, *Animal Liberation,* which has to date sold more than half a million copies.

Singer, who holds an endowed professorship at Princeton University's Center for Human Values, has provided compelling and rigorously thought out arguments about the immorality of animal agriculture. They center on the fact that, like humans, farmed animals are capable of experiencing pain and discomfort. Under Singer's utilitarian-based philosophy, any pleasure that humans derive from eating animal products is surely offset by the pain and discomfort that animals suffer to produce these foods. Given that a terrific variety of vegan foods is available, including not just convenience foods but also extravagant gourmet options, Singer holds that there's no ethical reason for consuming animal products.

One of the best things that can happen to farmed animals is when people start questioning the morality of raising animals for food. The animal rights movement inspires vast numbers of people to ponder the ethical implications of animal farming. Moreover, the movement is blessed with a range of arguments that are beautifully constructed and difficult to refute.

The Animal Welfare Movement

The third wrestler against that animal agriculture must contend is animal welfare. The goal of welfare efforts is to eliminate cruel farming practices.

Activists have made astounding progress by pushing for animal welfare. In 1994, the late Henry Spira successfully pressured the USDA to drop its requirement for face-branding cattle imported from Mexico. In 2001, PETA and others successfully convinced the top three burger chains to issue new animal welfare guidelines to their suppliers. And in 2002, Farm Sanctuary and the HSUS spearheaded a ballot initiative that banned the use of gestation crates at Florida's pig farms.

These achievements are only the start of what is possible, and the great potential of animal welfare is still largely untapped. Right now, in regard to welfare concerns, America's meat eaters are sitting on the sidelines. We need to get them involved.

One of the most unpleasant realizations I've had during my years in animal protection is that most Americans are simply unwilling to stop eating meat. They will often listen closely to the arguments supporting vegetarianism, but they will not change their diets. Despite this, most of these people do care about what happens to animals, and adamantly oppose cruelty. You won't find many nonvegetarians joining vegetarian societies or sending money to animal rights groups. But animal welfare is the one cause that everyone can get behind, regardless of diet. I think that anyone who eats meat, yet opposes cruelty to animals, faces a moral imperative to become involved in seeking welfare reforms.

Many factory farming reforms are initiated by animal rights-oriented groups. The welfare movement will truly realize its potential when it inspires the country's meat eaters to become active in seeking reform. When the day comes that the nation's meat eaters demand better farmed animal welfare, enormous improvements will happen overnight.

Limitations of the Three Movements

Each of the three movements we've just looked at carries unique strengths, and each plays a vital part in the struggle for animal protection. We have a vegetarian movement that awakens the public to the benefits of meat-free eating, and helps people to make the switch. We've got an animal rights movement that inspires people to question the ethics of eating animals. And last, we have a welfare movement that anyone can become involved with, to remove some of the cruelty from animal agriculture.

Yet animal agriculture is so big and powerful that it can probably survive the threats posed by these three movements. I therefore propose that an all-new fourth movement is necessary. And with four different movements on our tag-team, animal agriculture will ultimately fall.

I will devote the next chapter to introducing the fourth movement and explaining why it's necessary. But first, let's revisit the vegetarian, welfare, and rights movements. We've so far examined the strengths of each of these movements. Now, let's look at their weaknesses. An examination of these weaknesses will reveal why a fourth movement is so urgently needed.

Limitations of the Vegetarian Movement

The vegetarian movement, as it currently exists, is weak in two areas. One of these areas could easily be strengthened, while the other cannot.

The first weakness—the one that could readily be addressed—pertains to the arguments the movement makes to support vegetarian and vegan eating. Most of the best-selling vegetarian advocacy books published since the 1970s have devoted about equal space to the issues of health, the environment, and the animals. In consequence, when creating outreach materials, vegetarian societies usually give these three areas equal amounts of attention. Unfortunately, many of the health and environmental arguments presented in the movement's literature are of questionable accuracy.

For the vegetarian movement to gain credibility and persuasiveness, its leaders need to take a second look at the issues of health and the environment. Appendices A through D offer a lengthy examination of the health and environmental impacts of our food choices. The conclusion I draw in the appendices is that the vegetarian movement would do well to reduce the attention it gives to health and environmental concerns. There's no need for vegetarian advocates to renounce all claims regarding health and the environment, but these arguments need to be made with great care and they should be tailored to specific food choices and diets. With these appendices in mind, vegetarian activists can reshape their outreach arguments to achieve greater credibility.

The second weakness in the vegetarian movement is unlikely to be adequately addressed: the fact that most vegetarian groups emphasize celebration over action. One of the great strengths of the vegetarian movement is that it puts a friendly face on the idea of eliminating animal products from the diet. Around the country, most vegetarian groups are geared toward organizing social activities—potlucks, outings, turkey-free Thanksgiving celebrations, and so forth.

Every town needs a strong, vibrant vegetarian society. The situation confronting farmed animals no doubt improves whenever people gather to extol nonviolent eating. But there is only so much that can be accomplished through celebration. While vegetarian groups are terrific at organizing social events, they tend to be fundamentally unsuited to carrying out work that is more action oriented. It's not that vegetarian groups should be done away with—far from it!—but rather that they should be joined by groups that take a more activist role in undercutting the strengths of animal agriculture.

Limitations of the Animal Rights Movement

To the extent that the public understands animal rights philosophy, that understanding is probably embodied by the PETA slo-
gan: "Animals are not ours to eat, wear, experiment on, or use for
entertainment."

There are certainly activists who agree wholeheartedly with
this absolutist position. But the movement's literature actually
includes a number of books that take a more nuanced view of
matters. Chief among these is Singer's *Animal Liberation,* as well
as his other writings. Grounded in utilitarianism, Singer's philosophy seeks to shape a world with the least amount of suffering.
Doing so means paying attention to the times when the interests
of people come into conflict with the well-being of nonhuman animals. And nowhere is the conflict so evident than on the subject
of using animals for medical research.

Contrary to the views advanced in some animal rights literature, there are indeed occasions when animal testing can produce significant reductions in human suffering.* In consequence,
not all activists dismiss the use of animals in medical testing as
inherently immoral. Under Singer's philosophy, for example, it
would be morally desirable to painlessly kill a thousand mice if
the knowledge gained would spare tens of thousands of humans
from an agonizing death. Naturally, animal testing rarely produces such clear-cut results, and it's commendable that animal
rights philosophers wade into these murky waters in an attempt
to distinguish right from wrong.

Singer and other ethicists deserve enormous credit for looking
carefully at complicated issues like animal testing, and for crafting
sophisticated analysis rather than spouting simpleminded dogma.
Unfortunately, no good deed goes unpunished, and the general
public cannot be expected to read this material. As far as the
public is concerned, all animal rights activists are dead-set against

---

*Appendix G covers the ethical and practical issues surrounding animal-
based research.

any form of animal use, regardless of how little or how much humans stand to benefit.

All this makes animal rights philosophy poison when it comes to publicly debating animal agriculture. The battleground for public opinion is radio, television, and newspapers. None of these forums provides opportunity for protracted debate. When animal defenders and livestock producers trade jabs before the public or are quoted in articles, neither side has the opportunity to develop a sustained and coherent argument. All the public hears are sound bites. And it is here that the comprehensive nature of animal rights philosophy becomes a terrible liability for the defenders of farmed animals.

Time and again, in public debates, factory farm interests have been able to wrest the discussion away from the brutal practices of animal agriculture. The focus of debate is continually pushed into the thorniest thickets of animal rights philosophy. Activists are then left with the unenviable task of explaining why they are against animal testing, which could produce treatments for diseases that are currently incurable.

By all rights, factory farm representatives should constantly be forced onto the defensive during debates. At every turn, activists should demand agriculture interests to account for the suffering that occurs on factory farms. Unfortunately, it's impossible to hold the spotlight on this cruelty when animal rights philosophy is involved in the argument. Representatives of animal agriculture are smart enough to continually drive the discussion away from the ten billion farmed animals who die each year, and toward the contradictions that arise from the public's simplistic understanding of animal rights.

Animal rights philosophy has much to say about the ethical questions that arise when the interests of humans and animals come into conflict. Unfortunately, animal rights has proven a poor debating tool where farmed animals are concerned. People working against animal agriculture should read deeply in the animal rights literature, but they must also be aware that the arguments under consideration are often too complex to be productively put before the public. The argument against factory farming needs to be simple, easily understood, and primarily focused on the miseries suffered by farmed animals. Farmed animal protectionists would therefore do well to avoid debating philosophy in public. Instead, the public should be given a far simpler argument—that animal agriculture is inherently cruel, is uniquely resistant to reform, and therefore ought to be eliminated.

When it comes to making the case against animal agriculture, animal rights is generally a counterproductive line of argument. The philosophy is too complex to quickly explain, and its comprehensiveness allows the exploiters of farmed animals to hijack and win vital debates that the industry would otherwise lose.

Limitations of the Animal Welfare Movement

Welfare reforms have arguably produced greater gains for farmed animals than anything initiated by the vegetarian or animal rights movements. Yet, for all its potential, there are still severe limitations to what can be accomplished by the welfare movement. Welfare reformers have limited resources, and must focus attention on animal agriculture's most indefensible cruelties. Such a triage system leaves lesser cruelties unaddressed.

It's true that, over time, the welfare movement will work its way down to eradicating lesser cruelties. The trouble is that animal agriculture is a moving target and is continually developing new methods for raising animals. If there's one thing we can be sure of, it's that the people who brought the world beak searing, gestation crates, and battery cages are certain to dream up comparably cruel innovations in the future. So, while welfare reformists busy themselves getting rid of the worst of today's cruelties, the industry is rapidly devising new practices for tomorrow. What's worse, the rollout of new practices is usually gradual, and it may be some time before new cruelties become widespread enough to gain the attention of welfare reformers.

The trouble with welfare reform is that it is always behind the curve. However effective welfare reform may be at gradually getting rid of existing cruelties, it will always be powerless to prevent new cruelties from emerging.

Building a Fourth Movement

The three movements we looked at in this chapter each play an indispensable role in farmed animal protection. Each of these movements is ultimately defensive in nature, working to undo long-established social patterns and industry practices. The vegetarian movement seeks to wean people away from a lifetime of animal-centered eating. The animal rights movement works to modify society's exploitive beliefs about animals. And the animal welfare movement, piece by piece, puts an end to some of the worst cruelties carried out by animal agriculture.

While these three movements provide an excellent and much-needed defense of farmed animals, not one of these movements delivers much in the way of an offense. I believe we urgently need an all-new movement expressly designed to identify and strip away the primary assets of animal agriculture. The surest way to eliminate animal agriculture's cruelties is to seek to eliminate animal agriculture itself. To accomplish this, we need a new movement expressly designed to go on the offensive, with the purpose of ushering animal agriculture out of existence. As we'll see in the next chapter, it's within our power to build such a movement. While animal agriculture surely can't be abolished overnight, we need to begin taking the first steps down that road.

A movement that strives to weaken and one day topple animal agriculture will perfectly complement the work already being done by the vegetarian, rights, and welfare movements. For the first time, the animal protection movement will have an offense as powerful as its defense. Now, let's look at how such a movement can be constructed.

Chapter 6

Creating a Dismantlement Movement

In the previous chapter, I argued that an all-new movement is necessary, one that is specifically designed to weaken and ultimately eliminate animal agriculture.

I call this new movement the dismantlement movement, and it is built upon an audacious premise—that activists are capable of banding together to undercut and ultimately eliminate the industry of animal agriculture. Even the most radical elements of the animal protection movement have never set an explicit goal to eliminate animal agriculture.[1] I think activists have kept quiet about this matter because nobody wants to appear out of touch with reality. But until we begin working toward the goal of ending animal agriculture, the fate of America's farmed animals will remain sealed. The ten billion farmed animals who die each year need us to be brave enough to begin a grand task—one that will likely take several generations to complete.

The name "dismantlement" carries with it the underlying mentality of how animal agriculture can be overcome. Dismantlement is a word lacking any implication of hysteria or violence. Rather, the word suggests that animal agriculture can be taken apart in the systematic manner of a mechanic disassembling an engine—thoughtfully, calmly, and one piece at a time. The remainder of this book introduces the main ideas behind dismantlement. Believe it or not, despite animal agriculture's size and strength, there is good reason to expect that a concerted effort could one day topple the industry.

Before we consider what the dismantlement movement could accomplish, there's one point I must make about the varieties of animal protection work. In this book, I have so far analyzed what I see as the three existing farmed animal protection movements. But despite my separate treatment of each, animal protectionists commonly disagree about what constitutes a movement and what constitutes a strategy. For instance, some activists have persuasively argued that welfare and rights efforts are really a single movement. For that matter, other activists believe there is only one movement protecting animals—under this thinking, efforts to defend farmed animals by promoting rights, welfare, and vegetarianism are different strategies within a single movement.

In this book, I presented rights, welfare, and vegetarian activism as distinct from one another because I believe separate descriptions are more easily understood. For the same reason, I will describe dismantlement as an independent movement. I expect that some readers will decide that the dismantlement movement I propose is really just a strategy that fits into the existing animal protection movement, and that's fine with me.

Whether dismantlement is ultimately considered a movement or a strategy matters little—my primary concern is that dismantlement's goals and ideas attract the attention of activists, and inspire new people to become involved in farmed animal protection. Now, with that digression behind us, let's begin our examination of dismantlement by looking at its one obvious historical counterpart.

Comparisons to Abolition

Today's efforts to dismantle animal agriculture will doubtless be frequently compared to the abolition movement of the nineteenth century. These movements invite comparison, since each was conceived in order to rid the world of an oppressive but socially entrenched institution. It's tempting to say that the dismantlement movement is merely the abolition movement reincarnated. But there are important differences between the two movements that activists must understand.

These differences are reflected in the names given to each movement. As its name suggests, the abolition movement was all about convincing a third party—the federal government—to intervene and abolish slavery.[2] Abolitionists could reasonably expect to win help from the federal government. People seeking to overcome animal agriculture, by contrast, should have no similar hopes. Animal agriculture is one of the most politically powerful business interests in America, and there's no possibility that lawmakers will rush to outlaw this industry. In consequence, we can't expect the government to take a leadership role in stamping out animal agriculture. So dismantlement relies, not on government, but on individuals and organizations to take action against animal agriculture.

In contrast to abolitionists, who often lacked means to strike at the roots of slavery, animal protectionists can accomplish a great deal without help from the government. There are dozens of legal and effective actions that anyone can take on behalf of farmed animals, and anybody who joins the struggle against animal agriculture can create enormous change. In the years ahead, the dismantlement movement will doubtless undercut many of animal agriculture's strengths. With enough organized efforts on the part of activists, animal agriculture will lose its grip on government decision-makers. At that point, the industry and its thousand cruelties can at last be toppled.

Stopping Short of Perfect

The dismantlement movement is sure to develop differently than the abolition movement, but the two movements are identical in one respect: neither movement seeks perfection as its ultimate goal.[3]

After the Civil War, black Americans suffered ongoing hardships that included segregation and employment discrimination. These and other injustices persisted for over a century, until the rise of the civil rights movement. Surely, much of this post-slavery oppression could have been foreseen by the abolition movement's leadership. Why, then, was their agenda so limited?

The limitations of abolition's agenda were not rooted in laziness or complacency. These limitations were in fact the cornerstone of a brilliant strategy. At the time, slavery constituted the single greatest abuse of blacks at the hands of whites. This abuse was rooted in the fact that many Americans viewed blacks as an inferior race, and would never accept the notion that blacks deserved social equality. Abolition's great achievement was to recognize that, no matter what your opinions about race, you didn't have to be terribly progressive in your thinking to view slavery as an abomination.

The key to abolition's success lay in confining its objective to weakening and overturning slavery, thereby maximizing the number of people who would participate. Asking nineteenth century Americans to accept a doctrine of racial equality would have been poison to the abolition movement. Many of the people who fought and died to end slavery held beliefs that would today be judged as racist.[4] But, under abolition, people did not have to buy into the idea of there being full equality between the races. Abolitionists asked only that Americans recognize slavery as a grotesque evil and take action to end it. With slavery out of the way, it was only a matter of time before more subtle forms of oppression would be exposed and stamped out. But before any of these other advances could occur, slavery first had to go.

Giving Animal Agriculture the Priority It Deserves

Just as slavery was once America's most pressing human rights violation, there can be no doubt that the effort to eliminate cruelty to animals should focus on agriculture. Animal agriculture accounts for more than 97 percent of animals killed by humans in the United States.[5] Farmed animals therefore deserve priority, and arguments made on their behalf should not be weakened by lumping in rhetoric pertaining to hunting, medical research, or companion animals.

We live in a world where the majority of people have a highly exploitive attitude toward animals. It's therefore of the greatest importance to convince the public that animal agriculture is a vicious industry, and that regardless of one's feelings about other forms of animal use, the situation regarding farmed animals is intolerable. By continually drawing attention back to the harsh nature of animal agriculture, we can maximize the number of people willing to take action.

The Civil War was fought and won largely by people with racist attitudes, who nevertheless viewed slavery as an affront to human decency. Similarly, by confining our rhetoric and action to overcoming the injustices of animal agriculture, we will enable as many people as possible to participate.[6]

Advantages of the Dismantlement Approach

Both the vegetarian movement and the dismantlement movement depend upon outreach and advocacy—the act of talking about the issues to friends, family, and anyone who will listen. The remainder of this book offers numerous ideas to make the vegetarian argument more honest and appealing. But I believe that even the best vegetarian arguments will never rival the persuasiveness of the dismantlement argument. That's because the vegetarian argument has a critical flaw built right into its structure. The trouble with the vegetarian argument is that its opening premise begins: "You need to change your diet, and here's why..."

There's practically no way to advocate vegetarianism without suggesting up front that big dietary changes are required. Most listeners therefore gain the impression that cruelty-free eating involves enormous self-sacrifice. Consequently, few people are able to give the argument for vegetarianism a fair hearing, since they are preoccupied with thoughts of how difficult the diet will be. In my own long experience as an activist, I've often found it impossible to adequately assure people that cutting animal products out of the diet is a relatively simple and even enjoyable affair.

Dismantlement detours around this roadblock by making its opening argument about the inherently cruel nature of animal agriculture. Rather than suggest people become vegetarian or vegan, dismantlement seeks only to arouse a personal disgust for animal agriculture and a commitment to help get rid of it. Accordingly, dismantlement offers a way of encouraging veganism that does not scare people off. Once the public understands that animal agriculture perpetuates confinement and cruelty, the task of inspiring dietary change will become easier. For anyone who agrees with the arguments presented for dismantlement, a commitment to activism and veganism is almost inevitable.

What's more, people who agree with dismantlement are *much* more likely to become involved with activism than are people who are merely vegetarian. And the greatest threat to animal agriculture is that the general public will get off the sidelines and take action against the industry. Animal agriculture takes a small hit whenever somebody becomes vegetarian or vegan, but the loss of one customer is something the industry can live with. What the industry won't be able to endure is a steady stream of new activists seeking to put an end to animal agriculture.

The Force of Ideas

Animal agriculture is an enormous industry, one that possesses nearly limitless resources to defend itself. Yet for all its strength, the industry is supremely vulnerable. In order for meat, milk, and egg prices to stay as low as they are, the industry must rely on a number of cruel farming practices. To the extent that activists expose this cruelty, public opinion will increasingly turn against animal agriculture.

Since we can't expect the government to take the lead in abolishing animal agriculture, we need to construct a movement that inspires people to join the struggle to end farmed animal exploitation. The key to winning over the public is to have an honest, accurate message that primarily emphasizes the ethical problems with animal agriculture.

Our success will depend upon attracting the widest possible variety of participants. Some people, many of whom eat meat, will get on board to stamp out specific cruelties. Meanwhile, other activists will work toward weakening and ultimately eliminating the industry. But inspiring people to join the struggle against animal agriculture is only half the job. The other half is to ensure that there are effective organizations available to utilize the talents and efforts of incoming activists. The next chapter will examine how dismantlement organizations ought to be set up and run, to ensure that animal agriculture's remaining years are as few as possible.

Chapter 7

Organizing for Dismantlement

Tolstoy famously wrote that happy families are essentially alike, while every unhappy family is unhappy for a different reason.[1] The same cannot be said for dysfunctional animal protection organizations. Throughout the movement, animal advocacy groups fail in a few maddeningly consistent ways. These points of failure have a common origin. America's animal protection movement is made up mainly of progressives—and progressives are generally lousy at building effective organizations.[2]

In the next three sections, we'll look at what I regard as the three most common pitfalls in animal protection organizations: hostility toward hierarchy, publicity campaigns that alienate the public, and the ineffective use of money. Fortunately, each of these problems, once understood, can be remedied.

Hostility Toward Hierarchy

It's axiomatic that violent, heartless people are often ruthlessly efficient at uniting and carrying out their goals.[3] Progressive organizations, by contrast, tend to be hotbeds of internal bickering and failed leadership. And animal protection groups seem especially prone to develop problems related to leadership and hierarchy. I suspect that these problems arise because leaders in the animal protection movement aren't drawn from the ranks of business schools and corporations. Rather, these people enter the movement because they are unusually sensitive to the plight of animals, and they feel compelled to take action. Unfortunately, compassion toward animals does not necessarily confer the ability to manage people. Many of the people who start animal protection organizations lack the leadership skills required to run them effectively.

Mistakes made in leadership are often compounded by mid-level staff. Progressives are often hostile to structures of power, and they don't take well to the role of being subordinates. I've witnessed a number of prominent animal protection groups that generated more drama than the most unhappy of Tolstoy's families. Ineffective organizations generally have two things in common: leadership that lacks appropriate management skills, and subordinates who create a poisonous environment of behind-the-scenes second-guessing.

Fortunately, there is no reason why dismantlement organizations must fall prey to poor leadership and divisiveness. It's certainly possible to create well-run organizations that protect farmed animals. Leaders must understand that their work requires more than just enormous concern about animal suffering. Anyone who aspires to leadership needs to become immersed in the literature of managing people. Management is a skill that can be learned. And while there are a few born leaders who come into any movement, most leaders need to devote significant time to working on their management abilities. An excellent starting point for dismantlement leaders is to read Peter Drucker's books on managing nonprofit organizations.*

Just as leaders need to devote serious attention to learning management skills, so too must subordinates sharpen their abilities to contribute. In the role of a subordinate, it's vital to carry

---

*See Appendix I for a list of recommended reading, which includes a book by Drucker on managing nonprofits.

out responsibilities faithfully and without ever undermining the group's leadership. Many smart and talented people are nevertheless deeply unsuited to working in this capacity. So the first requirement for anyone wanting to work for dismantlement is to carry out a personal assessment. For people who don't think that working within an organization is a good fit, there are countless ways to participate in dismantlement by working independently. The activist essays that appear later in this book cover many ways that each of us, working alone or in groups, can make a difference.

Publicity Campaigns That Alienate the Public

The animal protection movement has become notorious for engaging in publicity stunts that outrage the public. It's true that these flames, once sparked by animal protectionists, are skillfully fanned by animal agriculture interests. But it's also plainly evident that if the animal protection movement exercised greater care in presenting its message, animal agriculture would find it much more difficult to turn public opinion against us.

Oftentimes, animal protectionists present their message in a way that seems gratuitously provocative. Strident publicity campaigns are certainly effective at publicizing some forms of animal abuse, since a stinging message can attract attention to an issue that would otherwise be ignored. In the case of farmed animals, however, it's counterproductive to present the dismantlement message in a confrontational manner.

Dismantlement was conceived on the premise that the arguments against animal agriculture are persuasive enough to win over ever-larger portions of the population. There is consequently no need to pose these arguments in ways that antagonize the public. At the same time, it's important that activists don't present these arguments in a half-hearted manner. Finding a balance can be tricky—it's admittedly impossible for everyone to agree on which messages are too wimpy, and which are too provocative. But too many times, the message is needlessly confrontational.

The animal protection movement, specifically PETA,* consistently outrages large portions of the public by choosing bizarre and abrasive messages.

It's the primary task of a dismantlement organization to frame its message in a way that arouses public support. Choosing the right words requires a good deal of vigilance. It's easy and appropriate to feel anger and disgust for how animals are treated. But it's important to keep anger from entering into the argument for dismantlement. Shortly after I began my work of writing about farmed animals, I had a dream that I had nearly bitten off my tongue. The symbolism of this dream struck me as obvious: there are many totally correct statements regarding the exploitation of animals that should nevertheless go unspoken. Working for dismantlement means continually biting your tongue, and striving to communicate only the most persuasive of messages.

Ineffective Use of Money

Compared to what animal agriculture spends to promote its products, the budget of animal protection organizations amounts to pocket change. Vegan Outreach, one of the farmed animal protection movement's best-known organizations, spent just $194,000 in 2003.[4] Even PETA, the world's largest animal rights group, spent less than $22 million in 2003.[5] Compare these figures to the $100 million that Tyson Foods committed to marketing and promotions that same year.[6] Meanwhile, McDonald's spends more than a billion dollars annually on worldwide advertising.[7]

Fortunately, effective activism can be done on a shoestring budget. Volunteers can do things like leaflet, write letters to newspapers, and organize local vegetarian events. These and other efforts can accomplish a great deal for farmed animals, at trivial expense. Corporations that profit from animal agriculture may

---

*Despite PETA's kooky attention-grabbing public profile, the organization employs some of the best people in the movement. PETA has carried out a number of campaigns that have won substantial changes for animals—but unfortunately the public never hears a thing about PETA's best work, since it's all overshadowed by the group's publicity stunts.

be able to significantly outspend animal protection groups, but their money cannot neutralize the volunteer efforts of thousands of dedicated activists.

While low-budget activism is immensely important, there is no substitute for cash. We cannot expect to overcome animal agriculture without raising enormous amounts of money. This money will initially be needed primarily for outreach and publicity. As the movement gains supporters and begins posing a credible threat to animal agriculture, it will become prudent to shift expenditures to hiring state and federal lobbyists.

Raising large amounts of cash must become one of the main jobs of the dismantlement movement. At the same time, it is dishonorable to do fundraising for animals if the money will not be spent to the greatest possible effect. Many participants in the animal protection movement worry about outsized executive pay packages that bleed organizations of money that could be spent helping animals. And it's true that there are several groups that show little restraint in executive compensation. For instance, in 1998, HSUS paid their CEO $570,325 in salary, expenses, and retirement benefits.[8]

I'm of two minds about executive compensation. On the one hand, I hate to see salaries go well into six figures, especially given the relative scarcity of resources possessed by the animal protection movement. On the other hand, I think there are times when the movement gets its money's worth from its high salaries. The top earners often have law degrees, years of specialization, and the capacity to work to great effect on behalf of animals. Many of these people have children and student loans, and must live in expensive metropolitan areas to carry out their work. Without relatively large salaries, some remarkably effective people would not be able to work on behalf of animals.

Executive compensation is a complicated issue that resists easy answers, but it surely ought to be one metric used for deciding which groups to support. With just a bit of research, it's possible to find out which organizations pay unreasonably high salaries. Each year, *Animal People* publishes a guide to salaries paid out by the nation's animal protection groups.[9] Anybody donating substantial amounts of money to animal protection ought to review a copy of *Animal People's* salary report.

Despite the abuses in executive compensation, it is nevertheless vastly more important to prioritize quality leadership than it is to worry about pay levels. That's because executive salaries usually account for only a small portion of a group's budget. And without good leadership, organizations often misspend most of their money. Years ago, I witnessed a well-known vegetarian advocacy group blow several hundred thousand dollars on a project that accomplished virtually nothing for animals. There was no dishonesty or sleaziness underlying what happened. Rather, there was a total breakdown of leadership, and the installation of a project coordinator who was almost comically unsuited for the job. It pains me to think of all the good this money could have accomplished, had it been designated for an effective campaign.

There's no clear answer to how the movement's money ought to be spent, and how much of it ought to be paid out in salaries. But we can certainly draw inspiration from others who have come before us, and who have struggled to save as many lives as possible. Perhaps the most moving film scene that I've ever witnessed occurred at the end of "Schindler's List." The movie concerned Oskar Schindler, a corrupt and deeply flawed industrialist, who nevertheless assumed a personal mission to save as many Jews as possible from the Nazi death camps. During the last years of World War II, he was personally responsible for keeping hundreds of Jews from the gas chambers. At the movie's end, the allies liberate Nazi Germany, and Schindler is surrounded by loved ones who praise his dedication. Schindler nearly collapses at this moment, sobbing that for all he did, he could have done more. He takes a gold ring from his finger and says that, had he sold it, the money gained could have saved another Jew.

Schindler was perhaps correct on this point, since there is always more that one person can do, but this kind of thinking can lead to counterproductive absolutism. Had Schindler sold all his stylish clothes and jewelry and dressed like a pauper, he would never have been able shmooze the Nazis, and he would have lost his ability to spare Jews from the gas chambers. In certain circles, bearing some trappings of luxury is the price of admission to doing vital activism. That said, there have been many animal advocates who've bled the movement of resources for the sake of indulging in luxurious lifestyles. Maintaining an appropriate balance here is not difficult, however, as long as the animals' interests are kept continually in mind.

Investing in Dismantlement

One of the animal protection movement's main problems is that, once a group reaches a certain size, it becomes self-perpetuating regardless of whether or not it's effective. All it takes is a long list of past donors coupled with a decent-looking newsletter, and a group's long-term survival is all but certain. In this way, some large groups steadily drain the movement of cash, yet accomplish next to nothing for animals.

Large but poorly run groups survive because most donors have no idea how organizations spend their money. It can be exceedingly difficult for a small donor to judge which groups most deserve financial support. It's understandable that few people take the time to research the organizations they support. Most donors just send off their checks and keep their fingers crossed that the money will be spent wisely.

When assessing an organization, there are five qualities I pay attention to. I favor groups that:

- Shun violence and property destruction.

- Keep salaries at reasonable levels, with no outrageous perks.

- Maintain dignity at all times, and refuse to generate publicity likely to antagonize the public.

- Strive for honesty and accuracy in the advocacy materials they publish.

- When possible, avoid duplicating work done by other organizations.

Donating is, after all, simply a form of investing—with the payback being social progress rather than money. And just as stock investors generally get burned when they don't do their homework, so too is money usually wasted when it's donated carelessly. When contributing money to animal protection groups, it makes sense to employ the same screening processes that wise investors use to evaluate a company's stock. In both cases, you want to look at the organization's track record and learn what it's accomplished recently. You also need to look at the people running the organization and assess their abilities to produce results. Close attention should be given to finances—how much money is the organization taking in, and what is it doing with its money? These are all simple things to examine, and it's easier to identify a well-run nonprofit organization than it is to invest wisely in stocks.[10] But donors who don't look into an organization's performance create the same situation as investors who purchase stocks at random—in both cases, money is likely being thrown away.

Fortunately, most of the facts an informed donor needs are easily obtained. Every nonprofit organization publishes an annual report that summarizes accomplishments, fund raising, and spending. The annual report is an essential document for determining which groups are most deserving of your money.

Moving Forward

This chapter looked at the problems of organizational structure, publicity, and finance that have plagued animal protection organizations. Activists face a tough job in cleaning up poorly run groups. But since the dismantlement movement is just coming into existence, we have the opportunity to keep past mistakes from being repeated by new organizations.

Of course, dismantlement organizations must do more than avoid mistakes. The real work involves coming up with strategies and executing projects that accomplish the movement's goals. The next chapter looks at where animal agriculture is most vulnerable, and evaluates the opportunities that exist for taking action.

Chapter 8

The First Steps to Dismantlement

As effective dismantlement organizations come into existence, the question turns to what these groups should accomplish. There are countless tasks that organizations can perform to benefit farmed animals. But one job stands above all the rest—reaching out to attract new people into the movement.

Outreach deserves priority for a number of reasons. The work to dismantle animal agriculture is in its infancy, and it will be many years before we have the numbers needed to create substantial change. So our first task is to promote movement growth as quickly as possible. The place to start is by winning over people who are already committed to vegetarianism and animal protection. With that accomplished, we need to bring our outreach efforts to the general public. We must do everything possible to double in size, then double again, and then double yet again.

As our outreach efforts expand, farmed animals will benefit in a number of ways. Demand for animal products will decline with each person who enters the movement. And as the movement continues to grow, we will be gaining the workforce and money needed to launch ever more ambitious campaigns. Attracting new activists must be dismantlement's top priority. In order to overcome animal agriculture, it's going to take huge amounts of money and millions of hours of volunteer efforts. The number of Americans who are vegan or seriously opposed to animal agriculture is currently far too small to get the job done. But an aggressive and carefully planned outreach campaign could rapidly gain us the numbers we need.

Methods for Growth

With the need for attracting new activists established, the question turns to deciding which kinds of outreach deserve priority. The answer here is straightforward: the most productive outreach is that which involves young people. It makes sense to channel most of our outreach efforts toward high school and college audiences.

Young people are *much* more open to concerns about animal suffering than older people. When it comes to outreach, Abbie Hoffman's 1960s maxim, "Never trust anyone over thirty," could fairly be rewritten as, "Don't expect people over thirty to change their diets." Of course, people become vegan at all ages, but anybody who's been in the animal protection movement for any length of time has seen that younger people have fewer inhibitions about making dietary changes.

A look around the animal protection movement shows just how resistant older people are to making a change of diet. Over the years, I've been lucky enough to make friends with many of the movement's leaders. These people know the arguments for vegan eating better than anyone else, and you probably can't find a more persuasive or passionate group of activists anywhere. Yet practically none of these leaders have been successful in getting their parents to stop eating meat.

Young people, by contrast, are especially open to vegetarianism because they are at a stage in life when they are questioning the values under which they were raised. I believe that if the right information were sufficiently publicized, perhaps 10 percent of college students might soon take up the cause of dismantlement.

Unfortunately, even among young people, the effort required to inspire one person to action can be substantial. Some people need only see a few pictures, or read a brief article, and they are willing to come onboard. But others require a whole lot more convincing.

In my own activism, I'm willing to make an extended effort to convince someone, but only if there are good prospects of success. I give priority when I see somebody who is already engaged in a number of compassionate causes, especially if that person has the intelligence and drive to be a significant asset to the animal protection movement. For instance, I was invited in 2003 to an interview on an Upstate New York radio station. My host was a twenty-year-old Cornell undergraduate named Rachel Wechsler. Rachel asked me some terrific questions, and in that hour-long interview I doubt I could have made a better case for being vegan. Yet after the show, Rachel told me that I still hadn't made a sale. She had grown up eating chicken every day, and while the things I said troubled her, she had no intention of changing her diet.

I then invited Rachel to accompany me to Farm Sanctuary in Watkins Glen so she could meet some animals who had been rescued from factory farms. She took me up on my invitation, and one sunny afternoon in March we drove up together. On the way back, we stopped at two commercial dairies and an egg farm. It was only upon personally witnessing the hens crowded into battery cages that Rachel had a change of heart. She had encountered photographs of factory farms before, but seeing the animals directly had a more powerful effect. Rachel decided that evening to become vegan, and she has since gotten heavily involved in activism that opposes animal agriculture.

Rachel is among the brightest and most selflessly engaged students I've ever met. I doubt that any amount of verbal communication could have gotten her to change her diet, but visiting a factory farm did the trick. And if it took that much effort to convince somebody like Rachel, I have to think that the majority of high school and college students are probably too resistant to be convinced to work for dismantlement. Nevertheless, students are by far the most receptive audience for dismantlement, and we need to do everything possible to direct our outreach toward high schools and universities.

In urging the movement to prioritize young people in its outreach efforts, I'm not suggesting that people over the age of thirty can't be reached. I've personally convinced at least a couple of people over seventy to become vegan. But we have to be aware that our time is limited, and activism directed towards young people delivers the largest payoff.

Choosing Dismantlement's First Campaigns

For many years to come, most of the dismantlement movement's efforts should be directed toward outreach. But it would be silly to neglect other attractive opportunities for action. Even with our current minimal resources, we can begin stripping away three of animal agriculture's most important assets. Right now, animal agriculture benefits tremendously from school lunch programs, grazing subsidies, and USDA nutrition guidelines. The dismantlement movement should seek reform in these areas, and the public will side with us if we adequately publicize what is at stake.

Reforming School Lunch Programs

Animal agriculture benefits enormously from the National School Lunch Program. In 2001, the program paid out $179 million for cheese, $171 million for beef, and $168 million for eggs and poultry. Together, this outlay for animal products amounted to $518 million—which dwarfs the $161 million that the program spent on fruits and vegetables.

Back in 1946, when Congress initiated the National School Lunch Program, it made sense to offer America's children subsidized meals that were loaded with fatty meats and dairy products. Malnutrition was a pressing problem, and what little was known about nutrition made it appear wise to feed children substantial amounts of animal products. But given what nutrition science has learned since the 1940s, there's no longer any justification for basing school lunches upon animal products. In America today, childhood malnutrition has been largely replaced by childhood obesity.

Not only does today's National School Lunch Program contribute to the childhood obesity epidemic, it also starts millions of children down the road to a lifetime of unhealthy food choices. I'm not at all suggesting that the program should be eliminated, and it's naive to think that it can instantly be made vegetarian friendly. But as it currently exists, the National School Lunch Program is nothing more than a dumping ground for animal agriculture's excess capacity. In the 1970s and 1980s, the people running America's school cafeterias began modeling their meals after the fast-food industry's offerings. They were under the impression that fast-food was all children would eat; the result of this decision is that many school lunch programs today resemble a second-rate McDonald's.

Today, our schools need an entirely different meal-planning approach. It's been demonstrated that children love to try interesting plant-centered meals, as long as schools make an effort to engagingly teach the importance of healthful eating.[1] Lunch programs that emphasize quality food preparation can start children on a lifetime of more healthful eating. What's more, since these revamped lunch programs would emphasize whole grains and vegetables instead of meat and cheese, significant savings in tax dollars would result.

Activists are now working to get the National School Lunch Program out of the hands of the USDA, and to assign the program to either the Department of Health and Human Services or the Department of Education. Dismantlement activists ought to contribute time and money to these efforts.

Ending Grazing Subsidies

Grazing subsidies constitute a second abuse of tax dollars that an informed public would never allow. A 2002 report estimated that federal grazing programs cost U.S. taxpayers at least $128 million per year.[2] But there are also a number of added costs that are difficult to tally, and the report's authors assert that annual government losses probably total somewhere between 500 million and a billion dollars.[3] The reason that the U.S. government loses money on its grazing program is that it rents land to ranchers at far below market rates. Given the health and environmental consequences of beef production, there's no reason to think that an informed public would tolerate the heavy grazing subsidies that currently exist.*

Putting the NIH in Charge of Nutrition Advice

The third, and perhaps most vulnerable, of government programs benefiting animal agriculture relates to the nutrition guidance issued by the USDA. There is simply no justification for the agency to offer nutrition advice to the public.

The USDA was formed in 1862 with the mandate to provide farmers with support, information, and productive seed varieties. During the Great Depression, the USDA initiated subsidies and other programs to benefit farmers. As farmers became increasingly dependent on the USDA, the agency was also given the task of formulating nutrition advice for the public.

From the beginning, the USDA's nutrition advice has been written with an eye to furthering the business interests of animal agriculture. Every five years, the USDA issues a new set of nutrition guidelines. And every time these guidelines are revised, the new edition is drafted by a committee made up largely of representatives of the meat, dairy, and egg industries. These people have no business sitting on government committees that make public health recommendations.

It was a betrayal of public trust when the government first handed the job of setting nutritional guidelines to the USDA. This task should be reassigned to the National Institutes of Health

---

*I've covered the health effects of beef consumption in Appendix A, and the environmental consequences of cattle ranching in Appendix C.

(NIH)—the agency that should have been given the job in the first place. The NIH ought to base its nutrition recommendations on the best science available. It's absurd that agriculture interests, whether dairy farmers or blueberry growers, are allowed to sit on boards that formulate the government's nutritional advice.

Looking Ahead

None of the three reforms I covered in this chapter will be easy victories. We can count on the meat industry to vigorously oppose sweeping changes to the National School Lunch Program. Reforming grazing fees will be equally tough, especially considering the clout the beef industry has with Congress. Finally, we can expect animal agriculture to do everything possible to keep the USDA in charge of issuing the government's nutrition advice.

The struggle to win each of these reforms will doubtless be long and difficult, but victory is obtainable. That's because, with each of these issues, the public good is currently being sacrificed to the interests of animal agriculture. As these injustices are brought to light, Americans will surely side with the dismantlement movement's calls for reform. By the time these reforms are won, the dismantlement movement will be large and powerful enough that a new range of opportunities will be plainly visible. Of course, the speed at which we make progress depends upon how many people become active in dismantlement, which is why outreach must remain our primary task.

Now that we've seen what the dismantlement movement must accomplish, the final two chapters of this book will look at what forms of activism are most—and least—productive.

Chapter 9

The Militancy Question

Throughout this book's presentation of dismantlement, I've focused on the value of outreach. In the previous chapter, I also put forth several goals—the achievement of which would substantially further the interests of farmed animals. In this chapter, I will look at militancy, and assess whether it is an appropriate tool for dismantlement.

Militancy can be defined in many ways—in this chapter I use the term solely to refer to acts that involve property destruction, but which do not put people in harm's way. There are strong moral and practical reasons for avoiding any activity that harms or endangers people for the sake of animals. The question of whether it is productive to destroy animal agriculture's property and equipment is less clear-cut, and this chapter will consider the matter.

I'm not a philosopher, and I'm not going to make any attempt in this chapter to argue whether property destruction is right or wrong. The questions I'll address here are: will the dismantlement movement attain its goals more quickly if some of us carry out nonviolent property destruction? Or are the consequences of these actions so severe that the dismantlement movement ought to shun militancy as counterproductive?

Can Militancy Further the Goals of Dismantlement?

Property destruction is a tactic that has repeatedly been used to counter numerous kinds of animal exploitation. Hunts have been sabotaged, fur farms have been raided, vivisection labs have been burned, and restaurants have been vandalized.

In November 2003, I attended a talk at Cornell University that featured a militant animal rights activist named Josh Harper.[1] During his talk, Harper cited several cases where vivisection labs and whaling boats were forced to cease operations when their property was destroyed by activists. It therefore appears that, leaving aside the troubling moral questions raised by militant action, property destruction can be effective in halting some kinds of animal cruelty.

Following Harper's talk, during the question and answer session, I expressed my opinion that even if militant action is an effective and morally sound tactic against some forms of animal abuse, it should never be used against animal agriculture. That's because keeping the public on our side is enormously important. And it's unreasonable to expect the public to support militant action on behalf of farmed animals—even though much of the public *does* support militancy on some animal protection issues.

For instance, many Americans who have no qualms about eating meat nevertheless view whaling as despicable, and have no problem with the notion of sending whaling vessels to the bottom of the sea. Similarly, many of the abuses that occur in animal research are horrifying, and the public often shows little sympathy to certain vivisectors whose labs are destroyed during raids.

By contrast, the overwhelming majority of the U.S. population eats meat, and sees nothing wrong with doing so. Most Americans are therefore unsympathetic to property destruction on behalf of farmed animals. In consequence, carrying out raids against animal agriculture plays right into the industry's hands. The industry is all too happy to pin us with the "terrorist" label.

Whenever activists destroy the property of factory farms and restaurants, we lose the moral high ground, and the public becomes uncertain about who the real villain is. At all costs, we need to keep the public's attention on the horrific cruelties that are perpetrated by animal agriculture.

After making these points to Harper, I argued that it's imperative to think twice about taking militant action on behalf of farmed animals. Activists who support militancy must offer clear evidence that property destruction can cause greater damage to animal agriculture than can outreach. And, as far as I can see, outreach is by far the more damaging tool. In fact, even the largest and most audacious illegal raids produce comparatively trivial gains compared to what can be accomplished through outreach.

I then provided Harper with an example that indicated why I think militant action can never compare to outreach in terms of saving farmed animals. Imagine, I said, driving a tractor trailer to a chicken farm on a moonless night, successfully loading the trailer with two thousand birds, and then making a successful escape. Then imagine driving those birds to an animal sanctuary, and shouldering their enormous feed, shelter, and veterinary bills.

Such an audacious act would surely do enormous good for two thousand chickens, but it would also create a number of difficulties for the movement. Animal agriculture would gain the opportunity to suggest that the perpetrator is a common criminal—and much of the public would likely agree with this assessment. The raid would give poultry producers one more reason to boost security, which would in turn limit the ability of dismantlement activists to photograph and publicize farm conditions. Most important, the activist would, if caught, be charged with multiple felonies and probably do substantial prison time. And it's difficult to help animals from a prison cell.

By contrast, doing outreach that convinces just one college student to become a vegan would save even more animals than the hypothetical raid I just described. An average twenty-year-old would normally eat two thousand birds over the next fifty years. There would be no negative repercussions that the movement would bear from convincing a twenty-year-old to stop eating meat. Quite to the contrary, the meat industry would lose a customer, and the dismantlement movement would gain an activist. With all this in mind, I challenged Harper to come up with a reason why militant action should ever be carried out on behalf of farmed animals, given the enormous potential of outreach.

I've yet to hear a militant activist make a convincing argument that property destruction can surpass outreach in delivering gains for farmed animals. And Harper did not attempt to make this argument. He did, however, explain why he believes that both outreach and property destruction should be used to protect animals. According to Harper, the animals benefit if the meat industry is forced to defend itself on as many fronts as possible— a coalition of militants and mainstream outreach activists would stretch the industry's resources and double its vulnerabilities.

Harper's assertion seems reasonable, but a closer look reveals a flaw in its logic. His argument assumes that the industry has an effective defense against outreach. But this is not the case. Indeed, outreach is a well that cannot run dry. On a per-hour basis, outreach offers a greater payback in terms of animals saved than any other form of activism. And each successful outreach effort strengthens the movement.

Militancy can certainly inflict damage upon animal agriculture, but its potential to do so is limited, while its capacity to turn the public against our efforts is unlimited. I therefore believe that militancy represents the greatest existing threat to the success of dismantlement. Animal agriculture desperately needs factions of the animal protection movement to resort to action that will alienate the public. And, even if a few barns get torched in the process, the industry comes out ahead. Indeed, I think it's possible that animal agriculture will one day launch phony attacks on its own property, in an effort to discredit animal protectionists.

For the sake of keeping the public on our side, I hold that

one of the primary tenets of dismantlement is to shun theft and property destruction on behalf of farmed animals. It's essential that the public perceives dismantlement correctly—as a movement that uses outreach in order to expose the injustices of animal agriculture. People committed to dismantlement should therefore vigorously oppose militant action carried out on behalf of farmed animals.

The animal rights movement is a big tent that contains activists from the most conventional to the most militant. Dismantlement, by contrast, is geared entirely toward legally permitted forms of action. There is only one exception in which activists can advance the dismantlement cause by breaking the law. We're about to see that this activity embodies moral and responsible behavior, and is therefore incapable of alienating the public.

Open Rescues

Merely setting foot inside a factory farm to witness how the animals are treated is enough to get a concerned observer charged with trespassing. Dismantlement is not the first movement to suffer from unjust laws. And here we should learn from Gandhi's Indian independence movement, the philosophy of which later guided the civil rights movement. During the struggle for independence, Gandhi advocated breaking a variety of oppressive laws. The key is that he urged people to break these laws openly and offer up themselves to legal prosecution.

In the 1990s, activist Patty Mark adapted Gandhi's approach by pioneering the concept of "open rescues." Using this technique, Mark and her colleagues entered Australia's factory farms while carrying cameras to document the conditions. Mark refused to damage property, and if she had to cut a lock to gain access to a building, she would pay to have it replaced. If she encountered any animals who were in dire need of veterinary care, or otherwise suffering enormously, Mark would perform a rescue and take the animals to a hidden shelter.

With this accomplished, Mark then notified the media and the police of her actions. The resultant press coverage was incredibly favorable. Rather than coming off as common criminals, Mark and the other activists involved in open rescues were tarnishing the reputation of animal agriculture.

Around 2000, several U.S. groups began doing open rescues in the United States, and the results have been as impressive as those attained in Australia.[2] The media has overwhelmingly taken the side of animal protection activists engaged in open rescues. Animals have been saved, and public opinion has consistently sided with activists rather than industry. Articles providing laudatory accounts of open rescues have appeared prominently in many of the country's leading newspapers.[3]

The key to open rescues' success is a Gandhian willingness to accept responsibility. People who engage in open rescues clearly break the law, but the offenses are minor and the rationale for committing these acts is something that the public can agree with. It may be wrong to trespass or cut locks, but it would be a far greater injustice to deny the public the opportunity to see how animals are being raised. Because people who engage in open rescues take responsibility for their actions and invite prosecution for any laws they have broken, they are more likely to be seen by the public as heroes rather than criminals.

For all these reasons, open rescues deserve to be held as an accepted and honored strategy toward dismantlement. Outreach and open rescues offer the two most effective ways for activists to gain ground against animal agriculture. Industry has shown itself wholly unable to mount a defense against either of these tactics. Militancy, by contrast, must be shunned by the dismantlement movement—the philosophical justification for militancy is too shaky, its ability to undermine animal agriculture too limited, and its potential to antagonize the public too great.

Chapter 10

Personal Action

One of my biggest regrets is that, even after I switched to a vegan diet, I took more than three years to become involved as an activist. Since I can't re-do those years, I can at least explain what kept me away from activism, with the hope that other people don't repeat my mistakes.

My main reason for not plunging quickly into activism arose from my belief that I was already doing enough. I told myself that my diet alone was making a solid contribution to preventing animal suffering. I reasoned that, since not one person in a hundred was vegan, I was way ahead of the pack in terms of what I was doing for animals.

I also allowed the media's negative view of animal rights activists to influence how I perceived the movement. I assumed that animal protectionists tended to be shrill and out of touch. Also, I thought their goals were hopeless in light of the financial strength of animal agriculture. I didn't see myself as an abrasive or clueless person, and I saw no point in joining a movement that seemed destined to go nowhere.

Despite my skepticism over what activism could accomplish, every now and then I felt pangs of guilt that I should do more than simply be vegan. But whenever I thought about becoming an activist, I had no idea where to begin. What was I supposed to do? Start an animal rights group? Meet with lawmakers? It all seemed way beyond my abilities.

As the years went by without my taking action, the sense that I had to do something began to gnaw at me. So I thought about the things I was good at, and asked myself how I could contribute. I had studied literature and writing in college, so I decided to start writing about vegetarianism.

I started modestly. My first project was developing a free software package of information and recipes. I put it on the Internet, and a few thousand people downloaded it. I even got a few letters from people who liked it. After experiencing that small success, I wanted to do more. So I contacted an editor at *Vegetarian Times* magazine, and, to my surprise, she hired me to write a few articles. I was gaining some confidence at this work, and I was starting to reach more people.

Dabbling

One of the lessons I learned from my first activist efforts is the importance of dabbling. You can't expect to start off doing world-shaking activism. Instead, begin with something modest that suits your interests and abilities. The great thing about dabbling is that small investments of time *do* produce results you can see. Once you start succeeding at little things, you get encouraged to try bigger things.

No matter what kind of activism you get into, it's important to start out by reading as widely as possible. As animal advocates, we're only as persuasive as we are informed. While I hope this book is an excellent starting point for dismantlement activists, there are many other books that merit attention.*

Even though I don't think that the health arguments for veganism deserve front-and-center attention, it's of great importance that activists read widely on the subject of nutrition. This is especially true because we need to make sure that new vegans thrive on their diets. There's nothing worse for the movement than when

---

*See Appendix I for a list of recommended reading.

people try a poorly planned vegan diet, and then go back to eating meat because they don't feel healthy.

Since books are by definition dated, it's important to stay current with what's happening in the world of animal protection. The website I publish, Vegan.com, is updated daily. And a number of other activist publications are also worth reading regularly. Vegan Outreach produces an email newsletter full of great material, and their website offers one of the best collections of archived writings in the movement. Compassion Over Killing also continually creates and distributes new material directed toward activists.*

Personal Outreach

It's important to read widely because, no matter what kind of activism you pursue, you'll also find yourself doing personal outreach. This form of outreach happens every time you engage family, friends, co-workers, or classmates in discussion. The more knowledgeably you present your point of view, the more compelling your arguments are likely to be.

Effective outreach is as much about listening as it is about providing information. The secret is to let the other person steer the conversation. There's no substitute for staying current on the topics of animal agriculture and health so that you can speak persuasively about whatever issues are brought up.

Since reading alone won't give you a degree in the health sciences, it's always important to preface remarks about nutrition by saying you don't have credentials in the field. But you can still knowledgeably summarize the most basic misunderstandings related to food and health, and refer your listener to books written by people with appropriate credentials.

In addition to reading widely, it's important to maintain a friendly and upbeat tone when speaking about diet and animal agriculture. When I'm doing personal outreach, I always try to

---

*Vegan Outreach is online at <www.veganoutreach.org> and Compassion Over Killing is at <www.cok.net>.

frame my main points in a positive manner, stressing all the advantages that come from making a change of diet and lifestyle. Outreach works best when it's a discussion rather than a monologue or argument. At all costs, avoid appearing as though you're judging the listener's choices on the areas where you remain in disagreement. People are exceedingly unlikely to change their opinions if they feel like they are being judged or scolded.

Many people will readily accept the case for dismantlement, but will nevertheless be apprehensive about a change of diet. For people who've spent their lives eating meals based mainly on animal products, the idea of giving up these foods can seem like an enormous hardship. These people need to be told repeatedly that it's surprisingly easy to stop eating animal products.

For some people, the idea of becoming vegan seems so overwhelmingly alien that it's helpful to use a vegetarian diet as a stepping stone. For people who are edging their way toward veganism by becoming vegetarian, it's important to understand the cruelties associated with commercial egg farms and dry-lot dairies. Free-range eggs and organic dairy products are far from perfect foods, but they are surely a step up from factory farmed meats.

I was vegetarian for more than a year before I became vegan, and I now regret that I spent a great deal of time learning recipes that called for eggs and dairy products. When I finally decided to become vegan, I had to toss out my vegetarian cookbooks and learn a new set of vegan recipes. With that in mind, I think it's smart for new vegetarians to try to cook mainly from vegan cookbooks. Vegan recipes are no harder to make, and no less delicious, than recipes that include eggs and dairy products.

The most effective way to persuade people about the pleasures of vegan eating is to let them experience it first-hand. If you've managed to interest someone in the idea of giving up animal products, consider going grocery shopping together, taking them to a restaurant with great vegan options, cooking them a meal, or finding some other way to get them to sample some terrific vegan food.

I find that most of the people who switch to a vegan diet, and then switch back, have one thing in common. They share the fatal belief that becoming vegan is all about willpower. In actuality, the need to exert willpower is a sure sign that a new vegan is taking the wrong approach. The most important task a new vegan can accomplish is to try a new food every day, or at least several new foods a week. The idea is that, over time, vegan foods will crowd out the animal-based foods that most of us grew up eating. When talking to potential vegans, it's helpful to stress that a successful switch has nothing to do with willpower, and everything to do with making an ongoing effort to discover new foods.

Finally, it's important to be sure that new vegans spend time reading about the basics of nutrition. It's likely that inadequate nutritional knowledge is the primary reason that some people fail to thrive on a vegan diet. In fact, many new vegans aren't even aware that getting a daily source of vitamin B_{12} is absolutely essential—a long-term deficiency of B_{12} can cause catastrophic health consequences, including irreversible nerve damage. There are several other nutritional pitfalls that new vegetarians and vegans must be taught to avoid, so it's urgent that anyone transitioning to a new diet invests the time to read about nutrition. A few hours with the right book is all it takes to learn the basics that will help you stay out of trouble.*

Immersion

After you've dabbled in activism for at least a few months, you will probably feel like you're ready for greater challenges. Many intermediate activists don't know how to make the next step—moving from dabbling into serious activism. I think the best way to move forward is to immerse yourself in the movement for several months, and then pull back and reflect on your experience.

Many animal protection groups offer internships that come with free housing. These internships involve some of the most

---

*See Appendix I for a list of recommended reading.

unglamorous work imaginable, like stuffing envelopes and answering phones. If you apply at a sanctuary for rescued farmed animals, you're likely to spend much of your time shoveling excrement. No matter what internship you take on, you won't have much idle time. Since animal protection groups often suffer from being underfunded, the unpaid labor provided by intern programs is immensely important to their survival.

Internships allow you to see the movement, warts and all. It helps strip away a lot of the idealism about how things work. In place of that idealism, you'll gain a first-hand understanding of how the animal protection movement looks from within. After spending at least a month or two as an intern, it's time to pull back and to reflect on your successes and frustrations.

In my own experience, I spent my mid-twenties dabbling in animal protection in one form or another. I wrote some articles, helped out with some groups, and otherwise eased my way into making small contributions. Over time, I felt a calling to do more. So I met with the executive director of a California group and accepted an intern position.

I wore a lot of hats with this group. I did things like write for their newsletter, upgrade their computer network, and create an information flier for tabling at events. Unfortunately, the group had its share of problems, both in human relations and in attracting new members. But the problem that disturbed me most had to do with the information the group passed out. Much of the material for the group's fliers and pamphlets was adapted from older books that weren't terribly reliable. I lacked the time and library access to personally re-research the organization's outreach materials.[1] And it bothered me that I was working for a group that printed tens of thousands of copies of pamphlets that were of questionable accuracy.

After spending six months interning with this group, I felt ready to leave and take stock of what I'd learned. I took a month off to visit a quiet place in the mountains and reflect on my experiences. I found my mind continually returning to my chief frustration as an intern—the fact that the organization's publications made improbable claims. As I sought the root cause of my frustration, I recognized that the problem extended beyond the literature put out by any one organization. There were simply no current books that dealt reliably with the advantages of being vegan. In consequence, much of the literature put out by the country's vegetarian groups was based on dated and debatable source material.

One night, while mulling over what kind of activism I could do in the future, I suddenly recognized that I could fill the gap in the vegetarian movement's literature by writing a book. This idea immediately intrigued me, so I started work right away. Over the next two years, I researched and wrote the manuscript and found a publisher. My book came out in 1997 and was titled, *Vegan: The New Ethics of Eating*. Looking back, I regard *Vegan* as far from perfect—I fell into the trap of over-emphasizing the health and environmental arguments supporting veganism—but I still think that the book helped to make the movement's literature more current and credible.

I've told my story here because I think it illustrates the three steps that would work well for anyone wanting to make a contribution to dismantlement. Start out by dabbling, and when you are ready to do more, immerse yourself in the movement. After at least a month or two of immersion, pull back and, if possible, go somewhere quiet where you can think hard about your experiences. Identify any frustrations you've had with the movement, and see if there are any intersections between your skills and these sources of frustration. You may find that you have a unique ability to make a contribution in an area the movement desperately needs.

Modeling and Goal-Setting

After you've passed through dabbling and immersion, and discovered your niche within the movement, there are two practices that will help boost your effectiveness: modeling and goal-setting.

Modeling is especially useful after you've been in the movement for awhile and have had the chance to learn about activists who are especially effective. Usually, these people are forthcoming about their methods, and you can read about their work or talk to them in person. When you find an activist whose work you admire, try to identify the key aspects to his or her approach, and then model your own work accordingly. By modeling appropriately, even new activists can gain the advantage of having many years of experience.

Along with modeling, goal setting is enormously important. Few activists set goals for what they intend to achieve. And even the activists who do set goals rarely set them high enough. Dismantlement activists are such a tiny minority of the population that we need to be sure that every person involved in the cause is as effective as possible. And I doubt it's possible to be highly effective without setting goals.

It's best to set short-term, long-term, and lifetime goals; that way, you're always in the process of finishing small projects that collectively build to larger ones. Let me tell you about my lifetime goal, which I set many years ago. When I was a teenager, my greatest ambition was to one day become a millionaire. In my twenties, as my primary ambition shifted away from making money and toward protecting animals, I adapted the millionaire concept for purposes of activism. I decided that I still wanted to be a millionaire, but not in terms of earning a million dollars. I wanted to be a millionaire in terms of keeping a million animals out of slaughterhouses.

Some people may scoff at the idea that one person can save a million animals. But I've met at least a dozen people in the movement who've achieved this level of success. I think saving a million animals is a lifetime goal that every serious activist would do well to adopt.

But is it realistic to think that a typical person could keep a million animals from slaughter? Absolutely! A twenty-year-old college student is likely to live for at least fifty years. And the average adult American eats more than forty chickens every year. So if you can convince a college student to give up meat, you've saved around two thousand birds, hundreds of fish, plus several pigs and cows. At two thousand animals saved per new vegetarian, this means that during your life, if you convince five hundred young people to become vegetarian, a million animals will be saved.

I believe that anybody who progresses beyond dabbling in activism will achieve significant results. Saving a million animals might be a bit beyond most people's capacity, but saving a hundred thousand animals is certainly not. At a bare minimum, any serious activist can be assured of saving tens of thousands of animals in the course of a lifetime of activism. Imagine how you'd feel knowing you have accomplished that!

Kindness

After you've figured out how you want to contribute, and set appropriately high goals, there's one last thing to keep in mind: it's vital to treat the people behind animal agriculture as opponents rather than enemies. Nothing good for the animals comes out of antagonizing or demonizing people. The dismantlement movement is already threatening the livelihoods of people who have precious few ways to make a living. So it's important to avoid needlessly insulting these people or regarding them as moral inferiors. Doing so will likely inspire them to fight even harder against our work.

My mentor, the late Henry Spira, emphasized the importance of not dividing up the world into saints and sinners. One thing he told me that I'll never forget is that "it's about creating social change, not giving people ulcers."

That's not to suggest that Spira was wishy-washy in choosing his objectives. He took on a number of tough campaigns in his life, nearly all of which he won decisively. But Spira always recognized that his main task was winning change, not humiliating opponents. Throughout his campaigns, he always sought to maintain cordial relations with the opposition, preferring to win concessions through negotiations. If discussions failed and he was forced to launch a campaign, it was well planned in advance and so devastating that the opponent usually gave in. Spira's response characteristically gave his opponent a chance to save face: he'd send a thank-you note congratulating them for taking the initiative to help animals.

Vulnerabilities in Animal Agriculture

People who seek to protect farmed animals are in a better position now than ever before. The modern animal protection movement has pioneered a number of effective strategies for eliminating cruelty. We now have three decades' worth of tactics from which to draw. With this in mind, let's take one final look at factory farming and consider where it's most vulnerable.

Throughout Part One of this book, we saw that factory farming has subjected animals to a number of hardships and cruelties. Wherever you look in factory farming, animals are being victimized. The spread of factory farming throughout agriculture appears to have brought only the most dire of consequences to animals.

And yet, in ways perhaps even the industry fails to understand, the rise of factory farming may ultimately play a decisive role in the animals' deliverance. This book opened with the story of the small family-owned egg farm across the street from my parents' house being pushed into a trench and set ablaze. Since the 1950s, millions of families who once had vested interests in perpetuating animal agriculture have been squeezed out of the business. Many who remain, performing the industry's grunt work, do so in the role of modern-day sharecroppers. They have been stripped of ownership, and are often deeply resentful of the roles they now occupy.

The consolidation of animal agriculture has provided animal protectionists with a remarkable opportunity. The poultry and livestock companies that remain today are incredibly wealthy, and they are also savvy about getting politicians to do their bidding. The trouble is, these companies have gained market dominance by being at the forefront of factory farming innovation. Their businesses are utterly dependent on the miseries associated with confining animals at the lowest possible cost. And, increasingly, activists are exposing the public to the realities of factory farming. For the first time, animal protectionists are becoming not just an irksome pest to the industry, but a genuine menace. The response of the animal agriculture giants is telling. They have too much invested in factory farming to change their ways. So they are resorting to lobbying politicians in an effort to keep the public in the dark about what goes on at factory farms.

Just as they did with Common Farming Exemptions, the industry is using its clout in state legislatures to prohibit photographing animals at factory farms and slaughterhouses. These laws apply, not just to activists, but to news and media organizations. In several states the penalties are so severe that it's doubtful that reporters will ever set foot again inside a factory farm for the sake of a story.

In 2003, state legislators in Texas introduced a bill that would have made it a Class-B misdemeanor to bring a camera into a slaughterhouse or factory farm.[2] Violators would have faced a $10,000 fine as well as jail time. In Missouri, state legislators drafted an even harsher measure. They introduced a bill that would have made it a felony to photograph or videotape "any aspect of an animal facility."[3] So much for Missouri being the "show-me" state.

Fortunately, both the Texas and Missouri bills died. But similar anti-activist measures have either been passed, or are pending, in a number of other states. Oklahoma lawmakers have enacted a $10,000 fine to be assessed against any activist who "disrupts" a slaughterhouse or factory farm operation. It's easy to imagine ways that this word could be creatively applied against anyone who set foot on a factory farm. In 2003, similar bills were drafted in New York, Ohio, Oregon, Pennsylvania, and Utah. A tough anti-trespassing law specifically directed toward animal farms in California went into effect in 2004.[4]

By pushing for the creation of these laws, animal agriculture has tipped its hand about its greatest fear. The industry has decided that, at all costs, the public must remain ignorant about how farmed animals are treated.

There's no doubt that animal agriculture interests will succeed in passing additional anti-trespassing and anti-photography laws. I wholeheartedly wish them great success in this task, and I hope that the industry manages to get draconian anti-photography laws passed in all fifty states. Decisions made out of fear often result in unintended consequences, and this strategy of outlawing photography, and imposing outrageous penalties for trespassing, will backfire on the industry.

Not only are these laws clumsy and heavy handed, animal agriculture is making the outrageous claim that its legislation is intended to guard against terrorism. This assertion is so blatantly false that neither the press nor the public is going to buy it. Perpetuating cruelty under the guise of combating terrorism is certain to incite public outrage. As one lawmaker who voted against the California anti-trespassing law put it: "This was really just an attempt to continue to hide from public view the deliberate cruelty to living things that goes on in industrial agriculture."[5]

No matter how severe the penalties or how rigorous the enforcement, these laws are incapable of accomplishing the industry's objectives. Camcorders are cheap, and most factory farms are unstaffed and unmonitored for many hours each day. There will always be activists willing to brave fines and risk jail time for the sake of documenting what happens in animal agriculture facilities. And these activists will happily provide professional-quality footage and photography to any news station or publication that wishes to use it.

The only way to stop cruelty from being photographed is to stop the cruelty itself, and this is the one thing that today's animal agriculture industry is unwilling to do.

Closing the Meat Market

Above all else, animal agriculture fears exposure. The industry can exist in its present form only as long as the public is kept in the dark about animal treatment.

For too long, animal protectionists have pushed the wrong messages. The vegetarian argument often seems to claim that vegan eating is a panacea for all health and environmental ills. Such overstated claims have cost us credibility, as well as the opportunity to adequately focus on the cruelty inherent in animal agriculture. Nor has animal rights philosophy been an effective way to turn the general public against animal agriculture. As we've seen, animal rights philosophy is simply too complex and comprehensive to be an effective means of winning over the public.

In working to shield factory farms from public view, animal agriculture has shown that it has something to hide. Activists must therefore stick relentlessly to exposing cruelty on farms, and seeking out the audiences who are most likely to respond. The animal protection movement must prioritize high schools and colleges, and do everything possible to inform young people about how farmed animals are treated.

Many people, especially the young, who learn about factory farming will come to one of two decisions. Some will recognize the urgent need to support alternative animal agriculture, and to convince free-range poultry farms and organic dairies to initiate meaningful welfare standards. Others will become lifelong opponents of animal agriculture, and will do everything possible to drive this industry out of existence.

The days are ending when animal agriculture can evade responsibility for its cruelties. Activists are currently adopting a variety of measures to hold the industry publicly accountable for its treatment of animals. No industry can prosper in the face of rampant public distrust, and there is the possibility that, within our lifetimes, animal agriculture will be thrust into an irreversible decline. Whether or not this happens will be decided by the strategies that we choose today.

The speed at which dismantlement occurs depends on how effectively we activists can recast our image. We must take every opportunity to win over the public, so that we are correctly perceived as caring people who are legitimately outraged over cruel farming practices. Too many times, in the conflict between activists and factory farming interests, it is the farmers who win public support and are regarded as victims. We can't allow this misinterpretation to continue, so we must turn the tables by speaking compassionately while making clear that factory farmers are not victims, but victimizers.

It is essential that we cultivate a public disgust for animal agriculture. But on top of this work, the dismantlement movement must be recruitment-oriented. We need to continually recruit new volunteers, while we build effective groups that let talented people pursue activist work full-time.

Not only must we attract people into activism, we need to inspire them to stick with it. One of the greatest problems confronting the animal protection movement is that many new activists participate for a year or two, and then their commitment fades. Our high drop-out rate probably stems from the lack of good communication networks within the movement. If volunteers could interact more easily, and be inspired by one another's successes, we would surely have fewer people abandoning activism.

In building our organizations, we must find ways to avoid the animal protection movement's usual pitfalls. We need well-funded, skillfully organized groups that use proven approaches to weaken animal agriculture. As the dismantlement movement gathers force, new opportunities for action will frequently arise.

So we must strive to continually identify and engage in promising new methods of activism.

Already, there are hundreds of activists across America who can serve as the core of this new movement. Our success will be determined by our commitment, and by our willingness to collaborate in innovative ways. In my own life, I intend to devote the bulk of my energies to inspiring people to work for dismantlement. Together, we can direct our collective abilities to ensure that animal agriculture's remaining years are as few as possible.

Epilogue: The Unluckiest Ones

Throughout the eighteen months I spent writing this book, I immersed myself in news reports related to animals and agriculture. And over this time, I encountered innumerable stories about farmed animals who suffered cruelty or neglect. Yet in this book, I wrote almost nothing about specific cases of animal cruelty.

My reason for not focusing on cruelty cases was two-fold. First, I didn't want to scare off readers who would otherwise have finished the book. Second, I wanted to avoid muckraking. My point in writing Part One of this book was to provide a fair and accurate description of how animal agriculture operates. Although cases of farmed animal cruelty are frequently reported, they are often not representative of how most of these animals are treated.

Yet over the course of writing this book, three cruelty cases came to light that I found too appalling to put aside. Together, these cases illustrate what animal agriculture, at its worst, is capable of doing to animals.

White Dairy Farm

What happened on Timmy White's dairy farm involved far fewer animals than the other two cases I'll describe. But in some ways, White's story bothers me the most, perhaps because he operated his farm just fourteen miles from where I wrote this book. In fact, had I not happened to glance at a headline in a local newspaper,

I'd have never known about this case.[1] So, in this respect, the White case embodies the thousands of cruelty cases that go unreported except by local newspapers—if they even get reported at all. This just happens to be the one that occurred in my backyard.

In July of 2003, Timmy White rented a dairy farm in Spencer, New York. White had worked at one of the research dairy farms operated by Cornell University and, on the strength of this experience, he was able to obtain a bank loan that covered the farm's rent and the purchase of 59 dairy cows. As we've seen throughout this book, animal agriculture favors the largest and most efficient producers, and smaller operators are continually getting squeezed out of the business. It only took a month or two before White's dairy ran into money problems. White responded to his financial difficulties by moving back to his hometown of Genoa, 36 miles away. As for the cows, he simply abandoned them. And since the Spencer farm had an absentee landlord and was located in a remote area, nobody had any idea White had left 59 cows to starve.

It's likely that every one of the 59 cows would have starved to death—but luckily, about three weeks after he abandoned the animals, White was arrested on a firearms charge. This arrest prompted the police to look into White's past residences, and to discover that he had recently been living at the Spencer farm. In early November of 2003, the police visited the Spencer farm in search of illegal guns. There, they discovered White's cows—who were by then suffering from advanced starvation. Six cows had already died, and their carcasses were decaying in plain sight.

The typical weight for a dairy cow is from twelve to sixteen hundred pounds. At the time they were discovered, White's cows weighed between three and six hundred pounds. Upon being notified by the police, the bank foreclosed on White's loan, seized the cows, and sold fifty of them for a pittance at auction—the three remaining survivors were euthanized after being judged too malnourished to recover. Timmy White was taken to jail and charged with 59 counts of animal cruelty, a charge that could have landed him in prison for up to 59 years.

Prosecutors had an airtight case against White; nine cows had died from his neglect, and fifty more had been brought to the brink of death. An animal cruelty investigator had visited the scene, compiled a report, and offered to give testimony at trial. The bank's representatives had photographs of the starved cows that could be used as evidence.

For abandoning 59 cows and leaving them to starve, White surely deserved harsh punishment. But tragically, many prosecutors don't view animal cruelty as a serious crime, no matter how great the suffering nor how many animals are involved. Most of the charges against White were dropped during plea bargaining. In the end, he was allowed to plead guilty to just two counts of animal cruelty. He was sentenced to 365 days in the county jail, and he was allowed to serve this time by coming in on weekends. He was also fined and ordered not to own animals in the future.

Although White's punishment was mild, at least he was sentenced to jail time. The two other cases I'll describe both ended in far greater miscarriages of justice.

Cypress Foods Egg Farms

For many years, overcapacity has plagued the egg industry. It's a business of razor-thin profit margins. Egg farms routinely lose their competitive edge and are forced out of business.

In March of 2002, a large egg company owned by James R. Biggers faced financial ruin. Wholesale egg prices had declined to the point that his facilities were hemorrhaging cash from one day to the next. It reached the point that Biggers had no money to buy feed for the million hens he kept in Florida and Georgia.

At this point, Biggers had two options that could save his birds from starvation. He could either have his employees euthanize the animals, or he could give the birds away to other egg farms. Biggers chose neither option.[2] Instead, he decided to hold onto the birds, even though he had nothing to feed them, while he attempted to sell his business.

Days went by, and Biggers didn't manage to close a deal. As the days turned into weeks, twenty thousand hens starved to death. About 980,000 hens remained, practically all of whom were on the brink of dying from starvation. They were then euthanized.[3]

Biggers' decision-making led directly to this mass-starvation. This would seem to be one of the largest, most appalling, and most clear-cut cases of animal cruelty imaginable. Unfortunately, the district attorneys in Florida and Georgia didn't see things that way. They declined to press charges.[4]

In comments to the media, Biggers' attorney said, "No crime or any wrongdoing occurred."[5]

Ward Egg Ranch

In early 2003, newspapers reported one of the most gruesome animal cruelty cases imaginable. California at the time was suffering from an outbreak of Newcastle Disease. While posing no danger to humans, Newcastle Disease can rapidly spread from one chicken farm to the next, stunting the birds' growth and playing havoc with poultry producers' profitability. In order to contain the disease, California ordered dozens of poultry producers to kill and discard their entire flocks. As a result of this order, 3.1 million birds were killed over a period of several weeks.[6]

In February of 2003, the owner of the Ward Egg Ranch decided on a cheap and quick method to satisfy the state's order to get rid of his chickens: he ordered the birds put—while still alive—through a wood chipper. About thirty thousand hens were fed into the chipper.[7]

The farm's owner, Bill Wilgenburg, claimed that his action did not constitute animal cruelty because he had gotten approval from a veterinarian.[8] But a local animal control officer, Mary Kay Gagliardo, investigated the case and urged the filing of cruelty charges. After reviewing Gagliardo's complaint, the local district attorney decided not pursue the matter. According to Gail Stewart, the district attorney's spokesperson, no charges were pressed because the department decided that using a wood chipper to kill chickens was "a standard industry practice."[9]

Upon learning that he wouldn't be charged, Wilgenburg told the media, "I got approval for everything that I've done from the right people and I'm sticking by it. We just want [the issue] to go away."[10]

Redemption

Every now and then, I think of James Biggers and Bill Wilgenburg, and what they did to those chickens. The orders they gave strike me as so bereft of compassion that I doubt whether anybody could have successfully intervened on behalf of those birds. I think there will always be people like Biggers and Wilgenburg, and they have their own conscience to deal with; their own peace to make.

Nevertheless, I think every one of us shares a measure of responsibility for what happened. We collectively live in a society that allows people like James Biggers to starve a million hens; a society that allows Bill Wilgenburg to shred 30,000 living and unanesthetized chickens through a wood chipper. And while you and I couldn't have stopped Biggers and Wilgenburg from doing what they did, we certainly carry some moral responsibility for living in a society that allows this to happen.

Certainly, laws can be changed, and we can each add to the push for industry accountability. But throughout this book, we've seen that animal agriculture is fundamentally resistant to reform. The only sure way to put a stop to the horrors inflicted onto farmed animals is to seek, not just reform, but dismantlement. As long as animal agriculture exists, people like James Biggers and Bill Wilgenburg will find their way into the industry and inflict unfathomable amounts of suffering without showing the slightest remorse.

Perhaps the agonies suffered by all these animals can be redeemed and given meaning. That redemption begins when one person looks at the rampant injustices fundamental to animal agriculture, feels horror, and begins working for dismantlement or reform.

Supplementary Material

Activist Essays and Appendices

Introduction to the Supplementary Material

Wait! Don't go yet! It's true that the supplementary materials and appendices of many books consist of a bunch of tables and other odds and ends that seem gratuitously added to kill trees and boost page count. That's not the case here. I wanted to keep this book as short as possible, so I've only added the following material because I regard it as vital.

I wanted this book to include some detailed advice about personal activism. But I realized that I had no business writing this material. Activism is about specializing, and there are dozens of distinct ways that one person can make a difference. I decided that my writing about the different forms of activism would amount to giving out secondhand information. I realized that, instead of personally writing about specific kinds of activism, it would be far better to ask a number of activists to briefly describe their work in their own words.

So, in the following essays, I invited nine of the most effective activists I know to write about their specific brands of activism. No matter what your personality or skills, there's a form of activism that's right for you. I hope that the following essays will inspire you to work in one way or another to promote dismantlement.

After these essays come this book's appendices. On several occasions in this book, I basically said "trust me" regarding certain arguments I was making. Whenever I did this, I pointed to an appendix in which the material was addressed. I also covered some important topics in the appendices that aren't addressed in the main text.

Finally, if you are serious about activism, please spend some time reading through the endnotes of this book. Many entries in that section articulate points that I could not make in the main text without sounding pedantic. At all costs, I wanted to keep the main text of the book readable, and this sometimes meant burying some important information and ideas in the endnotes. I think that spending an hour reading through the endnotes will provide a substantially better understanding of this book and its arguments.

As activists, we need to be as well informed as possible. The following material rounds out the information presented in this book, and provides a more nuanced explanation of the issues surrounding animal protection and dismantlement.

Activist Essays

Leafleting for Vegan Outreach

By Joe Espinosa and Marsha Forsman

Several years ago, we learned of the harsh realities that animals endure in the agricultural industry. We were moved to stop consuming meat, milk, and eggs as a result of this realization. Soon thereafter, we became involved in the animal rights movement because we wanted to do more to end the abuse of animals. It was not enough for us to simply stop supporting such violence ourselves. Knowing that billions of animals suffered so horribly year after year compelled us into action on their behalf.

We contacted one of the world's largest animal rights organizations for advice and contacts, and were put in touch with one of the animal rights organizations here in Illinois. We enthusiastically began what turned out to be several years of work with these organizations.

In order to grab media attention for the animals, we wrote letters, made signs, held protests, and donned costumes (cows, pigs, chickens, fish, clowns, cave people, even Jesus). We were successful in getting media attention for most of our projects, from simple letters to the editor to extravagant demonstrations featuring a pig turning the tables by barbecuing a human. But what was the result of our years of work and hundreds of dollars spent on behalf of the animals? This was a question that we did not feel qualified to answer, as the leaders of the movement were telling us that media coverage was the way to bring about animal liberation, and we were relative newcomers to the movement.

After many experiences of getting media coverage, yet feeling increasing doubts about whether we were truly helping the animals' cause, the question had to be addressed. We could not deny that many of our statements and actions were misconstrued in the reports given by the media, and wondered why this might be. Why would the media not give the straight story about what animals endure when used to feed or clothe people, to entertain people, or in the name of science? After giving the matter some thought, we realized that it was not in the media's financial interests to publicize farmed animal suffering. The animal exploiting industries advertise their products daily through various media outlets. It is in the best interests of media companies not to alienate their high-paying clients by reporting on the brutality behind their products. Waiting for the media to help bring about animal liberation is akin to asking the fox to guard the chicken coop. Although the media could potentially be a good tool for advancing animal liberation, simple politics makes this quite unlikely.

Although we were becoming aware firsthand of the ineffectiveness of our efforts, we were at a loss for what to do. By chance we noticed an advertisement in an activist magazine for an organization that was taking a different approach in their work on behalf of animals. Rather than struggling against the companies that profit from animal exploitation, or trying to generate media publicity, Vegan Outreach was distributing booklets that detailed what animals go through to produce meat, milk, and eggs. Their target audience consisted of those who expressed an interest when asked if they wanted a booklet.

Vegan Outreach seemed to be offering a better, smarter, and more cost-effective approach. We therefore decided to put down our signs, take off our costumes, and take up the work of distributing booklets. In our years of work for Vegan Outreach, we have personally distributed over 54,000 booklets because we believe that it is essential to give people thorough and accurate information on what animals endure on today's farms, in order to inspire them to stop supporting such cruelty. Distorted sound bites and dancing chickens will not do. Reaching people one at a time seems more labor intensive than using the media to reach hundreds of thousands of people at a time, yet the second scenario has been more illusionary than real. The number of people the media can reach is immense, but the quality of the message is usually lacking. Offering someone a copy of *Why Vegan?* allows them to read and witness the brutality of agribusiness, and to think about their own role in it. *Why Vegan?* and *Try Vegetarian* are the strongest pieces of vegetarian advocacy literature that we have seen. The detail, accuracy, and strong citations are vital to reaching the reader—shorter pieces of literature typically lack these qualities.

We strongly support Vegan Outreach financially because we know that our money goes further toward advancing animal liberation with their method of outreach. We distribute *Why Vegan?* on college campuses, at charity events, at train stations, even on busy streets—any location that offers many passersby who can be asked if they would like some information on vegetarianism. Keeping cooperative restaurants, health food stores, and bookstores stocked with booklets is the other distribution route we pursue. We urge others to undertake these actions because doing so supports an incredibly efficient and effective path to reduce animal suffering.

It can be difficult to contain oneself and think about being effective when faced with the urgent knowledge that animals are suffering today in the circus, in labs, on fur farms. But it is essential that we do stop and think. When we put forth our efforts in a struggle to save one or a few animals in such situations, we are not putting forth an effort that would have been much more powerful.

By contrast, distributing copies of *Why Vegan?* to interested

The FaunaVision Approach

By Eddie Lama

One of the first pieces of advice on animal advocacy that I received came from a wonderful fellow named Howard Lyman. Howard advised me to "plant a seed and walk away."

When I started doing animal activism in 1996, I learned that planting seeds depends on two items: the planter and the soil. And the tougher the soil, the more work the planter must do for the seeds to take root. New York City has concrete for soil and much of my potential audience wears pinstriped suits. Clearly, this is not the easiest soil for sowing seeds of activism. Yet I can't think of any other city where activism is more important. So I set my mind to exploring ways to make my seeds penetrate concrete. Part of this required that I look good while planting my seeds, because first impressions matter.

Cruelty is difficult to witness, and many people feel repelled by watching it. Yet it is precisely this act of witnessing that often inspires people to take action. I asked myself how I could expose people to the widespread nature of animal cruelty without causing them to recoil. Thinking along these lines led me to invent FaunaVision—a multimedia van built to roam the streets of New York, educating the public about animal rights issues. Equipped with large color monitors, speakers, computerized message boards, and a wireless PA system, the van displays footage of animal exploitation to awaken people to the hidden world of animal abuse. When I took FaunaVision on its maiden voyage to the old steakhouse I once dined at every week, it was an immediate hit. If a picture is worth a thousand words, color video presentations with high-fidelity audio are priceless.

People congregated around the FaunaVision, mesmerized by the visuals and audio. Passersby stopped in their tracks to ask questions about the horrors they were witnessing—the abuses that had been so cleverly hidden from them by the meat and dairy industries! It was a total departure from the traditional methods of outreach in which I had once participated. Normally, at the end of a long day of pamphleteering, most of us felt discouraged and frustrated. We sincerely wanted to get our message out, yet we would continually hear the same old lines about our "wearing leather shoes" (we weren't) and "what about the children?"

When we passed out our pamphlets, people would often scold us for "disturbing" them on their commute home. Passing out pamphlets opened us to ridicule, and it seemed as though peoples' only interest was to make us feel bad about ourselves and the inefficacy of our activism. But with FaunaVision, these difficulties evaporate. Through high-quality video, the message about the plight of the animals comes across loud and clear. What's more, our polished presentations give the matter legitimacy since they embody what people in this MTV visual age respect—a high-tech piece of equipment attended to by a couple of well-dressed, well-groomed people. The public responds to our presentations with interest, inquiry and discussion. With FaunaVision, the message is never confused with the messenger.

In the years since I invented FaunaVision, many other groups have emulated the concept. It's inspiring to me that people are using this technology to help the animals. Building a FaunaVision van isn't cheap: it can cost anywhere from $15,000 to $150,000 depending on its features and equipment. Obviously, not every activist or group can afford a FaunaVision-style van. So, in 1998, I created a more affordable activism tool called a Faunette, which can be built for $300 or less. The Faunette is a multimedia kiosk version of the FaunaVision van. Like the van, it features sound, a computerized message board and a color monitor; however, it is easily transportable and fits into the trunk of a car. A handy feature of this unit is that it runs on a rechargeable battery, so no external power source is needed. Additionally, the Faunette can go many places where the van cannot, including busy street corners and indoor concerts and events; in fact, some of our most successful activism has occurred by using a Faunette in New York's Grand Central Terminal.

If you wish to get your own Faunavision or Faunette you can do one of the following:

- Do it yourself. We animal people have always been resourceful, so why not build one with some friends? You can find assembly plans at <www.oasissanctuary.org>, or at <www.cok.net>.

- Contact us. In 2004, we totally redesigned the faunette and re-named it the Lil' Eddie. This new version of the Faunette features two screens (as opposed to one), a DVD unit instead of a VCR, and a telescoping pole to raise or lower the screens. All this equipment is contained in a unit that's even more compact than the original Faunette. We're making pre-assembled units available to interested animal protection groups and to individuals.

- Cut corners if necessary. If you can't currently build or buy one of these units, another alternative is buying a 13" TV/VCR unit. While you won't get the message boards or the option to run it without external power, for events where power is accessible these will work nicely, and they should drastically change your entire tabling experience. Plus, they can be purchased new for about $100.

Undoubtedly, once you have your own Faunavision, Faunette, or Lil' Eddie, you'll find that activism as you know it has completely changed. No longer will you be standing at your event hoping people come over and take a piece of literature. You'll find that at crowded events you'll have more people watching and transforming before your eyes than you ever thought possible.

So what are you waiting for? Buy or build yourself one of these great units. You'll gain an effective tool than can be used to help the animals for years to come. And remember, there are many seeds that still need to be planted.

Eddie Lama is the founder of the Oasis Sanctuary, which is online at: <www.oasissanctuary.org>.

Starting a Local Vegetarian Society

By Sukie Sargent

In 1988, my son Alex, then seventeen, announced that he was becoming a vegetarian for ethical reasons. OK, I said, and started to prepare vegetarian food for him. I respected his wishes but I wasn't ready to quit eating meat myself. It bothered me, however, to think of the slaughterhouse—but like everyone else, I was conditioned not to give it much thought. Over time, Alex's interest in animal protection became my interest too, and I joined a national animal rights group and started reading about factory farming. After reading their news magazine and learning about how farmed animals are treated, I decided to become a vegetarian myself. As I discovered more about animal agriculture, I decided to become vegan. And upon retiring in 1991, I decided to dedicate the rest of my life to helping animals.

Together with a friend, I started tabling at malls. People who came to our table often left us their contact information, and in September 1992 we had our first animal rights meeting with about fifteen people attending. This was the start of the first-ever animal rights group in El Paso. However, during our meetings I became aware that not everyone was interested in vegetarianism. It struck me as odd that I was surrounded by people committed to

147

helping animals, yet who saw no contradiction in eating meat. I realized that farm animal protection deserved to take top priority in my work, given that farmed animals constitute more than 95 percent of animals who suffer at the hands of humans. With that in mind, I decided that what my town needed was a vegetarian society.

With a list provided by a national vegetarian organization, as well as the names collected during our tabling, I sent a letter to about ninety El Paso residents. This contact led to our first meeting in February of 1993. One of our members predicted that the vegetarian society was going to be a success and that I was going to need help. He was right—the first membership roster had 39 people, and only five of those were active volunteers. Our present roster has 221 members, and now eighteen of these people are active volunteers.

When I attended the Texas Conference for Animal Rights in 1993, I met members of the Lone Star Vegetarian Network. Upon founding the Vegetarian Society of El Paso, we joined this network. They have done a remarkable job of coordinating statewide gatherings that have been attended and sponsored by local vegetarian societies like ours. Their annual Lone Star Vegetarian Chili Cook-Off is hosted in a different city each year, and consistently attracts favorable publicity and media attention about vegan eating.

One of our members volunteered to do the newsletter and this project has grown from a stapled twelve-page edition to our present bound 24 pages. In my opinion, a newsletter is the best tool to keep members involved and to reach nonmembers. With the development of the Internet, I also recommend registering a ".org" domain, and putting basic information about your group online. Some of your members will prefer to receive newsletters and event announcements by email or on your website, so it's helpful to find somebody with your group who can set up a website and list server.

Apart from newsletters, the other thing that brings a sense of cohesiveness to a group is regular meetings and events. Many groups in the United States rely mainly on potlucks, which I think is a flawed approach. People often lack the time to cook a special meal for a potluck, so they avoid such events. Others, particularly the aspiring vegetarians we strive to reach, may not have the cooking skills to participate.

In order to maximize our audience, our bimonthly dinners are always fixed-price buffet-style dinners hosted in restaurants. In seeking out restaurants that can host our events, we communicate extensively with restaurant owners to make sure they clearly understand the vegan concept and can cook buffet-style meals that are 100 percent vegan. Additionally, we only approach restaurants that have a special banquet room for gatherings. That way, we can carry on our events without having to disturb—or be disturbed by—other restaurant patrons.

We require advance payment from people attending our dinners. We learned this lesson the hard way, after getting stuck paying the restaurant for many no-shows. By requiring advance payment, we're financially covered regardless of attendance. And since our guests have already paid us, nearly everybody shows up at the event.

Our dinner events always include a speaker. In our early days, it was usually somebody local. But today, we are able to bring in top speakers from across the United States. I'm convinced that these speakers have reached the public and gained converts in a way that dinners alone could not accomplish. I consider the cost of these dinners to be a terrific bargain. When we started doing these dinners in 1993, the restaurant charged us $10 including drinks and gratuity. And we charged the same to members and nonmembers alike. As of 2004, our cost for the meals is $13, and we charge members $14 and nonmembers $15.

Over the years, the Vegetarian Society of El Paso has enjoyed strong and steady growth. When we first started, our attendance was about thirty five. Today, attendance typically is around a hundred. So far, our best-ever attendance for a dinner is 237 people.

As our numbers have grown, a strong group of volunteers has emerged to take on various tasks. Where once I worked mainly alone, today our volunteers carry a huge part of the load. I've been to a number of national animal protection conferences, and it's clear that our organization is one of the most active and successful. This is despite the fact that El Paso is not a first-tier city, and is by no means a haven for vegetarians. So, what explains our success? I think the most important factor is that I've been there from day one, and a steady force.

I believe that my working experience has helped me run a group such as ours. Years dealing with deadlines has given me the management skills to make sure things don't slip. In the decade that we've existed, our organization has never missed a newsletter and never missed a dinner. Breaks in established routine are a downfall for local groups because they convey the impression that the group is poorly run and not worth putting effort into. That's why I regard continuity as all-important. When I've looked at other groups around the country, I've seen that local vegetarian societies continually come and go. Almost always, it's because the leadership comes and goes as well. Often a group gets a vigorous start with great leadership, but shortly thereafter, the leader loses interest or leaves town. And almost always, the group either dies a quick death or gradually withers away.

I think every town needs a local vegetarian organization. If you have five or ten hours a month, and are good with people, I think you should consider starting a group of your own. I strongly believe, however, that these groups need to be started by people with deep local roots, and who have every intention of remaining in town and running the group for several years.

The future for farm animals will be dim until the day comes when every city and large town has a thriving local vegetarian society. As I write these words, I think that there are fewer than fifty towns and cities in the United States in which vegetarian societies have a strong, effective, and lasting presence. If you like working with people, have the ability to wear many hats while you get things started, and have a commitment to remain in your area long-term, you could well be the ideal person to start a local vegetarian society.

Sukie Sargent is Founder of the Vegetarian Society of El Paso.

Promoting Vegetarian Diets as a Nutrition Expert

By Virginia Messina, MPH, RD

When I first became a dietitian, vegetarianism wasn't on my mind at all. As I became interested in animal protection and vegetarian diets, I began to look for ways to further these causes through my career. For many years, I worked in traditional dietetics positions, and I frequently found myself amazed at all of the opportunities I had to talk about vegetarian diets. No matter where you end up working, the field of nutrition offers wonderful opportunities for promoting vegetarian and vegan diets.

The first step toward deciding if a career in nutrition is right for you is to think about whether you have the desire and ability to study science. You'll need to take classes in chemistry, biology, food science, biochemistry, physiology, microbiology, and more. There is no way to gain a solid understanding of nutrition without this background. Your education will continue throughout your career as you read scientific papers and attend seminars. Do you have enough interest in reading about nutrition to make this your job?

If you want to work in an educational capacity—counseling, creating educational materials, writing books and articles, and so forth—the best career path is in dietetics. To become a Registered

Dietitian (RD) you'll need to graduate from a four-year college, followed by an internship and a national exam. Many dietitians work in hospitals. For people who prefer a more community-oriented career, it's increasingly common to get a master's degree and sometimes a doctorate. I chose to get my master's degree in public health nutrition, and this credential set me on a career path to work in a variety of community programs. I've never actually worked in a hospital and don't have much knowledge about clinical dietetics. Instead, I've focused on diet needs throughout the life cycle.

When you consider where to go to school, know that there are many dietetics programs in the United States, but few that offer course work specific to vegetarian nutrition.* For the most part, becoming knowledgeable about vegetarian diets is something you must do on your own, but you can start this learning process at whatever school you decide to attend. You'll have plenty of opportunities to write papers or do research projects on the topic of your choice—in these cases, you can make a point of exploring vegetarian-related issues. In addition, as a dietetics student, you can join the Vegetarian Nutrition Dietetic Practice Group of the American Dietetic Association. This will put you in touch with others who are interested in vegetarian nutrition.

As you pursue your education, you may find that your classmates and instructors know comparatively little about vegetarian nutrition. While you may at times be frustrated by how the profession regards vegetarianism, the fact that you have chosen to enter this field means that you are creating the possibility for change.

After gaining your academic credentials, you'll want to find work that allows you to make a difference in people's lives. Many dietitians who are vegetarians aspire to become a "vegetarian dietitian" or to find employment in which they are practicing only vegetarian nutrition. These kinds of jobs are rare, but they do exist. For example, nonprofit organizations that promote vegetarian diets regularly hire dietitians. Some universities, such as those

---

*For a list, see: <www.eatright.org/Public/Careers/94_13280.cfm>

associated with the Seventh-day Adventist church, promote vegetarian diets. But there are definitely fewer of these jobs than there are vegetarian dietitians. That's OK though, because you are likely to have just as great an impact if you end up working in a traditional nutrition position. In these situations, you'll be bringing a positive perspective on vegetarian diets to people who might hear completely different information from a more "traditional" health professional.

Here are some examples of how you can promote vegetarian diets in your work:

- **Fitness Consulting.** If you are self-employed as a consultant, consider the opportunities at local health clubs and spas. They might welcome a professional to develop diets for clients or give classes. People who work out several times a week are often supremely motivated to eating healthfully, and they are likely to pay close attention to your advice.

- **Teaching at a College.** If you have the opportunity to teach in a college dietetics program, you can incorporate solid information about vegetarianism into your classes—something that other instructors may be unlikely to discuss in depth. After you become established as a vegetarian expert, you may be called upon by other teachers in the university to be a guest lecturer in their classes.

- **Letter Writing.** Any activist can write letters to the editor of a newspaper, but when the subject is diet, your letter and perspective on vegetarianism may carry a little more clout if you position yourself as a trained expert on the topic.

- **Teaching of Cooking Classes.** Many adult education programs offer cooking classes. As a nutrition expert, you have a chance to teach people not just how to cook, but how to plan healthful plant-based diets.

- **Consulting with Vegetarian Societies.** Share your expertise with others who are working to promote vegetarianism by acting as a consultant to a local or national vegetarian society.

- **Working with Mainstream Dietetic Organizations.** Become involved in professional organizations like the American Dietetic Association or with a regional dietetics group. These organizations tend to promote more traditional kinds of activities and advice. Your involvement can be crucial to ensure that materials produced for consumers and health professionals present vegetarianism in a balanced way.

- **Assisting Government Decision-Making.** Various government agencies regularly seek the advice of nutritionists to formulate vegetarian-oriented meals. Dietitians often have a chance to testify about these programs either before government groups or in writing. Again, as a professional and an expert, your opinion may carry far more weight than a consumer's.

- **Writing Books or Articles.** If you possess good writing skills, being a Registered Dietitian will give you an edge when it comes to attracting the attention of book and magazine publishers. Perhaps the best way to break into print is to start locally. Many hospitals and clinics offers a health newsletter. You can approach the editor, and ask about contributing a column on nutrition. Or, you might contact the editor for your local newspaper and inquire about the prospects of writing a health and nutrition column.

The wonderful thing about these opportunities is that they require varying amounts of time and energy. Some are perfect for part-time volunteering, while others can lead to full-time careers. In my professional life I've had the chance to work in many of these areas. As the circumstances of my life have changed or as I've developed new skills, I've always found new volunteer or employment opportunities.

In summary, while many people can speak out on behalf of vegetarian diets, people with scientific expertise carry special influence. You definitely don't need a science background to be a superb activist. But if you obtain solid credentials in nutrition, you'll have added opportunities to make a difference.

Virginia Messina has written numerous books on vegetarian nutrition, and was a co-author of the "ADA Position Paper on Vegetarianism," published in 1997 and 2003. Her website is: <www.VirginiaMessina.com>.

The Activist Chef

By Robin Robertson

I'm passionate about animal rights, yet I've never exposed a re-search lab, don't participate in demonstrations, and have never lobbied lawmakers. Thankfully, there are others who do those things well. My activism plays out in a different way: by being a vegan chef. This may seem an indirect method of supporting animal rights, but in reality, it goes right to the heart of the matter.

Everyone has to eat, and the eating of animal products is the root cause of farm animal suffering and death. All we have to do is convert meat and dairy eaters, and there will be no need for slaughterhouses. It's as simple as that. The hard part, of course, is convincing people to give up the taste of animal products. What better way than to provide sensational plant-based alternatives that are healthy and taste great?

As a vegan chef, cookbook author, and cooking teacher for many years, I like to think that I play a part in reducing animal suffering by virtue of my ability to create delicious vegan cuisine. Many people have told me that my recipes have influenced their decision to give up meat and dairy, and that's precisely why I chose to work in this field. When I first tried to become vege-tarian in the 1970s, there were few ingredients, fewer cookbooks, and practically no vegetarian restaurants anywhere. It was hard enough to cook vegan at home, let alone learn the craft of fine vegan cooking. These days, however, opportunities for aspiring vegan chefs are numerous.

You can prepare for a job in the food-service industry either through professional training or by learning on the job. My own early culinary training was on the job. I started out as a line cook, worked my way up to sous chef, and then later worked as a chef at a number of traditional restaurants. Food preparation can be demanding and exhausting, with constant standing and sweating through long days and longer nights—but if you love it, the discomforts won't stop you. Situations vary, depending on where you work. For example, if you can luck into cooking at a vegan café with a short menu and limited hours, your road will doubtless be smoother than mine.

On the other hand, with a culinary education, you are less likely to start at the bottom, and you will have a wider range of employment options. Jobs in vegetarian food-service still aren't as plentiful as those in nonvegetarian circles, but times are changing, and a vegan chef can enjoy a number of fantastic career opportunities. I know offhand of more than a dozen great career possibilities.*

If you're considering culinary school, visit as many campuses as you can before making a choice. There are a number of superb schools worth considering.† You can learn a lot attending weekend workshops, but accredited programs that award certificates or diplomas will give you training and credentials that can rapidly advance your career.

If possible, try to hold down a part-time kitchen job while you are going to culinary school. By doing this, you'll not only make your education more affordable—you'll also gain experience that will be of great use to you after you graduate.

---

*Jobs that demand cooking experience include: caterer, personal chef, celebrity or corporate chef, natural foods café chef, restaurant chef, spa chef, vegetarian restauranteur, specialty food company owner, baker, new product development, food writing, recipe development, cookbook author, magazine writer, cooking teacher, consultant.

†I maintain a current list of vegetarian-friendly culinary schools on my website at <www.robinrobertson.com>.

Many people who eat meat would become vegan right away, if only they knew how easy it is, and how delicious vegan cooking can be. As a vegan chef, you will gain unparalleled abilities when it comes to inspiring people to eat more humanely. One great meal can forever change how a person regards vegan foods. Although being a chef may not appear to be related to activism, there may be no more important work where farm animal protection is concerned.

Robin Robertson is the author of Vegan Planet and numerous other cookbooks.

Becoming a Medical Doctor

By Stephen Kaufman, MD

A number of educational paths lead to special opportunities to protect animals. While many careers are worth considering, I think that becoming a medical doctor is a wonderful idea for people committed to animal protection. In this essay, I'm going to discuss what it takes to become an MD, and why this is a terrific field to enter if you want to prevent animal suffering.

I have always been fond of animals. I had misgivings about working in an animal research laboratory as a tenth grader, which seemed at the time like a good "pre-med" thing to do. I initially convinced myself that vivisection was a necessary evil, but time and again I witnessed animals suffering more than the research required. I remember a beagle being slapped hard on the head because he was shaking while the technician struggled to place an intravenous catheter. I was deeply disturbed by seeing that dog punished for being a "bad" victim of animal experimentation.

Everything clicked during my sophomore year of college, upon reading a *New York Times Magazine* feature article on animal experimentation.* After next reading Peter Singer's *Animal Liberation*, I felt obligated to help stop the massive institutionalized

---

*Patricia Curtis. *New York Times Magazine*. January 14, 1977.

abuse of nonhuman animals. So, I contacted Eleanor Seiling, president of United Action for Animals in New York City. I told her I was pre-med and wanted to be a doctor, but I also had a passion for animal advocacy. She offered astute advice. She told me that going to medical school would dovetail nicely with my interest in animal advocacy. The animal protection movement needs doctors, because people trust and respect physicians, especially when it comes to receiving advice on diet and lifestyle issues. The animal protection movement also needs doctors to speak out about vivisection.

She added that becoming a doctor would help make me financially independent. I could therefore avoid the money-related conflicts and bickering that are widespread in the animal protection movement. With all this in mind, I resolved to stay pre-med and follow through on my original ambition to become a doctor. I graduated medical school in 1985 and have since specialized in ophthalmology.

In late 1985, Dr. Murry Cohen recruited me to the Medical Research Modernization Committee. The scientist in me has found the MRMC particularly appealing, because the MRMC has demonstrated compelling evidence that vivisection is often based on poor science. The group has maintained that ethical research with human subjects is a better way to advance human medicine. Many MRMC members have little interest in animal protectionism, and the MRMC has never taken a stance on the moral status of animals. Consequently, we have avoided being dismissed by the scientific community as an animal advocacy group, which has encouraged debate on animal experimentation's scientific merit. The MRMC has produced the monograph series "Perspectives on Medical Research" and the booklet *A Critical Look at Animal Experimentation,* which activists have found helpful. In recent years, I have become more involved in working to protect farmed animals, because of the number of animals abused and the degree of misery that they typically suffer. I've worked with a number of groups, and I've been able to offer some financial support to groups that I think are winning substantial change for the animals.

Advice for Activists Wishing to Study Medicine

Preparing for a medical career is, of course, challenging. First, you must perform well in pre-med courses and other schoolwork. Then, medical school's burdens usually include long hours, stressful learning situations, and substantial costs. Fortunately, many medical schools don't offer animal labs, and of those that have animal labs, at most one or two require participation. Instead, medical schools rely on dissection of cadavers, computer models, and hands-on clinical experience, which I think is most appropriate.

After medical school, it can be difficult to pay off loans, because training after medical school generally ranges from three to eight years, depending on which specialty is chosen. I would only recommend a medical career for someone with a genuine interest in medical science.

I advise those applying to medical and veterinary school to keep a low profile on their animal concerns. In particular, many pre-vet students think that veterinarians are animal lovers, but, in truth, vivisectors and people dedicated to increasing productivity of "food animals" dominate veterinary school faculties. Veterinary scientists generally see animal liberationists as potential trouble-makers.

Surprisingly, medical schools generally dedicate little attention to nutrition. Students who wish to gain a firm foundation in nutritional science usually need to pursue this on their own. Physicians, comfortable reading scientific literature, have little difficulty learning nutritional basics and, if so inclined, they can eventually gain expertise in the field.

Integrating Activism into Your Career

Scientific degrees enhance credibility. A background in science, particularly medicine, provides great advantages when communicating about diet. Whether you're talking personally to one person or communicating through the media to a wide audience, a degree in medicine greatly increases the receptiveness with which people greet your message. People usually listen carefully whenever they get a chance to receive nutrition advice from a medical doctor. And, in my personal activism, the majority of my letters to editors are approved, even when submitted to newspapers far from my home town.

As an ophthalmologist, I can sometimes recommend that my patients move toward a plant-based diet. In particular, recent research has shown that antioxidants appear to protect against severe forms of age-related macular degeneration. Primary-care physicians usually have more opportunities to encourage plant-based diets for disease prevention and management, particularly since so much chronic disease is related to elevated lipids and obesity. And, primary care doctors can offer solid nutritional advice among their office reading materials.

Looking back on my activist work, I think Eleanor Seiling was right that pursuing a career such as medicine offers compelling advantages. The money I make as an ophthalmologist funds my personal activism and gives me free reign to choose my goals and strategies. Additionally, people with well-paying careers generate resources with which to support worthy organizations and activities.

Stephen Kaufman is co-chair of the Medical Research Modernization Committee, <www.mrmcmed.org>, and the Christian Vegetarian Association, <www.christianveg.com>.

Making Food-Service Operations Vegan-Friendly

By Johanna McCloy

A new chapter in my life began in April 2000, when I was among tens of thousands of fans attending a baseball game at Dodger Stadium. After a few innings I headed to the downstairs cafeteria where they sold salads and veggie burgers. Upon reaching the area, I discovered that the cafeteria had been replaced by VIP suites. I proceeded to walk the stadium in search of a vegetarian meal. Endless concession stands and a full inning later, I had come full circle, with no success. The menu boards at each stand displayed hot dogs, burgers, pepperoni pizzas, barbecued meats, and meat-based submarine sandwiches. Nowhere on the menu was there a viable meal option for vegetarians.

Having been exposed to the realities of factory farming, I knew what these menu options meant in terms of animal suffering. I settled for peanuts and returned to my seat, but I could barely eat. In nearly every row, I could see fans cheerfully scarfing down hot dogs. What was there for me to do? Boycott the stadium? Who would care? I felt nothing but anguish, futility, and grief. The impact of the experience was so profound that when I returned home that evening, I was moved to tears.

Fast forward to April 2002. Again, I was at Dodger Stadium

with a packed and cheering crowd. This time, however, I was excited. Veggie dogs were making their debut—and my actions had made it possible! I went to the appropriate stand and stood in line. I heard someone in front of me ordering veggie dogs.

"I didn't know you sold those here," he commented.

"It's our first day," came the reply.

"Cool," he said, handing over some bills in exchange for two dogs. The concession manager met me there and we shook hands over our accomplishment. When I returned to my seat, I took a minute to look upon the thousands of fans and to absorb the realization of my dreams. Once again, I was moved to tears. This time, the tears came from feelings of hope and the realization that one person's voice can make a difference.

So, what happened? After my frustrating attempt to find vegetarian food at Dodger Stadium, I gave a lot of thought to the fact that I represented a consumer base that wasn't being tapped. I could easily do what others were doing and bring my own food or eat before the game. But that would not address the underlying problem—that concessions like Dodger Stadium needed to change their menus to reflect the growing numbers of consumers like myself, who would prefer to eat vegetarian options. Concession foods needed to start reflecting the times.

I resolved to contact the concession manager and express my ideas for improving Dodger Stadium's food offerings. I decided that my strategy would be to explain that the stadiums food business was leaving a substantial market untapped. All kinds of people prefer healthful, organically grown, tasty and meat-free options. As a profit-seeking business, wouldn't the stadium be interested in generating sales from these people?

With my background as a TV commercial actor, I was keenly aware of image and marketing. Messages that are positive, fun, and enticing usually win people over. Despite my nervousness, I communicated in a friendly and confident manner during my first call to Dodger Stadium's concession manager. As we spoke, I gave him some basic facts documenting the increasing demand for organic, vegetarian and kosher foods. I then made the point that none of these foods were available at the stadium. I emphasized that veggie dogs would be ideal for baseball stadiums and would satisfy the eating requirements for a diverse group of people.

I also noted that the stadium didn't sell vegetarian submarine sandwiches. I figured that these sandwiches would probably be easy to add to the menu. It made sense to give the concession manager as many options as possible, and to include at least one idea that could be likely be implemented without delay.

The concession manager respected my approach and decided to act on my suggestions. He added a vegetarian sub to the menu the next week! Unfortunately, the veggie dog proved problematic because of contractual obligations with the hot dog supplier at the stadium. So I continued to work with the manager to find a way around the problem. After two years of ongoing fan requests, accompanied by my persistent efforts, we were finally able to make veggie hot dogs available.

As a result of my communications with the concession manager, I became inspired to initiate efforts on a wider scale. I contacted every Major League Baseball stadium and solicited follow-ups from supportive fans and consumer groups in representative cities. I named my advocacy efforts "Soy Happy" and created a web site offering reference information and cheerful encouragement for all involved. I also offered my services as a liaison between stadiums and manufacturers. Hundreds of supportive baseball fans contacted their stadiums, and I began communicating with concession managers and manufacturers all over the country. Media coverage also helped to expand awareness and support.

By the end of the 2000 baseball season, three Major League Baseball stadiums had introduced veggie dogs. By spring of 2004, that total reached eleven—and counting! Restaurants, entertainment arenas, schools, hospitals, fairs, and many other vendors have consulted with Soy Happy in an effort to incorporate vegetarian alternatives into their menus.

Consumer activism is the key to our success. When we decide to use our power as consumers to speak up, we help to raise the collective consciousness. And this raising of consciousness is a precursor to creating tangible change. For example, think about soymilk or veggie burgers. Remember how strange and unappetizing they recently seemed to the mainstream? Not any more. It took persistence from manufacturers, both in terms of marketing and the formulation of increasingly tasty products, but all this work paid off. These foods have entered the mainstream psyche and are no longer considered unusual.

When enough consumers request alternative foods, vendors start to believe that these food choices are viable and in demand. We consumers may not succeed in getting items on the menu every time we ask, but it's still essential to raise consciousness, no matter what the immediate results. Even when a call results in no immediate positive action, there's still a chance our ideas will be implemented later, as more customers make their preferences known. Psychologically, the more visibility we bring to vegetarian food options, the less unusual these foods will seem. This is how consumers can propel massive change in a short amount of time.

To maximize our success when communicating with food vendors, it helps to know a bit about the food industry's structure, so here is a brief overview. The food business has two distinctive sides. There is retail, such as your local grocery store, and there is food-service, which is supplied by commercial vendors who sell ready-to-eat food for public consumption. These two sides of the business require different packaging, sales staff, and distribution channels. It's therefore often cost prohibitive to sell a given food through both retail and food-service channels. This is why some of the foods you purchase at the supermarket may not be feasible options at your local ballpark, music festival, or cafeteria.

Keeping in mind that retail and food-service products rely on different distributors, it helps to do as much of the legwork as possible before contacting a venue's food-service manager. If you can demonstrate that the item you're requesting is popular and easy to purchase, your chances of success are measurably increased. To find out whether an item you favor is available in food-service channels, you can contact the manufacturer directly. If you get this information in advance of making your pitch, you are likely to have an impressive amount of success.

There are some final things to keep in mind that will increase your effectiveness. On my website, <www.soyhappy.org>, I offer statistics showing the dramatic increase in the annual sales of vegan and organic foods. It's helpful to get a copy of this information, and to make it part of your initial presentation whenever you reach out to a food-service manager. It is important to note that *mainstream consumers* are responsible for the surging sales of these plant-based foods.

When you communicate to a food-service manager, stress the fact that the menu items you are suggesting will be in demand by a wide audience—not just vegetarians. Many people are opting for meatless alternatives because of health reasons, cultural inclinations, or religious affiliations. Speak for everyone who wants them. Your communication with a food-service manager is not an appropriate time to talk about the benefits of a vegetarian or vegan lifestyle. Remember that this is a food business, looking to make a profit, so focus on the wide scope of sales that new menu items can generate. Statistics and research studies will support you every time—I've posted these at <www.soyhappy.org>—so do a little homework on the latest sales statistics before making your presentation. Finally, if you know that competitors are offering these items, be sure to mention this when you make your suggestions. The psychology of the domino principle is useful when making your presentations.

In all situations, stay friendly, upbeat and courteous. Always thank the people you contact for their consideration. You need to extend your appreciation for their time and attention, especially when items are still on trial and are considered "new." Go out of your way to generate business for a vendor when they add new alternatives. Be the model consumer they want to please.

Working for School Lunch Reform

By Antonia Demas, PhD

America's school lunch program is the world's biggest feeding program. It has the potential to serve 53 million students every school day. I began my relationship with this program more than thirty years ago. I was living in Vermont and I volunteered at a Head Start center where I could bring my infant son to work with me. This enabled me to nurse him as I interacted with kids and food, the two great passions in my life.

While the Head Start program does many things right, I was alarmed at how they were feeding students. Most menu items were high in fat and sugar, with a heavy emphasis on refined carbohydrates and animal products. I focused my volunteer efforts on working with students to introduce nutritious vegetarian foods in a way that was fun, hands-on, and sensory-based. The students loved this type of interaction with foods as they learned to cook and eat a healthier diet. I also worked with the cooks and some of the families to teach them the pleasures of healthful cuisine.

The results were remarkable. Students devoured foods their parents swore they would never touch, and they even requested these items at home. While the students were eager to learn about healthful eating, teaching these same lessons to kitchen staff was far more difficult. But we made great progress on this front by holding cooking workshops. My volunteer work led to a paid position at Head Start. After that, I spent many years consulting and volunteering with a variety of educational programs.

No matter where my job took me, my strategy remained the same. I sought to make the experience fun while using food as a vehicle to teach science, math, social studies, language arts, and other disciplines. The kids loved this type of education and they eagerly ate anything they had a hand in preparing. I developed many lesson plans and curricula over the years on a wide range of topics. I frequently taught about the agricultural roots of holidays, food customs and rituals of traditional cultures, and how food affects our bodies and minds.

Through my work, I sought to demonstrate that it is possible to get kids to eat healthful foods in the school lunch program. In my view, the problem is not with the students—it is with the adults who determine what kids need to be educated about. Because family life has changed so dramatically in recent times, we can no longer assume that children are growing up with a basic knowledge about how to grow and cook food. Most families do not eat a majority of their meals together. We have consequently become a fast-food culture due to a perceived lack of time to prepare home-cooked meals.

To understand the challenges that confront school lunch reform, it's useful to know the history of this program. When public school attendance became mandatory in the late 1800s, teachers quickly recognized that many students were arriving hungry, not having eaten breakfast and with nothing to eat for lunch. As any educator knows, it is difficult to teach a hungry child—they have a difficult time concentrating and are easily distracted. For fifty years after compulsory education began, charitable groups worked to provide children with food during the school day. They lobbied for government support to make this effort feasible financially. It wasn't until 1946 that the government finally took action when Congress passed the School Lunch Act. From its inception, the School Lunch Act has served a dual purpose: to provide school children with food, and to support farmers by providing an additional market for surplus foods.

These surplus foods are known as commodity foods. The government buys them from farmers and makes them available to schools for free. The problem with the commodity program is that it overwhelmingly selects products from large-scale agribusiness and the meat and dairy industry. Given the size of the school lunch program, and the millions of dollars at stake, it's hardly surprising that large-scale agriculture lobbied heavily to rig the program in its favor.

The school lunch program purchases relatively tiny amounts of plant-based commodities. This has everything to do with the fact that the meat and dairy industry has had enormous success in getting the school lunch program to base its meals around animal products. Additionally, many people who run local school lunch programs believe that students will refuse vegetarian menu items.

The benefits that the school lunch program have delivered to animal agriculture have come at the expense of our children's well-being. The food that is served at schools not only affects student health, it also helps to shape behavior and academic performance. It is long overdue for educators to appreciate this fact, and to include nutrition-based study in every academic curriculum. Because there is clear evidence in the medical literature about the role diet plays in chronic disease, it is important that children are educated about this relationship so they are able to protect themselves from developing these diseases.

I returned to school at mid-life to document the fact that it is possible to get students to eat nutritious foods in a school setting. My PhD dissertation at Cornell University clearly demonstrated that students will consume healthful, plant-based foods—if only they receive the right instruction. The work I've done has repeatedly demonstrated that children enjoy and benefit from classes related to food and nutrition, especially when these classes involve cooking and tasting the foods under consideration. Students who receive this education usually bring the message home and have a positive impact on their families' eating behaviors.

Taking Action

America needs a school lunch program that celebrates the importance nutrients play in our physical, mental, and emotional lives. For a program like this to exist, local activists must become involved. The benefits of working on school lunch reform are far-reaching. Depending on the size of your district, you have the opportunity to improve the daily meals of hundreds, or even thousands, of students. And it's not hard to get started.

Before you begin, consider being trained by my organization, the Food Studies Institute, to become a Certified Food Educator. You can certainly accomplish a great deal without receiving this training, but with training you'll be better equipped to carry out your activism. Plus, you'll receive credentials that will increase your influence. Our three-day training teaches you to offer a curriculum, called "Food is Elementary," to students.

When you're ready to start work at a local school, start by contacting the principal and requesting permission to eat lunch in the student cafeteria. Observe how children move through the lines, what the noise level is, and how much time the children are given to eat. Determine what level of choice is given to the child about which foods their meal will include.

These cafeteria visits will give you a sense of how the lunch program operates, what kinds of foods are served, and what opportunities exist for improvement. Typically, the process of advancing reform is a long and protracted job. It helps to find as many allies as possible. So seek out people in your community who are likely to offer support. Get together with them, and come up with a plan that is upbeat and calls for constructive improvements to the lunch program. Outline a course of action that may begin with a PTA presentation or the formation of a nutrition advisory committee. It's especially helpful to bring to the classroom trained volunteers, who will educate students about nutritious foods.

With this work under way, you can then contact the Food Studies Institute for help in obtaining grants that will support your efforts. Our "Food is Elementary" program has been successfully implemented in more than 250 schools in seventeen states.

Working for reform involves a variety of tasks. No matter which efforts you undertake, they should all be geared toward awakening educators, parents, and students to the value of sensible eating. Winning over food-service employees and school administrators is key. With the right outreach, these vital people can be allies rather than opposition. Always remember to be positive and not political in your dealings with administration, teachers, and food-service staff.

Keep in mind that you'll continually have to confront decades worth of misinformation put out by animal agriculture. Currently, the main source of nutrition information that kids receive comes from the meat and dairy industries. Much of what parents, teachers, and students know about nutrition is based on industry propaganda, and this can take time to overcome.

There are many difficulties and obstacles you'll encounter on the way to introducing reform, but don't give up! This is extremely important work, and your energies can greatly improve the lives of thousands of children.

Antonia Demas is founder and President of the Food Studies Institute: <http://www.foodstudies.org>.

Appendices

Appendix A: The Health Argument

When you compare the nutritional profile of vegan foods against animal products, it's easy to come away with the impression that vegan foods are ambrosia, whereas animal products are slow-acting poison. Vegan foods tend to be low in fat, and extremely low in saturated fat. They are loaded with fiber. Additionally, over the past twenty years, scientists have discovered numerous antioxidants and phytochemicals in many vegan foods, which collectively are thought to reduce disease risk.

As for animal products, most of these foods are loaded with fat. What's more, the fat in red meat and dairy products leads to clogged arteries because it is highly saturated. Animal products contain no fiber whatsoever. And, in stark contrast to vegan foods, scientists have not found vast stores of anti-cancer compounds in foods of animal origin. In fact, the reverse is true: when meats are grilled, they produce heterocyclic amines (HAs) and other toxic chemicals. HAs are regarded as some of the most potent carcinogens commonly found in food. And while HAs are generated whenever meat is grilled, they do not occur when the same cooking methods are applied to plant-based foods.

Given the profound differences in the nutritional profiles of vegan foods compared to animal products, it's no surprise that vegans usually enjoy better health than the general population. Compared to the average American, vegans tend to have healthier body weights, and they rarely suffer from obesity.[1] Heart disease rates among vegans are markedly lower than the general population.[2] And there is some evidence that consumption of fruits and vegetables reduces the risk of several kinds of cancer.[3]

There are three distinct areas of the vegan health argument: the beneficial qualities of vegan foods, the harmful qualities of animal products, and the clear tendencies of vegans to experience better health than the general population. With this information in mind, it seems commonsense to conclude that a vegan diet is healthier than a diet that contains even small amounts of animal products. After all, every mouthful of chicken or beef swallowed (which is, at best, neutral in terms of impact on health), means one less mouthful of health-promoting vegan foods. But commonsense can lead to faulty conclusions. And the claim that a vegan diet is healthier than any diet that contains animal products is, surprisingly, not borne out by the best evidence.

The reason an *appropriately planned* vegan diet is so much healthier than the standard American diet is that vegans avoid the main pitfalls of the American diet. Most of the health advantages that accompany a vegan diet stem from the fact that, in closing the door to animal products, you're eliminating the possibility of eating excessive amounts of the most unhealthful animal-based foods. It's impossible to damage your health by eating excessive amounts of hamburgers or ice cream if you never eat these foods in the first place.

Different people have different thresholds for risk. Some people can smoke two packs of cigarettes a day for fifty years and show no ill effects. Yet, for most people, even a few cigarettes a day are enough to significantly raise lung cancer risk. Similarly, it's impossible to determine how many animal products a given person can safely eat. No matter what your personal threshold at which animal products become risky, you are always certain to be beneath this threshold if you're vegan.

The best evidence unfortunately indicates that most people can afford to eat significant amounts of fish or poultry and small amounts of beef, eggs, and dairy products, with little or no added health risks. Matters change for people who have developed heart disease—for them, a vegan or near-vegan diet offers clear advantages. But the general public can afford a weekly burger and a few ounces of fish or poultry a day, with no detriment to health. As an activist, I wish this was not the case. But since there's no convincing evidence that small amounts of animal products pose substantial health risks, it's important that the vegetarian movement faces up to this fact so that we can maintain the highest credibility.

There are, of course, a hundred health reasons to avoid animal products that have nothing to do with the long-term risks of disease. Some of these include:

- Antibiotic residues commonly found in meats, dairy products, and farmed fish

- Increased risks among regular meat eaters of suffering food poisoning

- Hormones that are used in cattle feedlots

- Possibility of adulterants, spoilage, or unlawful feed additives

These food safety risks are worth knowing, but none is terribly severe. Taken together, the short-term food safety risks of eating animal products will never rival those of getting in your car and driving on the highway.[4] In consequence, vegans need to show restraint when talking about food safety, and take care to avoid overstating the facts.

Just as the food safety arguments for veganism aren't breathtaking, the long-term health advantages of being vegan are also frequently overstated. While it's true that vegetarians have lower risks of heart disease, diabetes, and a few other conditions, these health advantages don't seem to translate into extended lifetimes. The limited research done so far indicates that vegans live longer than the general population, but this is mainly because vegans tend to avoid tobacco.[5] Among nonsmokers who don't drink excessive amounts of alcohol, the mortality rates of vegans are comparable to those of meat eaters.[6]

What, then, should be the vegetarian movement's position on health? It's fair to say that vegetarian activists tend to overemphasize the health arguments supporting a vegan diet. This is probably because most activists have had little or no formal education about nutrition. Without training in the field, or a scientific background, activists are prone to wholeheartedly accept health claims that rest on shaky ground.

If the vegetarian movement choses to contend that a vegan diet is markedly superior to any other diet, then it must face the burden of proving this claim. And unfortunately, the best scientific evidence does not put vegan diets significantly ahead of well-planned omnivorous diets. There are, nevertheless, excellent reasons to become vegan that are purely grounded in the health argument. Perhaps the best of these reasons is that a vegan diet eliminates all possibility of consuming unhealthful amounts of animal products. People are prone to temptation and lack of moderation. While small amounts of animal products are unlikely to significantly elevate disease risks, it's all too easy to end up eating unhealthfully large amounts of animal products.

There are at least two effective ways to deal with animal products so they don't compromise your health. The first is to consume animal products in the traditional Asian style, where meats are used as a garnish rather than as a main course. The second way, which is perhaps easier and more effective, is to strive not for moderation, but rather to make a clean break with animal products. By putting energy into exploring the enormous range of vegan-friendly cuisines, it's easy to make a lasting dietary change for the better. And taking a vegan approach to eating avoids the possibility of backsliding, which tends to plague Americans who try to moderate their consumption of animal foods.

I've confined my discussion of human health to this brief appendix because I don't believe that health issues are worthy of being one of the core arguments made on behalf of farmed animals. There are too many complexities and ambiguities for health concerns to be worthy of occupying one-third of the vegetarian movement's argument. The dedicated activist, however, needs to read widely on the matter of health.

Although the health advantages of a vegan diet are limited, there are certainly times when they merit discussion. Nowhere are these advantages more convincing than in regard to weight control. In 1980, 47 percent of Americans were either overweight or obese.[7] By 2000, that figure had jumped to 64 percent.[8] Americans are increasingly desperate to control their weight. The fact that vegans are slimmer than the rest of the population suggests that this could be an effective approach to weight control. Neal Barnard, MD, has written two vegan-oriented books on weight control that cover the subject well.*

There are several health-related arguments that may convince people to reduce or eliminate their consumption of animal products. These arguments deserve to be mentioned by the vegetarian movement, but overall the health argument is not worthy of receiving the starring role it has long held. Similar cautions should also be raised in regard to the environmental arguments supporting veganism, which are even more prone to exaggerations on the part of activists. And that is the subject of the following appendix.

---

*Barnard, Neal. *Foods That Cause You to Lose Weight*. New York: Avon Books. 1999. Barnard, Neal. *A Physician's Slimming Guide: For Permanent Weight Control*. Summertown, TN: Book Publishing Company. 1992.

Appendix B: The Environmental Argument

Many vegetarian activists apparently believe that there is a resounding environmental case against all forms of meat production. Time and again, vegetarian advocacy materials make the point that if you're still eating meat, you have no business calling yourself an environmentalist.

The environmental argument for vegetarianism rests mainly on the assertion that meat production is wasteful of land and water resources, and it generates substantial amounts of pollution. These points are true, but when you look closely at the environmental damage necessitated by animal agriculture, the costs aren't nearly as high as they first appear. In fact, with the exception of beef and fish, a nonvegetarian diet need not use substantially more resources than a vegetarian diet. Appendices C and D explain why cattle production, fishing boats, and fish farms are genuine environmental menaces. But here, we'll look at the glaring weaknesses in the common environmental arguments put forth by vegetarian activists.

Cycling Grain Through Animals

There's no disputing the fact that whenever grains are fed to farmed animals, food is being wasted. Vegetarian advocates often focus their environmental arguments on beef production, since cattle are notoriously inefficient at converting grains to flesh. At the feedlot, it takes about thirteen pounds of grain, mostly corn, to produce a single pound of beef.[1]

There's something obscene about feeding all this grain to cattle and getting so little beef in return, particularly when people elsewhere in the world are starving. The trouble is that this feed conversion argument is prone to oversimplification. Cattle are indeed terribly inefficient at converting grain to flesh, but other farmed animals do much better. This is especially true regarding chickens, who take only about three pounds of feed to produce a pound of meat.[2] Pigs are also much more efficient than cattle, requiring about six pounds of grain per pound of meat.[3]

There's no doubt that a vegan diet is somewhat more efficient than an omnivorous diet. But it's misleading to bring up the beef industry's poor feed-to-meat conversion rates in order to imply that pigs and poultry are comparably inefficient. Beef excepted, the feed waste that occurs with animal products is not sufficient to make for a compelling argument. Meat may require more resources to produce than do feed grains, but the same is also true for fruits and vegetables, yet you'll never hear vegetarians argue that people should abstain from apples and carrots for environmental reasons.

Water Resources

If you look at the vegetarian movement's usual arguments against livestock production, the most problematic of its claims pertains to water use. It's true that many vegan foods can be grown using less water than it takes to produce meat. But the difference is hardly impressive enough to merit being one of the movement's primary arguments.

Yet the movement's books and pamphlets consistently refer to water use. Time and again, the claim has been made that it takes about 5200 gallons of water to produce just one pound of beef.[4] If this were indeed the case, water use would deserve to be one of the main arguments against beef production. But an examination of the issue reveals that the 5200-gallon figure has no real evidence to back it up.

The 5200-gallon claim first appeared in 1978 in a now-defunct journal called *Soil and Water*.[5] Given how heavily cited this article is in the vegetarian literature, I was eager to read it to see how the authors came up with their figure. The trouble was there are only a few libraries in the country that carry archives of the journal. When I finally obtained a copy of the article, I was surprised that something so poorly done could be accepted for publication, and I was astonished that anyone would have thought its figures worthy of being cited. Basically, the article amounts to two pages of tables indicating the water requirements of various foods. Along with the tables are a couple of pages of explanatory text. Nowhere does this article present data that shows how the authors came up with their claim that it takes 5200 gallons to produce a pound of beef. Nor does the article feature any citations to other literature that back up this claim. This article is the original source of the vegetarian movement's 5200-gallon claim, and there's nothing at all in its analysis that provides credible support for this figure.

Disturbingly, the vegetarian community has taken this 5200-gallon claim as gospel, perhaps because *Soil and Water* is so hard to find that hardly anyone has bothered to seek out a copy of the original article. There are other water claims commonly advanced by the vegetarian movement. And John Robbins' 2001 book, *The Food Revolution*, references two more of these claims. Robbins has played a pioneering role in the vegan movement, and his writings have been profoundly influential. Unfortunately, where water use is concerned, the analysis he presents is deeply flawed.

In *The Food Revolution*, Robbins lays out his argument in a way that makes the National Cattlemen's Beef Association look as though they are advancing an unreasonable claim about water. Robbins presents a table, which begins with the Cattlemen's assertion that a pound of beef requires 441 gallons of water. He then sets this figure against competing claims of 2500 and 2464 gallons. Robbins then concludes his table by including—without a word of criticism—the dubious 5200-gallon figure we just looked at.

Given the figures presented in Robbins' table, it is made to appear as though the Cattlemen are in dreamland with their low-ball claim of 441 gallons. But it turns out that the 2500 and 2464-gallon figures that Robbins cites are scarcely more credible than the 5200-gallon claim. Let's now look at both of these claims.

The 2500-gallon figure is taken from the late Professor Georg Borgstrom, who was chairman of the Food Science and Human Nutrition Department at Michigan State University. Given his impressive credentials, it would be interesting to see what kind of article Borgstrom could put together to support his estimate. The trouble is, Borgstrom never wrote such an article! The Robbins footnote refers, not to a peer-reviewed article, but to a talk Borgstrom gave back in 1981. No proceedings from this talk were published, so there's no record of any data upon which Borgstrom based his figure. For this 2500-gallon claim to be credible, it should point to a well-organized collection and analysis of the data—the amount of water used for feed corn, irrigated pasture, drinking water, and so forth. Borgstrom apparently never published any such data, so his 2500-gallon claim deserves to be treated as nothing more than a guess.

The 2464-gallon estimate is a different story. It's the only reference that Robbins cites (apart from the Cattlemen's) that rests on actual data. The 2464-gallon figure is taken from a 1991 book by Marcia Kreith, which was published by the Water Education Foundation.[6] In her book, Kreith offers a detailed analysis of how she derived her estimate. But even before we examine Kreith's methodology, there's a tremendous problem. Kreith confined her analysis to beef produced in California. Raising beef cattle in California requires more water than is needed in the leading beef-producing states.[7] And since only 2 percent of America's beef cattle are born in California—and many of these animals are sent to feedlots in other states—California's water use statistics are of highly questionable value.

California's inhospitable environment for beef production is only a small part of the reason why Kreith's water estimate is so much higher than the one put forth by the Cattlemen. The main reason for this disparity is that Kreith bases her estimate on several unwarranted assumptions.

Kreith's estimate includes a great deal of water that cannot justifiably be counted. Most of the water in Kreith's 2464-gallon figure comes from rain that falls on rangeland and is absorbed by plants that are eaten by cattle.[8] This is not water that, in the absence of the beef industry, could be used for any human purpose. Since the water in question cannot be used to fill swimming pools, flush toilets, or irrigate crops, it is misleading to count this water as though it is being lost to human use. About the only way this water could serve human purposes, apart from the grazing of cattle, is if the rangeland were converted to farmland—the rain that fell upon this new farmland would then be watering crops grown for humans. But even this scenario is exceedingly unlikely, since most rangeland is too dry, too remote, and too lacking in topsoil to be worth farming.

While it's true that the beef industry benefits from rainwater falling on rangeland, the whole point of this investigation is to figure out how much water the cattlemen are depriving humans of using. The rainwater absorbed by rangeland plants cannot be diverted for human use, regardless of whether ranchers are permitted to graze cattle. Indeed, the grazing of cattle represents the only practical way that the water in question can be extracted for human use. It's therefore unreasonable to count this water as though it's being lost due to beef industry activity.

Kreith's analysis makes a second significant blunder that further inflates her numbers. Her estimates concerning irrigated pasture are way off base. There's no doubt that the irrigation of cattle pasture is tremendously wasteful of water resources, but the practice is far less pervasive than Kreith indicates. She asserts that one-third of California cattle graze irrigated pasture, when in reality the figure is probably less than 10 percent.[9] Additionally, she estimates that cattle typically graze such pasture for six months, which is yet another overstatement.[10]

Despite its shortcomings, Kreith's work amounts to a sincere attempt to analyze the amount of water required to produce beef in California. Sadly, her work is based on flawed assumptions which result in a wildly inaccurate estimate.

A Rigorous Analysis of Water Use

Unfortunately, the truth about water use is on the beef industry's side. In 1993, two animal scientists at the University of California at Davis published an article examining how much water goes into a pound of beef. They carried out an exhaustive state-by-state analysis of the various water inputs necessitated by beef production. When I looked over the methods they used to calculate these numbers, I was awed that anyone would take on a task of such forbidding magnitude. They had to obtain data that included the average amount of rain falling on corn fields in each state, the average amount of water each animal drank, and the average amount of irrigation necessary to produce each pound of feed corn. Taken together, finding all this data amounted to an astonishing piece of scholarship. Their study determined that a pound of United States beef requires just 441 gallons of water.[11]

This 441 gallon figure is the number Robbins points to in *The Food Revolution,* setting it against the far larger estimates we just looked at. *The Food Revolution* was not the only time that Robbins wrote about the UC Davis study. A year before that book's publication, in the spring of 2000, he wrote an article titled, "2500 Gallons All Wet?"[12] In that article, Robbins defends his claim that producing a pound of beef requires 2500 gallons of water. While he mentions the UC Davis study, he makes no effort to pick apart its data or to criticize its analysis. Instead, Robbins suggests that one of the authors is biased because he wears a cowboy hat in his official university picture. Robbins then goes on to claim that George Borgstrom, the scientist who came out with the 2500-gallon claim, is "renowned" and therefore highly credible.

I believe that the way a scientist becomes renowned is by conducting carefully executed, rigorously thought out studies using reliable data. Unfortunately, where water inputs for beef are concerned, only the UC Davis researchers have proven up to the task of providing credible numbers, backed up by real data and thorough analysis. Until somebody can come along with a detailed critique of the UC Davis study that pinpoints specific mistakes in its data or analysis, the 441 gallon claim ought to be accepted as the most reliable estimate of the water requirements for beef.

Since it appears that the 441 gallon figure is fairly accurate, the vegetarian movement would be wise to avoid arguing water use statistics. When you consider how much water is needed to grow a pound of broccoli (42 gallons) or a pound of tomatoes (28 gallons), the water needed for beef production doesn't seem extreme.[13] And the water advantages of vegan foods become even less significant when you measure food yields by calorie, rather than weight.[14] It works out that a hundred gallons of water will get you about 296 calories from beef, or about 335 calories from tomatoes.[15]

Finally, water requirements for chicken and pork aren't much different than for beef.[16] The numbers for chicken and pork aren't quite as reliable as the beef estimate, but there's no reason to think they are far off the mark. With all this in mind, vegetarian advocates ought to think twice before bringing up the issue of water consumption. We need to maintain credibility at all costs, and continuing to advance dubious claims about water use will get us branded as liars.

Water Pollution

The other environmental argument concerning water and meat production has to do with pollution. The amount of manure produced on America's animal farms is staggering—1.37 billion tons each year.[17] Worse, as large-scale factory farming has established itself, much of this manure has concentrated in comparatively few

places. For instance, a one-thousand-cow dairy operation generates 86,000 pounds of manure every day.[18]

The trouble with manure is that, by weight, it's mostly water.
It is therefore exceedingly heavy and expensive to transport. In
consequence, most of the manure produced by factory farms is de-
posited on fields close to the facilities. It is more economical, and
perhaps more environmentally friendly, to use petroleum-based
fertilizers on fields far from factory farms than it is to use the
fossil fuels necessary to transport manure to the fields.

Over time, the manure applied to fields surrounding factory
farms saturates the soil with nitrogen. Rainfall percolates through
this soil, and increases the nitrate content of the water table. This
is an alarming occurrence, given the amount of manure each factory farm produces, but it's far too easy to jump to the conclusion
that the sky is falling. The federal government has put in place
relatively tough regulations on water quality, and factory farms
have the technological and financial ability to keep water pollution from getting out of hand.

Regulations aren't capable of totally protecting the water supply in areas where poultry and livestock are raised. Factory farms
have doubtless harmed water quality in hundreds of communities
around the United States. But the question is whether this effect
is so damaging that it deserves to be a prominent part of the argument for vegan eating. I don't think it comes close to crossing
that threshold. In fact, as water treatment technologies improve,
the effect of factory farming on water quality will probably diminish. The burden of proof falls on activists to show that animal
agriculture causes water pollution in a profound and irreversible
way. Until somebody comes along with a credible analysis showing this to be the case, vegetarian activists would be wise not to
emphasize arguments that pertain to water pollution.

Surf and Turf

Taken together, the environmental impact of meat production is far less costly than many vegetarian activists suggest. But there are two notable exceptions—foods that are enormously harmful to the environment, especially where biodiversity is concerned. It's beyond doubt that cattle ranching has damaged more square miles of land in America than any other activity. And the consequences of the world's appetite for fish have become ruinous to the oceans. The following two appendices cover these issues.

Appendix C: The Environmental Costs of Cattle Ranching

Nearly all American steak comes from cattle who graze the western states before going to feedlot.[1] America's beef cattle graze enormous expanses of land—taken together, it totals more than 832 million acres.[2] About 44 percent of all land in the continental United States is grazed by cattle or sheep.[3]

Ranching carries immense environmental consequences that are nevertheless difficult to appreciate. Many grazing areas are so desolate that, at first glance, it seems they might as well be stocked with cattle, since it appears that few other animals could survive in these areas. But the truth is that America's rangelands have become inhospitable precisely *because* they are grazed by cattle. Take away the cattle, and in a surprisingly short amount of time, most ranching areas become revitalized. Within just a few years, plant life makes a strong recovery, and this regeneration attracts wildlife to return.

Why are America's rangelands so degraded? Much of the reason relates to how poorly beef cattle fit into western landscapes. These animals were initially imported from Europe, where they were raised on lands that had abundant topsoil and plenty of rainfall. These large and ravenous animals are a catastrophic match to the fragile ecosystems that exist in the desert-like western United States. Cattle are voracious and indiscriminate eaters, and they play havoc with areas that have slow-growing plant-life surviving on small amounts of rain. When allowed to graze in sufficient numbers, cattle rapidly denude vast areas of the grasses and brush that wildlife depend upon for survival.

Even as cattle destroy habitat, ranchers often seek to kill any surviving wildlife. Ranchers have a long history of exterminating animals who could prey upon cattle or otherwise threaten their health. Just about any animal with a spine is considered a varmint and is liable to be shot, trapped, or poisoned. Ranchers have carried out a well organized and far-reaching extermination of wildlife. Over the past century, ranchers have killed billions of prairie dogs, as well as uncountable numbers of wolves, coyotes, and even bear.[4] America's indigenous cattle, the buffalo, have been nearly wiped off the continent to make way for beef cattle.

Ranchers don't do all this killing alone. The USDA's Wildlife Services division exterminates animals likely to prey on livestock. In 2002, this division killed 86,000 coyotes, 5000 foxes, 380 black bears, and 190 wolves.[5] A great many of these animals were taken at the request of cattle and sheep ranchers.

Barbed wire has functioned as another potent weapon against wildlife. It's impossible to walk anywhere in the back country of the West without coming across miles upon miles of barbed wire fences. Ranchers maintain at least a million miles of it.[6] While these fences are erected to keep cattle from straying, they have also devastated nearly every species of mammal inhabiting the western states that depends upon migration.

The environmental problems brought on by grazing are often compounded when ranchers put too many cattle on a piece of land. Overgrazing hastens the rate at which cattle degrade an area, but the added profits it creates can lead ranchers to succumb to the temptation of overstocking animals.

Beef industry representatives are able to muster a reasonable-sounding defense of cattle ranching. They typically claim that it's in the rancher's interest to maintain biodiversity, and that well-managed grazing actually benefits the land. The few pages I have here cannot adequately counter these arguments, but a number of books demolish the industry's claims. Perhaps the most convincing of these books is *Welfare Ranching: The Subsidized Destruction of the American West,* edited by George Wuerthner and Mollie Matteson, which features a series of photos comparing grazed land to areas that have been left untouched by cattle.[7] These photos, and their accompanying narrative, give a clear sense of the specious and self-serving nature of the beef industry's arguments.

Although the effects of ranching are frequently devastating, vegetarian and environmental activists sometimes push certain arguments too far. When this happens, ranchers offer effective rebuttals that include comforting descriptions of "sustainable grazing" and other success stories. But even though ranchers may offer reasonable defenses against specific criticisms, they cannot credibly dispute the overarching argument against ranching—if cattle ranching were abolished it would set the stage for a massive recovery of wildlife throughout the western United States. On this point, the cattlemen have no convincing response. The beef industry has been overwhelmingly responsible for the collapse of wolf, buffalo, and other wildlife populations in the West. The continued existence of cattle ranching is all that stands in the way of the western states recapturing their past magnificence as a habitat for millions of wild animals.

Appendix D: The Consequences of Fishing

There is a great deal of work that is continually put into assessing the environmental consequences of fishing and aquaculture, the factory farming of aquatic animals. Records are kept of annual catches, and governments continually pour resources into assessing the health of the world's fisheries. If the oceans are looked at as nothing more than a food-producing engine, then, from some accounts, the impact of commercial fishing appears relatively benign and sustainable. There's no sign that the oceans, as a whole, will lose their capacity to produce vast amounts of aquatic animals in the foreseeable future.

The premier organization that monitors the oceans' long-term ability to feed people is the Food and Agriculture Organization of the United Nations (FAO). Every two years, the FAO publishes a review on the status of the oceans. These reviews are the product of enormous study, and they consistently provide a soothing and well-informed counter-argument for people who worry that fish are rapidly being eradicated from the world's oceans.

While the FAO acknowledges that over-fishing has depleted great numbers of animals in wide expanses of ocean, the agency reports that long-term prospects are good for the majority of the world's fisheries. According to the agency, nearly half the world's fisheries are fully and sustainably exploited.[1] In other words, fishing boats are taking almost exactly the maximum catch possible without causing fish populations to decline year by year. And the agency says that a full 25 percent of the world's fisheries are actually under-exploited; that is, catches in these areas could markedly increase without threatening fish populations.[2]

The FAO's position is sensible, so far as it goes, but its analysis avoids examining the larger picture. The agency regards the oceans primarily as a food resource, and it makes little effort to assess how commercial fishing affects marine habitats and the oceans' biodiversity. On these points, we need to look beyond the FAO's limited analysis. It turns out that commercial fishing doesn't just kill fish; it also imperils nearly every ocean animal, from sea anemones to whales. The extent to which commercial fishing and aquaculture endangers ocean life is becoming increasingly apparent, and it has been documented by several large and prestigious studies.

One of the largest and most highly regarded studies to examine the health of the oceans was conducted by the Pew Foundation. In 2003, the foundation published a 166-page report titled *America's Living Oceans*. This study was funded by a $5.5 million grant and was carried out by top marine scientists, as well as political leaders representing both parties. Owing to the impressive credentials of the study's authors, and the thoroughness with which they carried out their research, *America's Living Oceans* did much to undermine the FAO's contention that the oceans are being responsibly managed.[3]

The State of the Oceans

The FAO's rosy view of the fishing industry is possible because the agency measures the oceans' health mainly by the prospect of future fish production. The FAO is probably correct that global fish catches can stay near their current tonnage for many years to come. Looked at solely from this perspective, there seems little reason to worry about the state of the oceans. Of greater interest is what happens to the oceans, year by year, at current fishing levels. What price is being paid for these enormous catches? It turns out that, despite the FAO's upbeat appraisals, commercial fishing is proving catastrophic to the world's fisheries. The worst damage is occurring in the waters off China, but the situation off the coast of North America is bad enough to make the point that commercial fishing has been wiping out fish populations left and right. Atlantic halibut were among the most widely caught fish in the waters off North America. But over-fishing throughout the twentieth century caused the population of this species to collapse. According to the Pew report, these fish are now "commercially extinct" in U.S. waters.[4] While they can still be found, they are present in such small numbers that it is no longer worthwhile for fishermen to try to catch them.

The situation off North America's Pacific Coast resembles that of the Atlantic. For decades, red snapper was one of the primary fish caught in western U.S. waters. These fish have not suffered the total collapse of the Atlantic halibut, but the decline has nevertheless been massive. The Pew Commission reports that the population of red snapper in Pacific waters has declined by 90 percent due to over-fishing.[5]

The fishing industry has rapidly purged other once-common fish from U.S. waters. Catches of cod, tuna, haddock, and flounder are all down more than 50 percent over the past half-century. These declines are all traceable to an American fishing industry that has the equipment, technology, and willingness to fish at unsustainable yields. Meanwhile, the government has consistently failed to enact sufficient regulations to prevent over-fishing.

The massive mistakes made by the American government nevertheless pale beside the incompetence of Canada's fishing ministry. Even more so than America, Canada has been blessed with several of the most magnificent and productive of the world's fisheries. The most renowned of these was Newfoundland's cod fishery. In this forbidding and unforgiving climate, where icebergs drift the oceans during the summer months and where the Titanic sank to the bottom of the sea, fishermen had supported themselves for more than two centuries. The cod were once so abundant that they seemed limitless. And Canada's fishing boats were permitted to take in massive catches year after year. In 1968 alone, Canadian fishermen pulled 810,000 tons of cod from Newfoundland's northeast coast.[6]

By the 1980s, over-fishing had put Newfoundland's cod population into a nosedive. Fishing nets were being hauled up nearly empty, and what few cod they contained were undersized juveniles. The sensible response would have been to curtail fishing for a few years, to allow the cod population to recover. Instead, Newfoundland's fishermen only intensified their efforts to catch what fish remained. It wasn't until the late 1980s, with the fishery by then in severe trouble, that the government stepped in to announce strong restrictions on commercial fishing. But by then, it was too late. The fishery never recovered, and the ecosystem off Newfoundland's coast has shifted to favor crustaceans instead of codfish.

In the waters outlying Canada's maritime provinces, codfish can still be found, albeit in far fewer numbers than in decades past. And Canadian fishermen remain intent on catching as many cod as possible. In order to maximize the catch, the fishing industry has pushed the Canadian government to authorize a massive seal hunt. Seals live largely on cod, so to Canadian fishermen, fewer seals mean greater codfish catches. In 2003, Canada's government bowed to fishing industry pressure and ordered a hunt intended to kill 975,000 seals over the next three years.[7]

Canada's seal hunt is just one example of how the fishing industry harms a wide variety of marine life. Much of this killing is unintentional, but the numbers are nevertheless staggering. Each year in U.S. waters, 2.3 billion pounds of unwanted marine life get hauled aboard fishing boats, then tossed back dead.[8] Worldwide, this inadvertent slaughter is enormous—the most recent studies estimate 60 billion pounds of by-catch per year.[9] And American consumers are responsible for a substantial amount of this by-catch, given that 80 percent of America's shrimp is imported.[10]

The taking of ocean shrimp causes more by-catch than any

other kind of fishing. Shrimp are bottom-dwellers, and they are caught by dragging nets across the sea floor. Since even jumbo shrimp are tiny, the nets used to catch shrimp are fine enough to scoop up nearly all life found on the ocean's bottom. Every pound of shrimp that is caught results in the killing of ten pounds of other marine life.[11] Most of the dead by-catch comprises tiny animals, which, although unwanted for human consumption, nevertheless contributes substantially to the oceans' biodiversity.

The animals who escape this dredging usually don't get much of a reprieve. The nets dragged across the sea floor breaks up fragile coral and otherwise destroys habitat for bottom dwellers. Shrimp are in such high demand that fishing boats revisit the same areas again and again, giving the habitat little time to recover. The Pew report indicates that in most U.S. shrimping areas, a given section of ocean floor gets dredged by shrimp nets at least once a year.[12]

Other segments of the fishing industry kill huge numbers of animals in all sorts of unlikely ways. For instance, the waters off Chile are heavily fished for sea bass, by boats towing fifty-mile longlines. These lines are pulled just beneath the water's surface, and seabirds continually mistake the baited hooks for food. In consequence, one hundred thousand seabirds are hooked and killed each year in Chilean waters.[13]

Fishing is a leading cause of death for some of the rarest animals in the ocean, including turtles and whales. More than twenty thousand sea turtles die each year after getting hooked on longlines.[14] And more than eight hundred dolphins and whales die every day as a result of getting tangled in fishing nets.[15] These victims include animals ranging from baby bottlenose dolphins all the way up to gigantic endangered blue whales. The researcher responsible for calculating these dolphin and whale deaths has gone on record predicting that "several species will be lost in the next few decades if nothing is done."[16]

Aquaculture

In the 1970s and 1980s, fish farming appeared to be a potential savior of marine life. Aquaculture raised the possibility of making the commercial fishing boat obsolete. No longer would wild fish species need to be caught and potentially endangered to satisfy the world's hunger for fish. Instead, the most popular seafood species could be specially bred for growth, with their offspring . raised in netted enclosures.

Aquaculture has grown tremendously since the 1970s. Its share of the world's seafood production grew from 4 percent in 1970 to 27 percent in 2000.[17] But with its increased size, the environmental costs of aquaculture have become all the more apparent. It has become evident that, in many respects, aquaculture poses a greater threat to the oceans than does commercial fishing.

The concept of fish farming certainly has its appeal. Consumers often choose farmed fish out of the belief that they are helping to keep wild fish populations intact. What the industry doesn't publicize is that most of the feed used by fish farms is netted from the oceans. Fish farming is therefore far from environmentally benign—it kills a large amount of marine life in order to raise a small amount of domesticated fish. Marine scientists have determined that for every pound of farmed fish produced worldwide, several pounds of marine life are caught to provide the necessary feed.[18]

Although it takes place underwater, fish farming is really just another form of factory farming. Both fish farms and factory farms operate by tightly confining animals who are specially bred for growth or productivity. Stocking densities on fish farms rival those of battery-caged hens at egg farms. As with pig and poultry confinement facilities, fish farm owners consistently have to deal with elevated risks of disease. The industry relies heavily on antibiotics to keep their crowded fish pens from becoming disease-ridden.

The crowded conditions at fish farms constitute more than just an animal welfare problem; they also pose a deadly threat to surrounding marine life. Many fish farms are thoroughly infested with parasites, the most common of which are called sea lice. Blood red and raisin-sized, sea lice are to fish what fist-sized ticks would be to deer. The crowding at fish farms provides ideal circumstances for sea lice to reproduce. The ocean waters surrounding many fish farms are heavily populated with sea lice, which can devastate local populations of wild fish.

To native fish populations, an even greater risk than parasites is the damage to gene pools caused by escaping farmed fish. The perils of genetic pollution are especially clear with salmon—the most heavily farmed fish species. Researchers have discovered that escaped farmed salmon possess a perverse advantage when it comes to reproducing, since wild salmon consistently seek out the largest possible mates. But the resultant offspring are poorly suited to carrying forward the species—they consistently show severe losses in their fitness to survive ocean conditions.[19]

Given that salmon breed by spawning thousands of eggs at one time, just one fish farm escapee can contaminate the gene pool of salmon inhabiting a wide expanse of ocean. The genetic consequences would be worrisome enough if only a few hundred farmed salmon escaped into the oceans each year. In actual practice, matters are much worse. Fish farms have proven themselves completely unable to prevent large numbers of fish from escaping. Between 1987 and 1992, more than a million salmon escaped U.S. and Canadian fish farms.[20] Norway's track record has been even worse—in 1992 alone, 600,000 hybrid fish escaped from the country's fish farms.[21]

Many environmental protection groups now view fish farms as an unequaled menace to the oceans. The World Wildlife Fund warned that fish farms may soon wipe out all wild salmon in Scottish waters.[22] In 2003, the Pew Commission urged a worldwide moratorium be imposed on the construction of new fish farms.

A Matter of Necessity?

The state of the world's oceans is a topic that attracts substantial media attention. Oftentimes, articles on the subject end by encouraging people to avoid eating the most endangered species of fish. This kind of advice is unquestionably beneficial, so far as it goes. A person who switches from swordfish to striped bass is taking an important step to protect the oceans. But there's more that can be done. Unfortunately, neither the media nor environmental organizations are apt to raise the possibility that people stop eating fish entirely.

When considering the desirability of doing away with commercial fishing, it's important to concede that a small amount of this fishing serves a vital human need. Fishing provides work and food for about 23 million impoverished workers.[23] Without fishing, or an alternative food and income source, many of these workers and their families would face starvation.

But most people don't eat fish due to poverty. The vast majority of fish is caught, not out of necessity, but to provide a luxury food. In industrialized countries, most kinds of seafood cost double, triple, and even tenfold the price of an equal quantity of chicken or beef. What's more, the seafood favored by Westerners tends to have far greater environmental consequences than the seafood eaten by impoverished people. Westerners tend to prefer large predatory species like swordfish and salmon, which are near the top of the food chain. These fish are comparatively few in number, and they are easily decimated by commercial fishing since they take years to grow to adult size.

It's certainly a step in the right direction for Americans to switch to eating more common varieties of fish, but the benefits of doing so are limited. Even the most abundant species of fish cannot be taken without impacting other marine life. Fewer fish in the oceans mean less food available for dolphins, sea lions, pelicans, and multitudes of other species. And finally, without personally going out to sea and watching the catch brought in, you can never know just how much by-catch is occurring.

Fish as Sentient Beings

Beyond the environmental impact of fishing, there is one more reason to avoid fish. Until recently, there was no scientific evidence that fish were capable of suffering. Fish can neither vocalize, nor can their eyes convey expressions. In consequence, people don't tend to feel especially troubled about fishing. But in 2003, Britain's Royal Society came out with a study that provided strong evidence that fish are indeed capable of feeling pain.[24] Given that nearly all commercially caught fish suffocate to death, it's alarming to gain evidence that fish are capable of feeling the agonies of suffocation.

It's also known that some fish keep long-term mates, and that they may even possess an ability to form emotional attachments. Two friends of mine, Steve and Chris McDiarmid, had a permanent change in outlook after a morning of spear fishing in the Bahamas. Twenty feet underwater, Chris encountered two large amber jacks swimming side by side. She speared one, and with help from Steve, was able to get the fish back to their sailboat. As they were eating, they spotted the second amber jack, swimming around the boat, and occasionally breaking the water's surface to look upwards. The fish lingered by the boat for the rest of the day. Knowing that amber jacks mate for life, the behavior of this animal made the McDiarmids so uncomfortable that they never again ate another bite of fish.

Eating with the Oceans in Mind

We've seen throughout this chapter that the world's oceans are in an increasingly precarious state. What's surprising is that, considering how heavily the oceans are fished, how little food actually comes from the sea. Despite the massive efforts of the world's fishing industry, seafood provides only about 1 percent of the total calories eaten by humans.[25] In this way, commercial fishing is akin to cattle ranching: both activities devastate huge expanses of space to produce relatively small amounts of food.

It's understandable that the media focuses on making small changes, and encourages people to switch to species of fish that are not threatened. But I think it's wrong to assume that people won't go the extra mile, and refuse to eat aquatic animals of any kind, if they are just told what is at stake. There are a number of persuasive reasons to avoid seafood entirely, and it's probably easier to avoid fish altogether than it is to stay reliably informed about which fish stocks are being sustainably fished.

Nearly all Americans could eat a diverse and abundant diet without ever needing to consume fish. I personally think that avoiding fish is a show of solidarity with marine life and the world's poor. Neither marine life nor impoverished people have much choice about what to eat. But for most people, giving up ocean animals results in no hardship at all; the main personal consequence is lower food bills. Avoiding seafood is an acknowledgment that the oceans are under tremendous pressure, and that we each have the ability to avoid contributing to the problem.

Appendix E: The Ethics of Hunting

Hunters and animal protection activists often have unkind words for each other. Naturally, it's difficult for one side to listen to what the other has to say. But the arguments raised by hunters deserve to be carefully considered by animal advocates. Overall, hunters are far better equipped than factory farmers to convincingly defend their practices.

The pro-hunting arguments follow two lines. One is that hunting is environmentally responsible and in fact necessary. The other is that hunted animals suffer far less than those raised in factory farms. There are truthful elements, as well as glaring shortcomings, to both these arguments.

Let's start by looking at the environmental side of pro-hunting arguments. Any hunter who claims there are environmental benefits to hunting rare animals like bears or mountain lions should not be taken seriously. But the vast majority of hunters are out for deer or birds. With the exception of geese, few birds pose overpopulation problems. In the case of deer, however, there are significant overpopulation problems in many parts of the United States. Deer overpopulation stems from the removal of natural predators—wolves, coyotes, and mountain lions. In the absence of such predators, hunters offer the only alternative to starvation and disease to keep deer populations in check.

Controlling deer populations is beneficial, both to humans and to deer. Too many deer inevitably increases the number who stray

211

onto roads and are killed by automobiles, and automobile collisions kill hundreds of thousands of deer each year in the most painful and gruesome ways. Dozens of drivers are also killed in the United States each year in accidents involving deer. National records of vehicle collisions with deer are not kept, but between 2000 and 2001, there were 136,000 such collisions in just five Midwestern states.[1] These collisions injured more than five thousand people, caused thirty human fatalities, and led to $232 million in property damage.[2] Nearly all the deer involved in these collisions suffered violent and sometimes protracted deaths.

Deer overpopulation is an ugly problem that lacks a gentle solution. Animal protection activists who oppose hunting deserve a measure of scorn if they fail to advocate some other method of population control. At least hunters offer an answer to the growing problem of deer overpopulation.

But hunters are not the ideal solution they claim to be. Deer hunters usually target males rather than females, which is the worst possible strategy for controlling population. One buck will mate with several does during rutting season, so selectively killing bucks does little to reduce overall herd size.

Another problem involves the kind of deer that hunters target. Many hunters seek to bring down a "trophy animal" worthy of photographs or taxidermy. They therefore seek out vigorous males with large antlers. Predatory animals, by contrast, usually chase down the weakest and sickest deer.

By going after bucks with the largest possible racks, hunters subvert natural selection. That is, they selectively target animals who have demonstrated an ability to survive for extended periods of time. And this preference for trophy game is reinforced by the culture surrounding hunting, which attaches bragging rights to killing animals who are in magnificent condition.

Native predators are being reintroduced to many regions of the United States, which I view as a positive trend for controlling deer populations. There are, however, some drawbacks to relying on predators instead of hunters. Hunting season lasts only a few months each year—in regions lacking predators, the woods can be enjoyed by people for the majority of the year without risk.

While wolves and coyotes pose little danger to anyone but children and domesticated animals, there is some genuine risk to adults brought about by reintroducing mountain lions and panthers to rural areas. Over the past twenty years, mountain lion populations have been increasing, and attacks on humans have become more common. One way to mitigate these dangers is to reintroduce wolf populations to areas inhabited by mountain lions. Wolves prey on mountain lions, and their presence causes mountain lions to change their feeding behavior in ways that reduce the threat to humans.

The most compelling reason to avoid reintroducing predators is that hunters can *potentially* offer an especially humane way of killing animals. It's unquestionably true that a well-aimed shot from a high-powered rifle brings a more humane death than what a pack of wolves would dish out. But if the case for humane hunting is to be made, it's important to consider the skill level that most hunters actually possess. In my opinion, many hunters lack the judgment, the eyesight, and the shooting skills to be allowed into the woods with a firearm. I've spent much of my life in rural areas, and the degree of incompetence I've witnessed among hunters is staggering. During hunting season, I don't usually hear a single shot coming from the woods. Most of the time, it's two or three shots in rapid succession—a likely sign the hunter has either missed his target or did not get a clean kill. There's no way of knowing how many thousands of animals each year are wounded but manage to escape, only to suffer lingering and miserable deaths from internal injuries.

These same hunters pose great risks to anybody who dares to step into the woods during hunting season. U.S. accident reports taken from 2001 show that hunters wounded 491 people and killed 56.[3] The hunting lobby is quick to point out that these deaths are a small fraction of the number of people who die while biking or swimming. But someone who gets on a bicycle or jumps into the water does so voluntarily and aware of the risks. No one chooses to be shot by a hunter.

Additionally, the number of innocent people killed by hunters would be far higher, if a great number of people weren't afraid to set foot in the woods during hunting season. The incompetence of hunters is the stuff of legend; some of these guys make Elmer Fudd look like a hardened woodsman. In 2001, only a few miles from where I was living in Central New York, a hunter was shot while sitting twenty feet up in a tree stand.

Fewer than 5 percent of Americans hunt.[4] And that small percentage of people who hunt renders woods and fields dangerous for everyone else for two months each autumn, during what is arguably the most beautiful time of year and the most comfortable time for hiking outdoors. The 66 million people who venture into the woods to watch wildlife, or to exercise, are put at risk by just 13 million hunters.[5]

I am not trying to argue that all hunting is wrong. I'd personally rather see a person hunt deer than dine on animal products raised on factory farms. I also concede that there are rare cases when a good environmental argument can be made for hunting. And I would never argue that poor people, who cannot afford to eat well, should be barred from killing deer to round out their diets.

But most Americans do not hunt because they are hungry. In many cases, introducing predators to rural areas would be a safer and more environmentally responsible way of dealing with deer overpopulation problems. No matter whether deer overpopulation is handled by hunters or predators, remote areas will always carry some danger to those who visit them. In my experiences in the woods, I've come face to face with a large mountain lion and within earshot of a bear. And while these experiences were frightening, I still don't find these predators to be half as dangerous as a hunter up in a tree stand who raises his gun at the sound of every snapping twig.

Despite their differences, animal protectionists and hunters can find some common ground. They can start by agreeing that factory farming is a horror story, and that hunting offers a more humane way of producing meat. Likewise, hunters and animal protectionists should also agree that there's no health-related necessity for eating meat. A well-planned vegan diet is at least as healthy as any diet that includes meat, and only a tiny percentage of hunters are so poor that they actually depend on hunting for food.

There's a second topic upon which hunters and animal protectionists should agree. If hunting is to be permitted, the animals should be killed instantly and as cleanly as possible. That would mean much higher standards governing who is permitted out in the woods with a rifle. As things stand now, most states impose trivial obstacles before awarding hunting licenses. In New York, all that's required is a ten-hour class. And shooting skills, the foundation of safe and humane hunting, are never assessed. There's no reason why society should allow people who are mediocre shots to bring their rifles into the woods. Standards ought to be raised for hunters so that, to receive a hunting license, you should have a degree of shooting proficiency that would qualify you as a marksman in the military. The need to avoid the deaths of innocent people, and to minimize the suffering of animals, demands nothing less.

Even if strong reforms were made to guard against hunting accidents, there would still be a significant social cost to legalized hunting. The mere existence of hunting rifles encourages a more violent society. In 2001, U.S. law enforcement recorded 434 cases of murder and manslaughter committed by people firing hunting rifles.[6] Shotguns were used in an additional 575 cases.[7] Together, hunting rifles and shotguns accounted for 6.3 percent of all cases of murder and manslaughter in the United States in 2001.[8]

Few people understand just how deadly a high-powered deer rifle can be. Rifle bullets travel at four times the speed of sound—better than half a mile a second. Given the lethality of a modern hunting rifle, there is one final area where hunters and animal protection advocates should find agreement. Tougher penalties should be enacted for "hunting accidents"—a term which ought to be gotten rid of, since it helps hunters to evade responsibility. Currently, in nearly all cases in which a hunter seriously injures somebody, he is given a free pass and serves little, if any, jail time.

State hunting bureaus often encourage people to wear "hunter orange" before heading into the woods. This is a clear sign that the norms governing hunters' behavior need to be changed. The fact that people must wear abnormally bright clothing to protect themselves in woods and fields shows that some hunters don't bother to hold fire before they are completely sure of their target.

Manslaughter laws exist to protect people who kill by accident from receiving the penalties doled out to murderers. But when these watered-down penalties are applied to careless hunting, it gives the most reckless hunters one less thing to worry about when firing their weapons. Too many hunters today are willing to fire at what they think *might* be a deer. And dozens of people each year end up wounded or dead in consequence. This needs to be stopped, and the hunting and animal protection communities ought to unite to see that careless hunters receive harsh punishment.

Appendix F: Why Red Meat Can't Compete

Among other topics, Part One of this book covered the chicken industry's transformation over the past half century. Hens today lay three times more eggs than they did fifty years ago, and meat chickens grow three times faster than their ancestors. This rapid progress is due to the fact that chickens are especially well suited to selective breeding programs.

It is quick and cheap to selectively breed chickens. A single hen lays four to seven eggs per week. If you put together a breeding pool of a hundred hens, you can breed well over a thousand chicks a month. Because these chicks reach maturity within months, breeders can cull the adolescent chickens who perform poorly, then use the survivors to breed an all-new generation even more likely to carry desired traits.

By selecting breeding meat chickens in this way, poultry geneticists can produce a new generation of mother chickens at least twice a year. The costs of raising these chickens for the sake of research are trivial compared to the cost reductions that more efficient birds bring to the industry. Getting chickens to grow faster and lay more eggs is big business, and the task has been largely outsourced to private companies that specialize in selectively breeding poultry.

Pigs are also selectively bred, but these breeding programs are far more expensive to operate, and vastly more time-consuming, than they are for poultry. That's because sows take almost four months to produce a litter, and then require an additional two months to go into heat again. And the usual litter size is fewer than twelve; compare this to the more than 150 chicks a typical hen will produce in six months' time. Further, it takes the piglets months before their growth traits become evident. So from the time a sow gets pregnant until the time her litter reaches adulthood, and is sorted for desirable breeding traits, at least nine months has elapsed—and farmers have fewer than a dozen piglets to show for it. Add in the vastly greater costs of feeding pigs vs. feeding chickens, and you can see why the pig industry has lagged behind the chicken industry in increasing the growth rates of their animals.

We've just seen that chickens are ideally suited for selective breeding. Pigs are less suited to these efforts, but since they at least give birth to litters instead of one offspring, it is still worthwhile to run large operations to selectively breed these animals. But with beef cattle, the costs and time involved for selective breeding are enormous. A cow's pregnancy lasts more than twice as long as a sow's.[1] And when a cow finally gives birth, she produces just one calf, rather than a litter. And that calf takes more than a year to reach maturity. Meanwhile, the mother can't be impregnated again for three months after giving birth.

The beef industry has always selected the fastest-growing cattle for reproduction, but their efforts have been halfhearted compared to what pig and poultry breeders have accomplished. There has therefore been relatively little improvement in how quickly beef calves grow while grazing the range. This is bad news for the beef industry, but it's terrific news for beef cattle. It means that you don't see beef calves falling prey to the growth-induced crippling suffered by modern pigs. Nor do beef calves develop the heart and lung problems that are widespread in broiler chickens. The slow progress achieved in breeding more efficient beef cattle has meant the animals live healthier and more comfortable lives. Until, that is, they hit the feedlots.

Appendix G: Animal Testing

The arguments both for and against animal testing are frequently overstated. Advocates of this research often imply that medical progress would grind to a halt without the ability to test on animals. Animal protection activists, by contrast, sometimes take the equally absurd position that animal testing has never produced any tangible gains for humans.

To buttress their arguments, animal advocates have throughly documented the most worthless tests involving animals in laboratories. There has been no shortage of appallingly brutal, repetitive, and utterly insignificant animal tests—for a background of these abuses, read *Animal Liberation,* by Peter Singer. In the 1970s, there were few safeguards in place to ensure that animal testing occurred for medically justifiable reasons, and countless animals therefore suffered excruciating ordeals for the weakest of reasons. Reforms since then, and the dramatic reduction in the use of bizarre tests like the LD_{50}, have diminished the number of pointless experiments done on animals.*

Even with recent reforms, there is still no shortage of animal testing that produces questionable gains. Some animal protection activists contend that it is the nature of all animal tests to produce

---

*The LD_{50} is an abbreviation for Lethal Dose-50. Under this test, a group of animals was fed or injected with a substance until half —50 percent—of the animals die. The amount ingested would constitute the LD_{50}. This test was once widely done to measure the toxicity of a given substance, even though the test results provided little knowledge of any practical value.

misleading and useless results. And it is certainly true that animal tests sometimes provide terribly misleading data. For instance, the anti-morning sickness drug thalidomide was tested on animals in laboratories, producing no sign of hazards. However, once the drug went to market in the early 1960s, thousands of babies were born with severe birth defects.

But to say that animal testing never advances medical knowledge is worse than naive—it comes across as delusional. Some animal research has yielded clear-cut reductions in human suffering. For instance, in 1958, Albert Sabin released an oral polio vaccine that was cheaper and easier to administer than the Salk vaccine. There's no doubt that the advantages of the Sabin vaccine allowed millions more people to be protected from polio. Thousands of animals were used in developing this vaccine. Near the end of his life, Sabin said, "There could have been no oral polio vaccine without the use of innumerable animals, a very large number of animals."[1]

In other matters, the benefit of experimenting on animals in laboratories is not as clear-cut. For instance, countless animals were used in the development of insulin. But while these tests were being conducted, non-animal research also made tremendous strides in understanding diabetes. It's difficult to know to what extent animal testing contributed to the creation of laboratory insulin. But the argument that animal testing did not help at all is feeble.

Overall, there have probably been thousands of instances in which animal testing helped diminish human suffering. At the same time, there have been countless horrifying animal tests that have produced nothing of any benefit. Incompetence and insensitivity are, after all, as common in medical research as in any other field of human endeavor.

It may well be that animal testing of any sort is immoral—that since animals cannot give consent for these experiments, we have no right to sacrifice their interests for human gain. Unfortunately, Americans are nowhere close to being ready to entertain this argument. As long as animals rank so lowly that it's considered morally acceptable to eat them to satisfy the cravings of our taste buds, there's no real hope that America is ready to give serious thought to most animals used in research. The one exception concerns monkeys and apes. Because the brain structure and behavior of primates and humans are so similar, many people are disturbed by the practice of experimenting on these animals. Organizations like the Great Ape Project are pushing to halt the use of apes in medical research, and this effort is gaining widening support.

As public concern for animal suffering grows, there's reason to hope that progress for research animals can be won on two fronts. The first consists of activists seeking to prohibit research on primates. These efforts will probably elicit increased public opposition to all forms of animal research. Meanwhile, on the second front, animals in laboratories benefit indirectly whenever activists publicly expose the injustices of animal agriculture. Once it becomes widely accepted that animal agriculture is an inherently brutal industry that needs to be eliminated, America will be ready to give thought to the more complicated issues that surround animal research.

As these struggles for social change play out, advances in research techniques will continue to make animal research a less attractive tool for scientists.

Appendix H: Back to the Jungle—Meatpacking in America

Prior to the 1906 publication of Upton Sinclair's *The Jungle*, Americans were oblivious to the treatment of slaughterhouse workers. Sinclair's novel movingly told the story of a generation of immigrant workers who were exploited at every turn, until they were too weary, injured, and emotionally broken to support their families. A massive public outcry arose upon the book's publication. Much to Sinclair's disappointment, however, this public outrage was not inspired by concern for worker exploitation.[1] Instead, what caught the public's attention was the book's revelations of unhygienic slaughterhouse practices. *The Jungle* failed to inspire reform of the meat industry's employment practices. But fortunately, for reasons having nothing to do with the book, the situation confronting meat-cutters was about to improve.

The Jungle was published just as inexpensive refrigeration machinery was reaching the market.[2] Refrigeration made it possible for Americans to make big changes in the types of meat they ate. In place of cured meats like hams and sausages, Americans increasingly purchased fresh cuts from local butcher shops. While cured meats were typically processed at slaughterhouses, fresh meat was usually cut up by local butchers. It took many months of training to become a butcher, but the work was less hurried and less dangerous than comparable jobs in large slaughterhouses.

The trend of moving jobs out of slaughterhouses and into butcher shops played a big part in improving the treatment of America's meat-cutters.

In the 1940s and 1950s, the rise of the labor movement delivered additional gains to meat industry workers. By 1960, slaughterhouse workers were earning about 15 percent more than the average manufacturing worker, and wages for local butchers were even better.[3] A half-century after *The Jungle,* conditions for meat-cutters had improved to the point that much of the book's argument had become inaccurate. Unfortunately, the pendulum was about to swing back.

By the 1960s, meat companies had lost a huge chunk of their revenue stream to local butchers. These butchers would buy sides of beef and pork, cut them up with a bandsaw, and sell these cuts to the public at a significant markup. It turned out that the real money wasn't in killing animals, it was in processing the meat into "value added" portions. Slaughterhouses understandably wanted to get in on this profitable action, and in 1967 industry giant IBP (Iowa Beef Processors) introduced "boxed beef." By processing sides of beef directly at the slaughterhouse, the company could reduce its costs—and do away with the need for the local butcher. IBP's business plan delivered enormous savings in production costs. The largest of these savings came from the use of assembly lines to maximize worker efficiency. America's first large-scale slaughterhouses had long ago demonstrated that one expert performing dozens of tasks can never work as efficiently as a team of people, with each member assigned a single task.[4] Boxed beef delivered additional savings by reducing transportation expenses, since fat and bone were trimmed from the product prior to shipping—and boxes are easier to transport than "swinging sides" of beef or pork carcasses.

The competitive advantages of boxed beef overwhelmed local butchers, whose financial straits further worsened once pork producers adopted the concept. During the 1970s, America's butcher shops rapidly gave way to supermarket meat counters, stocked with packaged meats. As local butchers were driven out of business, the game shifted to slaughterhouses seeking to outcompete one another. They all used the same strategy—slashing labor costs and boosting line speeds.

No industry has been better at busting unions than the meat industry, with IBP once again leading the way. Historically, unions have been most effective when they represent workers with hard-to-replace skills. IBP's founder admitted in a 1965 *Newsweek* interview that "we've tried to take the skill out of every step" of butchering.[5] IBP's boxed beef strategy put unions into a miserable position. Unions could no longer mount devastating strikes, since the unskilled nature of boxed meat production meant that replacement workers could be quickly recruited.

IBP dealt another blow to unions by locating its early plants in states with laws that discouraged labor unions from operating. The company's passionate anti-union stance was reinforced by several violent strikes at its plant in Dakota City, Nebraska.[6] IBP's success at undercutting unions forced other companies to follow suit in order to remain competitive. In the early 1980s, a number of companies embarked upon fierce wage cutting programs. Wilson Foods of Oklahoma City filed for protection under the bankruptcy code, repudiated its union contract, and slashed wages 40 percent from $10.69 an hour to $6.50. Another strike, this one at a Hormel plant in Minnesota, illustrates how aggressive the industry's anti-union tactics had become. In October 1984, Hormel announced it was reducing hourly base pay from $10.69 to $8.25—a 23 percent cut. When the union responded by going on strike, Hormel hired strikebreakers, and Minnesota's Governor called in the National Guard.[7]

Injuries

Improvements in equipment and better ergonomics have allowed America's slaughterhouses to make great strides in reducing injuries. But despite these advances, twenty out of every hundred meatpacking workers were injured in 2001.[8] This was two-and-a-half times greater than the rate for manufacturing workers.[9]

Although there's no disputing that slaughterhouse safety has markedly improved—the annual injury rate was 42 percent in 1990—the meat industry still has its share of grisly fatalities.[10] But the most troubling aspect of worker safety probably relates to widespread chronic injuries. Carpal tunnel syndrome and other repetitive motion injuries occur widely throughout the meat industry. One large study conducted in 1992 found that 13 percent of slaughterhouse workers had developed a chronic repetitive motion injury.[11]

Precious little is done for workers who are hobbled or sickened as a result of their work. Medical services provided by company nurses seem geared, not toward healing, but for dampening the pain so that work can continue. And, just as it was in Upton Sinclair's day, meat companies are once again well-known for firing workers whose job-related injuries have rendered them unproductive.

Considering that meat-cutting is one of the most hazardous jobs in America, health insurance for these workers is severely lacking. Most slaughterhouses provide no insurance benefits until a worker has been on the job for six months.[12] Workers who suffer work-related injuries in their first months of employment often find themselves out of a job, with no compensation and little prospect of getting back on their feet.

The Social Costs of Slaughterhouses

While stories of work-related tragedies at slaughterhouses are commonplace, the impact that these facilities have on communities is every bit as disturbing. For two decades, Don Stull, a professor of anthropology at the University of Kansas, has studied what happens to the quality of life in towns that host slaughterhouses. He has co-authored two books and written numerous academic articles on the subject. His research has taken him to one meatpacking town after another, and he has lived and worked in several of them for months at a time. In one slaughterhouse town, he even took a job as a bartender so he could talk candidly with the plant's employees in a comfortable setting.

Over the course of his career, Professor Stull has watched meat and poultry processing become a dominant force for rural job growth in the United States and Canada. But these jobs have been accompanied by what he and his co-author Michael Broadway have called the slaughterhouse blues.* Stull and Broadway's work emphasizes the Faustian bargain that large slaughterhouses thrust upon impoverished rural towns. Meat and poultry processors offer rural communities what appears to be an incredible prize: the creation of jobs, lots of them, not only in their plants but in related industries and services. But, in return, local communities face the overwhelming problems that accompany explosive population growth. Towns that decide to host a slaughterhouse often find out too late that they lack the tax base to provide a safety net for their rapidly expanding population. Hospitals, schools, and social service organizations find themselves under strain to keep pace with the influx of workers and their families. Some observers argue that the jobs and tax revenues meat and poultry plants create are essential if rural communities are to survive. But the industry's low wages and alarming rates of injury and illness ensure high employee turnover. The constant arrival of new workers and their families is felt in every aspect of community life—housing, health care, education, social services, traffic, crime, and more.

When seeking community approval to build a new slaughterhouse, companies like Tyson and Excel stress that they are motivated to hire local workers. But once the plant is built, the hard and dangerous work proves unappealing to most townspeople. Managers and clerical staff in slaughterhouses are mainly native-born Anglo-Americans. But production workers—the people who

---

*Stull and Broadway's book on the subject, *Slaughterhouse Blues,* was published in 2003 by Thomson-Wadsworth, Belmont, California.

make up most of each plant's workforce—are overwhelmingly immigrants, primarily from Latin America.[13]

Small towns are seldom remotely prepared for the problems brought by a meatpacking plant and its immigrant workforce. Local and state governments often hand meat and poultry companies huge tax incentives in exchange for the jobs they promise. But the large influx of low-income workers and their families inevitably strains what are already meager public resources. A severe housing shortage usually accompanies plant openings, as new workers flood into town. Rents rise dramatically, making mobile homes the primary source of affordable housing. Slaughterhouses sometimes enter into agreements with trailer park owners and landlords to house their workers, with rent often deducted directly from workers' paychecks. It is common for workers who live in such accommodations to be assigned roommates and to sleep in shifts.

Few rural communities have homeless shelters to serve the needs of the many poor people who come seeking work. Newcomers often have no option but to sleep in rundown motels or trailers. People lacking money for such housing often end up sleeping in public parks, or even in their cars. As demand for public assistance mounts, social workers must accommodate an increasing diversity of language and culture. Booming small towns, filled with low-income workers, require a number of social service programs that aren't needed in traditional rural towns. Yet social service agencies in meatpacking towns find it increasingly difficult to fund existing programs, so starting new programs is usually beyond their reach.

There is a clear connection between the meatpacking industry's labor demands and the elevated social and economic difficulties host communities face. The industry has done little to remedy the situation. And while there are indeed state and federal laws that would force slaughterhouses to be more accountable to their communities, these laws are rarely enforced.

Meatpacking Then and Now

Over the past century, meatpacking has come full circle—it is once again one of the nation's most exhausting, hazardous, and poorly paid jobs. Since few Americans are willing to accept this kind of work, the industry targets immigrants for its needs. Industry observers believe that about 25 percent of slaughterhouse workers are illegal aliens; most of the remainder are first-generation Latino immigrants.

In the 1950s, unions wielded great power to protect the interests of slaughterhouse workers, but those days are over. Slaughterhouses have transformed meat-cutting into a job that requires nearly no training. As the need for skilled workers has been eliminated, unions have lost their bargaining strength. And despite the weakened stature of unions, meat companies remain as hostile to them as ever. When seeking sites to build new slaughterhouses, management consistently favors cities and states where unions are weak, and where "right-to-work" laws are strong.

Market forces have compelled meat companies to cut their operating costs to the bone. The glory days of America's meat-cutters were in the late 1950s, and ever since, conditions have gone downhill. As long as meat-cutting remains an unskilled job, and slaughterhouses have access to a steady stream of impoverished immigrants, the situation confronting meat-cutters and their communities is unlikely to improve.

I am indebted to Don Stull and Michael Broadway for the enormous help they provided me in preparing this meatpacking appendix. I carried out a lengthy correspondence with them as I researched and wrote this material. They were each unstintingly generous of their time, and supplied me with most of the information appearing here. Finally, with their kind permission, I adapted several paragraphs from their emails to me for publication in this appendix.

Appendix I: Recommended Reading

There are numerous sources of information related to vegan eating and farmed animal protection. This appendix lists some of the best starting points for further reading.

- **Robin Robertson. *The Vegan Planet*. Harvard Common Press, 2003.** Learning to cook quick and delicious vegan meals is a great help to successfully changing your diet. With more than a hundred vegan cookbooks currently in print, I think that *Vegan Planet* is the obvious one to buy first. It's cheap, giant, and the recipes are fantastic. Many vegan cookbooks are filled with uninspired recipes, but nothing mediocre made the cut for this book. With four hundred recipes, this book can cover all your cooking needs for years to come.

- **Virginia Messina. <www.VirginiaMessina.com>.** A top authority on vegetarian and vegan nutrition, Virginia's website is a superb resource for all the latest information about eating well.

- **Peter Singer. *Ethics into Action*. Rowman & Littlefield, 1998.** I consider this biography of the late Henry Spira to be Singer's most important book on animal protection. Unlike Singer's earlier books on the subject, *Ethics into Action* offers proven and practical advice for stopping as much animal suffering as possible. By showing what Spira accomplished during his activist career, and how he accomplished it, Singer provides countless lessons for effective activism.

- **Peter Singer.** *Animal Liberation.* **Ecco, 1975, 2001.** *Animal Liberation* helped to bring the modern animal protection movement into existence. This book provides a rigorous yet readable philosophical argument against animal exploitation.

- **Peter Drucker.** *Managing the Non-Profit Organization.* **HarperBusiness, 1990, 1992.** This classic text on nonprofits should be required reading for anyone starting or working for an animal protection organization. It would also be a helpful book to read before participating in an internship. The book is a collection of interviews and essays, which together provide enormous insight into the workings of a successful nonprofit.

- **Matthew Scully.** *Dominion.* **St. Martin's, 2002.** Animal protection has long been embraced primarily by people who are to the left politically. By contrast, few conservatives or Christians have spoken up against the meat industry. Matthew Scully served as a speechwriter for George W. Bush, and his book condemns modern animal agriculture by invoking the values of conservatism and Christianity. While Scully's book has inspired controversy within the animal protection movement, it's beautifully written and impeccably researched. *Dominion* deserves to be read by activists of every political orientation.

Acknowledgments

I received an enormous amount of help while I researched and wrote this book. To everyone mentioned here, I offer my most heartfelt thanks.

Advisors:

I am deeply grateful to the following people for giving this book so much of their attention:

Neil Switz convinced me to rewrite four of the book's middle chapters, and he provided me with a number of insightful comments.

Alec Shuldiner likewise gave me a large number of useful comments, many of which dovetailed with Neil's suggestions, which helped me to work out a strategy for making revisions.

Jack Norris and Matt Ball each gave the manuscript a close review, and offered numerous suggestions and comments.

Don Stull and Michael Broadway provided me with many hours of assistance as I wrote Appendix H. Don also commented extensively and helpfully on Appendix E.

Stephen Kaufman read the manuscript and provided many suggestions.

Virginia Messina advised me on the material presented in Appendix A.

Paul Shapiro and Gaverick Matheny offered helpful suggestions related to my analysis of the animal protection movement's activities.

Jarurat Ousingsawat and Venkatesh Rao shared their expertise as I typeset this book in LaTeX.

Wendy Skinner proofread the final text of this book.

I especially thank Beth Geisler and Miyun Park for separately copyediting this book, and also for offering many style-related editorial suggestions.

Activists:

In researching this book, I turned to a number of people within the animal protection movement for help related to their areas of expertise.

Lorri and Gene Bauston provided much useful information related to farmed animal care. Patrick Cartwright, Jr. supplied me with the facts and sentencing details related to the Timmy White cruelty case. Simon Chaitowitz obtained for me the latest USDA spending information concerning school lunches. Merritt Clifton provided me with an analysis of the animal protection movement's finances. Mary Finelli kept me informed of new state laws intended to bar activists from factory farms and slaughterhouses. JP Goodwin supplied an estimate of the number of animals killed by America's fur industry. Karen Hirsch referred me to estimates of downer cattle numbers. Julia Lehner sent me statistics and analysis of euthanasia at America's animal shelters. Christine Ketter McDiarmid shared her fishing story that I included in Appendix D. Reed Mangels provided me with information on the growth of the natural foods industry. Donna Maurer helped me to better understand the progress made by the animal protection movement. Lauren Ornelas and Juliet Gellatley's article, "When Pigs Cry," referred me to much of the source material I used in my section on pig welfare. James Weishaupt researched Tyson Food's historical stock performance. And last, David Wolfson kindly reviewed my material related to Common Farming Exemptions—all of which was based on his pioneering research.

Mann Library Reference Staff:

I feel a special debt to the entire reference staff of Mann Library, Cornell University. Their cheerfulness and professionalism was a great inspiration to me as I carried out my research. Of this reference staff, I give special thanks to:

Michael Cook, for working with me to locate source documents related to water use in animal agriculture.

Greg Lawrence, who contacted USDA staffers on several occasions to help me pin down elusive information.

Nathan Rupp, for taking it upon himself to find several references in this book that I could have never found by myself.

Essay Contributors:

I thank everyone who contributed activist essays to this book:
Antonia Demas
Joe Espinosa and Marsha Forsman
Stephen Kaufman
Eddie Lama
Johanna McCloy
Virginia Messina
Robin Robertson
Sukie Sargent

Supporters:

The following people have extended support to my work at pivotal times, and have helped my writing reach a wider audience: Dan Eckam, Warren Havens, James Weishaupt, and others who wish to remain anonymous. Finally, I thank the hundreds of people in the United States and Canada who have organized my past speaking events, and the thousands of people who've traveled short and long distances to attend. It's because of the support of local activists that this book has been possible.

Notes

Introduction

[1]On December 31, 1959 there were 2,170,265 farms on which hens were being raised for eggs. By December 31, 1969, the number of these farms had dropped to 471,284.

Department of Commerce, Bureau of the Census. *1964 United States Census of Agriculture*. Volume II, Chapter 2. 1967. p. 44

Department of Commerce, Bureau of the Census. *1969 United States Census of Agriculture*. Volume II, Chapter 5. 1973. p. 9

Chapter One

[1]The number of animals dying in the animal agriculture industry in 2002 fell just short of 10 billion. For 2003, preliminary numbers show the ten billion threshold was exceeded by about 63 million animals. Of these animals, 9.15 billion were slaughtered. The remainder died of illness or injury, or were culled male layer chicks.

USDA/ NASS "Poultry Slaughter 2002 Summary," February 2003. USDA/ NASS "Livestock Slaughter 2002 Summary," March 2003. USDA/ NASS "Chicken & Eggs," March 2003. USDA/ NASS "Turkey Hatchery," April 2003. USDA/ NASS "Meat Animals Production, Disposition, & Income 2002," April 2003. USDA/ NASS "Chicken & Eggs," August 2003. USDA/ NASS "Poultry Slaughter," August 2003. USDA/ NASS "Livestock Slaughter," August 2003.

[2]1980 totals taken from Agricultural Statistics, Washington DC: USDA, 1981. In 1985, US farmers raised 4 billion meat chickens, 289 million layer hens, 34 million cattle or veal calves, and 96 million pigs. See tables 584, 586, 460, 471, and 409.

1940 totals taken from Agricultural Statistics, Washington DC: USDA, 1941. In 1950, US farmers raised 696 million meat chickens and layer hens, 33 million turkeys, 24 million cattle or veal calves, and 77 million pigs. See tables 622, 633, 354, and 496.

[3]"The New Rich." Forbes October 13, 1997: 328.

[4]Unlike Wendell Murphy, Don Tyson had been on the Forbes list since 1986. But 1997 was the first time his net worth exceeded a billion dollars (the October, 14 1996 Forbes, on p. 203, reported his net worth at 950 million.) In 1997, Forbes set his wealth at 1.2 billion: "The Forbes 400," Forbes October 13, 1997: 224. By 1997, Tyson was nearing the end of his career at Tyson Foods. He was the company's CEO from 1967 to 1991, and he retired as Senior Chairman of the Board in 2001.

[5]Figures reflect a purchase made at close of trading on January 2, 1973, and a sale of all stock at close of trading on January 2, 2003. During this thirty year period, Tyson produced an annual average return of 18.81 percent.
Weishaupt, James. Buttonwood Capital Management, New York. Personal Communication. February 2003.

[6]Singer, Peter. Personal Communication. November 18, 2003.

[7]Quote taken from Tyson Foods' website on October 1, 2003.
<www.tyson.com/chicken/faq/default.asp>

[8]Quote taken from the National Cattlemen's Beef Association website on October 1, 2003.
<www.beef.org/dsp/dsp_content.cfm?locationId=887&contentTypeId=1&contentId=1653>

[9]The purchasing power of a dollar in 2003 amounts to just thirteen cents in 1950 dollars. That represents a total inflation of 769.2 percent over 53 years. US Department of Labor. Bureau of Labor Statistics. Inflation Calculator.
<http://data.bls.gov/cgi-bin/cpicalc.pl>

[10]The average price of a new house went from $11,000 in 1950 to $175,200 in 2001. The 1950 figure comes from:

Rose, Judy. "Houses have Doubled in Size Over 50 Years," *Detroit Free Press,* July 19, 2002.

The 2001 figure comes from:

US Census Bureau, Department of Commerce. Statistical Abstract of the United States 2002. Austin, TX: Hoover's Business Press. 2003. Table 924, page 592.

[11]In 1950, the US produced 6.666 million autos, at a wholesale value of $8,633,272,000 dollars. This comes to an average wholesale price of $1295.12. Adding 10 percent for transportation to the dealer and for dealer markup (this is probably a bit on the high side) yields an average retail price of $1424.63 for each new car sold in the US.

The way the government reports car sales has since changed, as the government now estimates average resale price per car. The average new car sold in the US in 2001 went for $21,605.

So, between 1950 and 2001, the average car price increased by 1416 percent.

Statistical Abstract of the United States 1952. Statistical Abstract of the United States 2002.

[12]The increase in milk prices between 1950 and 2003 amounts to 352 percent.

A gallon of milk purchased in Los Angeles cost 76 cents in 1953. In January of 2003, milk had a US retail price of $2.68 per gallon.

Scott Derks, ed. The Value of a Dollar: 1860-1999 Millennium Edition Lakeville, CT: Grey House Publishing, 1999. p. 280.

Bureau of Labor Statistics. Average Price Data. US City Average. Milk, Fresh, Whole, Fortified, Per Gallon.

[13]A dozen eggs purchased at retail in Los Angeles cost 62 cents in 1950, while a pound of chicken cost 58 cents. In January of 2003, a dozen eggs cost $1.18, and a pound of chicken cost $1.00.

Derks, p. 279.

Bureau of Labor Statistics. Average Price Data. Large Grade A Eggs, and Chicken, Fresh, Whole, Per Pound.

[14]This giant Los Angeles farm is called Egg City. In 1972, Newcastle Disease hit Egg City's flock. To halt the spread of the disease, all 3.4 million hens on the premises were slaughtered and incinerated.

[15]"Top Company Rankings." *Egg Industry.* 108.1 (2003): 19-20.

[16]Cal-Maine Foods had 20,600,000 hens as of December 31, 2002.

"Top Company Rankings." Egg Industry.

[17]Exact drop was 92.4 percent USDA.

Census of Agriculture. 1952 and 1982.

[18]NASS recorded 91,990 dairies as of 2002.

USDA, NASS, Agricultural Statistics Board. Statistical Highlights of US Agriculture 2002-2003. p. 35.

[19]Farms raising pigs fell from 240,150 in 1992 to 73,350 in 2002.

USDA, NASS, Agricultural Statistics Board. Statistical Highlights of US Agriculture. 1995-1996, p. 9, and 2002-2003, p 35.

[20]Gunderson, P., et al. "The Epidemiology of Suicide Among Farm Residents or Workers in Five North-Central States, 1980-198" American Journal of Preventive Medicine 9 (May/June 1993): 26-32.

U.S. Public Health Service, The Surgeon General's Call To Action To Prevent Suicide. Washington, DC: 1999.

<www.surgeongeneral.gov/library/calltoaction/calltoaction.htm>

Accessed December 4, 2003.

[21]Pounds are a finer unit of measurement than gallons, so the USDA records milk yields by the pound. To provide gallon measurements, I divided the USDA's pound figures by 8, and then rounded to the nearest five gallons. The USDA's measurements were: 5314 pounds milk in 1950; 10360 pounds milk in 1975; and 18,571 pounds milk in 2002.

Milk production statistics for 2002 came from: USDA, NASS Fact Finders for Agriculture: Milk Production. February 14, 2003. 27 pages. p. 1.

Milk production statistics for 1950 and 1975 were taken from the USDA's website. NASS Quickstats. Agricultural Statistics Database. "Annual Milk Production, Milk Cows, and Milk per Cow." Years 1950 and 1975.

<www.nass.usda.gov:81/ipedb/>

Accessed December 4, 2003.

[22]Pigs are slaughtered at about 176 days of age, and average slaughter weight is 264 pounds.

USDA Grain Inspection, Packers, and Stockyards Administration. Assessment of the Cattle and Hog Industries, Calender Year 2001. June 2002. p. 33.

USDA. Agricultural Statistics 2002. Table 7-36.

[23]Conatser, Glenn E. et al. "Performance Testing." (Table 5).

<http://animalscience.ag.utk.edu/docs/PERFORMANCETESTINGConatser.doc>

Accessed January 2, 2004.

[24]Chickens had a market weight of 3.08 pounds in 1950, as opposed to five pounds in 2000. Tyson 2001 Investor Fact Book. Tyson Foods, Inc. Investor Relations Dept. Springdale, AR. p. 7.

[25]This is, of course, with the overall inflation rate taken into account.

[26]Xin, H. et al.. "Feed and water consumption, growth, and mortality of male broilers." *Poultry Science* 73 (1994): 610-616.

[27]USDA. Part I: Reference of Dairy Health and Management in the United States, 2002. USDA, APHIS. p. 54, 55.

Additionally: "A correlation between retained placenta, mastitis, and milk fever to milk yield during the previous lactation was found to be probable and for ketosis and displaced abomasum such a correlation was found to be possible. A connection to the yield in the current lactation was shown for ovarian cysts, claw diseases, and milk fever." P. Fleischer et al. "The Relationship Between Milk Yield and the Incidence of Some Diseases in Dairy Cows." Journal of Dairy Science 84 (2001): 2025-2035.

[28]USDA. 2002. Part I: Reference of Dairy Health and Management in the United States, 2002. USDA: APHIS:VS, CEAH, National Animal Health Monitoring System, Fort Collins, CO. p. 43.

[29]I'm being conservative with this 100,000 downer claim. Industry and government make no effort to count downer cattle. The *Bovine Practioner* survey referenced below put the annual number of downed cattle in the US at 195,000. The USDA has been repeatedly referenced as having put forth a 130,000 downer estimate, but this number doesn't check out and nobody at the USDA will stand behind it. Clearly, the USDA ought to require the reporting of downed animals, so that a reliable count can be made.

Hansen, Don and Bridges, Victoria. "A survey description of down-cows and cows with progressive or non-progressive neurological signs compatible with a TSE from veterinary-client herd in 38 states.' *The Bovine Practitioner* 33.2 (1999): 179-187.

[30] Yahav, S. and Plavnik, I. "The Effect of an Early Age Thermal Conditioning and Food Restriction on Performance and Thermotolerance of Male Broiler Chickens." *Br. Poult. Sci.* 40(1999): 120-126.

Chapter Two

[1]Walter Jaksch, "Euthanasia of Day-Old Male Chicks in the Poultry Industry." Int J. Stud. Anim Prob. 2.4 (1981): 203-213.

[2]This number is gained by getting the number of female layer pullets added to America's chicken flocks in 2002, and assuming an equal number of males were born. USDA, NASS, Agricultural Statistics Board. Chicken and Eggs 2002 Summary. p. 14 table: "Disposition: Number Slaughtered, Lost, and Added During the Month." 2003.

[3]Michael Gentle et al. "Behavioral Consequences of Partial Beak Amputation (Beak Trimming)." British Poultry Science Journal. 30 (1989): 479-488.

Michael Gentle et al."Behavioral Evidence for Persistent Pain Following Partial Beak Amputation in Chickens." Applied Animal Behavior Science. 27 (1991): 149-157.

[4]The beak searing process will likely improve in the years ahead, as hatcheries are installing camera-equipped devices that ensure a uniform cut.

[5]Investigations carried out by Compassion Over Killing found that, among the egg farms the group visited, stocking density was typically about eight birds per cage, and sometimes as many as eleven. The new United Egg Producers welfare guidelines should drop the average birds to cage to seven.

Shapiro, Paul. Person Communication. January 13, 2004.

[6]McDonald's requires 72 square inches per bird. Burger King requires 75 square inches. This is set against the previous recommendations by the United Egg Producers, which had advocated a minimum of 48 square inches per bird. In 1999, most egg farms gave each bird no more than 54 square inches.

Mench, Joy A. "Consumer Voices, Dollars, are Changing Animal Welfare Standards." Sustainable Agriculture. Davis, California: University of California Sustainable Agriculture Research and Education Program. Summer 2002.

The United Egg Producers now calls for egg farms to gradually decrease stocking density, so that, by 2008, each chicken will have 67 square inches.

"UEP Outlines Certification" Egg Industry. Mt. Morris, IL: Watt Publishing. 107.4 (April 2002): 5.

[7]Park, Miyun. Personal communication. July 14, 2004

[8]There are numerous companies that supply conveyor belts and other machinery for egg farms. Lubing Systems of Cleveland, TN is the manufacturer of "Soft Ride" conveyors. They ran an ad for this product in *Egg Industry*, January 2003, Watt Publishing. p. 2.

[9]I went back more than a decade in several leading poultry industry journals, and could find no significant discussion of broken bones among layer hens, apart from the following footnote.

[10]T.G. Knowles. "Handling and Transport of Spent Hens." World's Poultry Science Journal. 50. (1994): 60-61.

[11]The average age of layer hens at slaughter is 101.5 weeks.

USDA. *Layers '99—Part II: Reference of 1999 Table Eggs Layer Management in the US*. January 2000. USDA/APHIS Veterinary Services. National Animal Health Monitoring System. p. 29.

[12]At their laying peak, 100 hens will yield about 90 eggs each day. *Layers '99—Part II*. p. 26.

[13]In chickens, the body part through which the egg passes is called the cloaca. Part of the cloaca always prolapses each time an egg is laid. But it usually retracts shortly thereafter. In the severe cases that I refer to in this passage, the entire cloaca comes out with the egg, sometimes accompanied by the lower digestive system.

[14]Don Bell informed me that ready-to-lay pullets (about 17-weeks of age) are available from growers, costing between $2.50 and $3.00 each.

In reference to the point I'm making in the text, I'm not suggesting that a 17-week-old hen is purchased from the hatchery and stuck in the cage to replace a dead hen. Since all hens in a cage are sent to slaughter at the same time, it would be foolish to mix in new hens with old. My point here is that the money that could be spent on veterinary care for treating prolapsed hens is more economically spent toward purchasing a new batch of hens from the hatchery.

In response to the footnoted sentence, and the above entry, Don Bell writes: "Veterinary care is expensive and difficult to obtain and is used for population health problems, not individual bird conditions. It's just like it is with humans—many people self-diagnose their problems and treat themselves with off-the-shelf medications. Many people just live through a disease or health problem without availing themselves of professional assistance."

My response to Prof. Bell: Humans can certainly decide to self-medicate or to ignore a given condition. But when an illness or injury crosses a certain threshold of pain, or becomes life-threatening, most people have the option to obtain individualized medical care. As Prof. Bell acknowledges, commercial chickens never receive individualized veterinary treatment. And I think that's immoral. There's no doubt that millions of birds suffer needless and protracted suffering, that could be eliminated with individualized veterinary attention.

Bell, Don. Poultry Specialist (Emeritus), University of California, Riverside. Personal Communication. February and November 2003.

[15]Prolapses are not rare, but neither the government nor the poultry industry has kept reliable numbers on deaths from prolapse. For the sake of being conservative, I've based this calculation on a prolapse rate of one percent of birds. Don Bell, one of America's foremost poultry experts, estimates that about 1 to 2 percent of layer hens dies from prolapse. Since America's egg farms stock about 270 million hens, this brings about 2.7 million prolapse-related fatalities per year, if we are selecting the low end (1 percent) of Bell's estimate. In the text, I've made my guess even more conservative by rounding down the figure of 2.7 million.

Don Bell's comments to the footnoted sentence and the above text: "Concentration on one cause of death without mentioning (or knowing) the corresponding amount of death by the same reason or a different reason in nature inappropriately places bias on the commercial or domesticated condition. It is totally biased to focus only on one aspect of mortality that happens to be studied without placing an equal amount of emphasis on predation, internal parasites and other diseases and problems associated with non-confined systems as if they were free of mortality problems."

My response to Prof. Bell: There's no doubt that prolapses occurred with wild chickens in the past, but it's unreasonable to suspect that they occurred with anywhere near the same frequency. For one thing, wild chickens laid far fewer eggs than today's domesticated chickens; for another thing, the eggs laid by wild chickens were far smaller than today's commercial eggs. The size of today's eggs, coupled with the frequency of laying, surely drives up the rate of prolapses to a level far above what occurred in nature. Prof. Bell does have a point that wild chickens certainly suffered from a range of health and predation problems. But, visiting commercial egg farms, I have to think that the moment-by-moment conditions the animals endure are far nastier and more unpleasant than the day-to-day life of any wild animal I've ever witnessed. And, in any case, humans don't bear a responsibility for the disease and predation of wild animals—that's something beyond our control. We do have a moral responsibility, however, to address clear-cut cases of protracted suffering that occur with the animals we raise for food.

Bell, Don. Poultry Specialist (Emeritus), University of California, Riverside. Personal Communication. February and November 2003.

[16]Two million hens, at two days each, equals four million days. Four million divided by 365 days (one year) equals 10,954. I suspect this two-day claim is conservative, and that many hens linger on for more than two days, which makes at least 11,000 birds suffering at any moment a reasonable assumption.

[17] USDA records indicate that 14.6 percent of layer hens die before slaughter.
Layers '99—Part II. p. 29.

[18] *Layers '99—Part II.* p. 25.

[19] *Layers '99—Part II.* p. 29. (This information indicates that force-molted flocks produce 38 more weeks than non-molted flocks, but it's important to remember that a minority of flocks are force-molted twice. Since this reference lumps all force-molted birds together, it does not give a clear indication of how long a single forced-molting will extend production.)

[20] The length of time that food is withdrawn depends upon the weight loss that occurs among the hens, as well as their mortality rate during molting. These molting guidelines have been written up by the United Egg Producers.

Bell, Don. Poultry Specialist (Emeritus), University of California, Riverside. Personal Communication. February and November 2003.

[21] During forced molting, hens may suffer up to a 30 percent loss of body weight, and a mortality rate of up to 1.2 percent.

Don Bell responds to the footnoted sentence and the above text: "Your choice of words always bears a bad connotation to the reader. If you have a choice of words, you always pick the harshest words: "heavy cost," "kills the weaker," "suffer," and so on. I challenge you to say the same things without shading the discussion to your generally negative views. Do you really believe that the flock gains nothing by being molted by the farmer. Do you really believe that a short life is better than a longer one? Have you ever heard of a flock molting in nature? Have you ever heard abut humans fasting for health reasons? And don't fall back on the argument that, 'taking the feed away is not fasting.'"

My response to Professor Bell: I have used negative words because, when I see suffering, I write about it. Having spent time at egg farms, I think that, if anything, my writing about the conditions is overly restrained, and unfair to the birds because it barely even hints about the extent of their suffering. To answer your questions: yes, I believe a flock gains nothing by being molted by the farmer, apart from added months of misery. I think that a long life is usually better than a shorter one, unless it's a cramped and painful life in which case shorter is better and not being born is better still. I've certainly heard of flocks molting in nature, and there's no doubt that wild chickens faced cold and hunger during the winter; it's one of the unpleasant things that wild animals experience, which is one reason why I'm not at all envious of wild animals; but one visit to any commercial egg farm will confirm my assertion that the fate of a battery hen is far, far worse. And while I've heard of, and for that matter have personally experienced, fasting for health reasons—people who fast do not experience a 30 percent loss of body weight or a 1.2 percent likelihood of dying from the fast. I don't see how it's relevant to compare a voluntary and generally harmless human decision to something vastly harsher, that's forced on animals for the sake of generating profits.

Bell, Don. Poultry Specialist (Emeritus), University of California, Riverside. Personal Communication. February and November 2003.

[22] *Layers '99—Part II.* p. 29.

[23] *Layers '99—Part II.* p. 17.

[24] A typical broiler house is 40' x 500' (20,000 square feet), and contains 22,200 meat chickens. Ernst, Ralph A. "Poultry Fact Sheet No. 20." University of California Cooperative Extension. June 1995.

<http://animalscience.ucdavis.edu/Avian/pfs20.htm>

Accessed February 9, 2004.

[25] Higgins, Kevin T., "Tools of the New Trade." Food Engineering 4.1 (January 2002): 46.

Some further background information not in the Higgins article: in 1997, the USDA introduced a pilot program called HIMP that increased permissible line speeds in new chicken slaughterhouses to a maximum of 10,740 birds per hour. As of 2004, the HIMP program is being rolled out nationwide. To gain HIMP eligibility, chicken slaughterhouses must make a number of equipment and procedural changes.

[26]Mieszkowski, Katharine, "Would You Like Spinal Cord with That?" (Interview with Eric Schlosser) Salon.com. February 8, 2001.

<archive.salon.com/tech/feature/2001/02/08/schlosser_interview/print.html>

Fast Food Nation author Eric Schlosser states that the US cattle slaughterhouses process between 300 and 400 animals per hour.

[27]Gregory, N.G. and Wotton, S.B., "Effect of Electrical Stunning Current on the Duration of Insensibility in Hens," British Poultry Science 35.1 (July 1994): 463-465.

[28]Kang, I.S. and Sams, A.R., "Bleedout Efficiency, Carcass Damage, and Rigor Mortis Development Following Electrical Stunning or Carbon Dioxide Stunning on a Shackle Line." *Poultry Science* 78 (1999): 139-143.

[29]An industry article summarizes the problem of administering lasting poultry stuns without damaging the carcass: "Evidently, there is some conflict between animal welfare and meat quality."

Z. Turcsan Z. et al. "The Effects of Electrical and Controlled Atmosphere Stunning Methods on Meat and Liver Quality in Geese." Poultry Science 80 (2001):1647-1651.

[30]Yearly consumption of chicken increased by 26 pounds per American between 1970 and 2001, while consumption of red meat dropped by 21 pounds.

USDA Economic Research Service. "Red Meats: Beef, Veal, Pork, Lamb and Mutton, and Total. Boneless, Trimmed (Edible) Weight, Pounds per Capita per Year. Poultry: Chicken, Turkey, and Total. Boneless, Trimmed (Edible) Weight, Pounds per Capita per Year." Statistics accessed through the website of USDA's Economic Research Service.

<www.ers.usda.gov/Data/foodconsumption/DataSystem.asp?ERSTab=3>

Accessed December 4, 2004.

[31]According to Tyson Foods, the average steer weighs 1150 pounds, of which 715 pounds are beef.

Also, according to Tyson's Investor Fact Book, the average meat chicken weighs five pounds. Tyson Foods does not indicate the average resultant carcass weight of deboned chicken, and finding this number in the literature was surprisingly difficult. The one figure I found, 61.7 percent, dates all the way back to 1979.

61.7 percent of five pounds amounts to 3.08 pounds. I suspect this 61.7 percent figure is likely too low by several percentage points. For purposes of being conservative with this claim, I have rounded up to 3.25 pounds deboned meat from each chicken. With these assumptions, it would take 220 chickens to equal the meat provided by a single steer.

Tyson Foods. *Investor Fact Book 2001.* Springdale AR. p. 4, 7.

[32]2.987 billion "broiler" chickens were slaughtered in 1970, and 8.284 billion were slaughtered in 2000.

USDA *Agricultural Statistics,* 1972. Page 482, table 595. USDA *Agricultural Statistics,* 2003. Page VIII-36, table 8-53.

[33]Smith, Lewis W. "Observing Swine Behavior to Lower Piglet Mortality." *Agricultural Research.* USDA/Agricultural Research Service. June 2001: 2.

[34]Kelly, HRC et al. "Limb Injuries, Immune Response, and Growth Performance of Early Weaned Pigs in Different Housing Systems." *Animal Science.* 70 (2000): 73-83.

[35]Kelly, HRC: 73-83.

[36]By contrast, at traditional family farms, the cost of straw was trivial. There weren't many pigs being raised at any one time, and most farmers had a ready source of straw from nearby fields.

[37] In factory farms, 11.7 percent of piglets who survive birth die before weaning. Of these deaths, 55.7 percent were the result of the mother accidentally lying on the piglets, and either smothering or crushing them.

USDA. *Swine 2000—Part III: Reference of Swine Health and Environmental Management in the United States, 2000.* USDA: APHIS: VS, CEAH, National Health Monitoring System, Fort Collins, CO (2002): 6, 7.

[38] Donald C. Lay, an animal behaviorist at the USDA's Agricultural Research Service, believes that uncomfortable flooring in farrowing crates causes sows to frequently get up and shift position. Each time they do this, their newborn piglets are apt to squirm into the farrowing pen, and be crushed when the sow lies back down. Since dozens of sows are kept in the same farrowing building, these sheds are terribly noisy. Lay thinks that sows kept in these facilities might grow accustomed to the noise of squealing piglets, and disregard the squealing that occurs when they are accidentally crushing their own offspring.

Smith, Lewis W.: 2.

It's not surprising that sows sometimes don't respond appropriately to squealing if one of their piglets is being crushed. These breeder facilities are so noisy that employees wear earplugs. Daniel Roth. The Ray Kroc of Pigsties. Forbes. October 13, 1997. p. 115-120.

[39] *Swine 2000—Part III: Reference of Swine Health and Environmental Management in the United States:* 6, 7.

[40] Surprisingly, as of December 4, 2003, Murphy Family Farms had this damaging information on their website breeder farm information available by hitting the "tour" button at: <http://www.e-murphyfarms.com/>.

[41] This figure is calculated by doubling the rate of culled breeder sows in the six-month period between December 1, 1999 and May 31, 2000. Of these culled sows, 41.9 percent were culled because of age, 21.3 percent because of reproductive failure, and 16 percent because of lameness.

USDA. *Swine 2000—Part I Reference of Swine Health and Management in the United States.* National Animal Health Monitoring System. August 2001. p. 8.

[42] This figure is obtained by doubling the rate of breeder sows found dead in the six-month period between December 1, 1999 and May 31, 2000.

Swine 2000. Part I Reference of Swine Health and Management in the United States. p. 8.

[43] *Swine 2000. Part I: Reference of Swine Health and Management in the United States.* 2000. p. 16.

[44] Touchette, KJ et al. "Effect of spray-dried plasma and lipopolysaccharide exposure on weaned pigs: I. Effects on the immune axis of weaned pigs." *Journal of Animal Science.* 80 (2002): 494-501.

[45] I'm referring here to pigs raised for the commodity-level pork that ends up in most supermarkets and restaurants. For the few farmers who are able to get premium prices for pork sold to natural food stores and at farmer's markets, it's doubtless financially viable to avoid the practice of tail docking.

[46] Of the piglets who die in the nursery, 28.9 percent succumb to respiratory disease. This is a clear indication of how bad the air quality in nurseries tends to be.

Mortality figures taken from: *Swine 2000—Part III: Reference of Swine Health and Environmental Management in the United States.* p. 8.

Time spent in nursery taken from: *Swine 2000—Part I Reference of Swine Health and Management in the United States.* p. 20.

[47] Additionally, fewer than 5 percent of farrowing and nursery piglets are allowed outdoors.

Swine 2000—Part I: Reference of Swine Health and Management in the United States. p. 26.

[48]*Swine 2000—Part I: Reference of Swine Health and Management in the United States.* p. 21.

[49]Swine 2000—Part I: Reference of Swine Health and Management in the United States. p. 22.

[50]Lung problems are the top killer of pigs living in finishing sheds. Of finishing pigs who die before slaughter, 43 percent of deaths are caused by lung problems. *Swine 2000. Part III. Reference of Swine Health and Environmental Management in the United States.* p. 8.

[51]Thorne, P.S. et al. "Occupational Health." In: Thu, KM, Mcmillan, D and Venzkem H, *Understanding the Impacts of Large-scale Swine Production,* Iowa City, IA: University of Iowa. 1996.

[52]*USDA/NAHMS. Swine '95: Part II: Reference of 1995 U.S. Grower/Finisher Health & Management Practices.* p. 19.

[53]*Swine '95: Part II: Reference of 1995 U.S. Grower/Finisher Health & Management Practices.* p. 19.

[54]Of these 80,000 dead pigs, 70 percent were found dead when the trucks were unloaded, and the other 30 percent died of injuries before they could be slaughtered.

   Grandin, Temple. "2001. Livestock trucking guide: livestock management practices that reduce injuries to livestock during transport."

   <www.animalagriculture.org/pamphlets/Livestock%20Trucking/LTG.htm>
   Accessed December 4, 2003.

[55]Weise, Elizabeth. "Food Safety Chief Scolds Inspectors." *USA Today.* November 11, 2003.

[56]"Field Operations: The Heart and Soul of FSIS." Remarks prepared for delivery by Dr. Garry McKee, Administrator, FSIS, before the Office of Field Operations' Supervisory Conference, Nashville, TN, October 27, 2003

   <www.fsis.usda.gov/oa/speeches/2003/gm_ofo.htm>
   Accessed November 11, 2003

[57]The USDA's number is for 2002 is 123,677,000. USDA/NASS "Hogs and Pigs: Marketings, Price, and Cash Receipts"

   <www.usda.gov/nass/pubs/stathigh/2003/tables/livestock.htm#hprcpt>
   Accessed February 9, 2004.

[58]Warrick, Joby. "They Die Piece by Piece," *Washington Post.* April 10, 2001; Page A01.

[59]Gregory, N.G. and Wotton, S.B. "Sheep slaughtering procedures IV: Responsiveness of the brain following electrical stunning." British Veterinary Journal 141 (1985): 74-81.

[60]Food Safety Inspection Service, USDA. Module 12: Swine Inspection (305). March 2000.

   <www.fsis.usda.gov/ofo/hrds/slaugh/redmeat/swininsp.pdf>
   Accessed December 4, 2003.

[61]Agricultural Statistics Database. "Annual Milk Production, Milk Cows, and Milk per Cow." Years 1970 and 2001.

   <www.nass.usda.gov:81/ipedb/>
   Accessed December 4, 2003.

[62]One of the largest of outdoor dry-lot dairies I've ever seen is located about 30 miles west of El Paso, and straddles Interstate 20 for several miles. The welfare conditions at this dairy are appalling, and can easily be witnessed by passing motorists. The stench generated by thousands of cows kept closely together is enough to force you to roll up your car windows. Incredibly, this particular dairy makes no effort to conceal its corporate identity. It has even installed large signs on its property, facing the Interstate, that advertise its brand of milk.

[63]In the year 2000, the average annual production of a US dairy cow was 18,201 pounds of milk per year. At eight pounds per gallon, that totals 2275 gallons of milk.

USDA-NASS Agricultural Statistics 2003. Chapter 8, p. 7.

[64]In 2001, the US dairy herd amounted to just over 9 million cows. 26.5 percent of dairy cows are culled due to reproductive problems, and 27 percent are culled for udder problems or mastitis. Additionally, 22 percent are culled for lameness or disease, and some of this figure has to be due to the stresses arising from milking and repeated pregnancies.

<http://usda.mannlib.cornell.edu/reports/nassr/livestock/dairy-herd/specda02.txt>

USDA, APHIS. *Dairy 2002—Part I: Reference of Dairy Health and Management in the United States.* January 2003: p. 40. *Dairy 2002—Part I: Reference of Dairy Health and Management in the United States.* p. 43.

[65]The mortality rate of dairy calves born alive, and prior to weaning, is 8.7

Dairy 2002—Part I: Reference of Dairy Health and Management in the United States. p. 57.

[66]*Dairy 2000—Part I: Reference of Dairy Health and Management in the United States.* p. 43.

[67]Contrary to the claims in much animal rights literature, veal calves (at least some of them) do get a small amount of iron in their diet. But this iron is withdrawn as the calves get older, in order to keep the calves' flesh from turning a healthy red color. Here's the veal industry's take on the matter, in which they go so far as to claim that veal calves have a healthy diet: "Veal calves receive a highly nutritious diet designed for optimum growth and good health." Taken from: "The American Veal Industry: Facts About the Care and Feeding of Calves." American Veal Association, Middletown PA. (This flyer is undated but was part of the AVA's veal information kit in 2003.) It is available online at:

<www.vealfarm.com/education/pdfs/calf-care.pdf>

Accessed December 4, 2003.

[68]The rather unappetizing words "grayish pink" are taken from: "Safety of Veal from Farm to Table." USDA, Food Safety and Inspection Service. February 2003.

<www.fsis.usda.gov/OA/pubs/veal.htm>

Accessed December 4, 2003.

[69]There were 9.11 million dairy cows in the US in 2001. That year, 88.8 percent of these cows gave birth to live calves, for a total of 8.08 million live calves (the actual number is a bit higher because of occasional births of live twins.)

Dairy 2002—Part I: Reference of Dairy Health and Management in the United States. pp. 53, 81.

[70]I've been to calf auctions and seen injured newborn calves go for under $30, but $50 is probably on the low side of what most veal farms pay for a healthy animal. A budget put out by Iowa State University in 1998 assumes a $50 purchase price, but also makes provisions for calf prices of $100 or $170.

"Veal Enterprise Budget—First Quarter, 1998, Base Budget." Iowa State University, Dairy Science Extension. 4 Kildee Hall, Ames, Iowa.

[71]Veal consumption per American has declined strongly since the 1950s. The average American ate: 5.6 pounds of veal in 1950; 4.2 pounds in 1960; 2 pounds in 1970; 1.3 pounds in 1980, .89 pounds in 1990; .55 pounds in 2000; and .49 pounds in 2001. Data Taken from USDA Economic Research Service. Food Consumption (per Capita) Data System. "Red Meats: Beef; Veal; Pork; Lamb and Mutton: and Total Boneless Trimmed (Edible) Weight, Pounds per Capita Per Year."

<www.ers.usda.gov/Data/foodconsumption/DataSystem.asp?ERSTab=3>

Accessed February 9, 2004

[72]In 2002, the USDA reported the previous year's calf slaughter at 1.01 million animals.

USDA/NASS. Livestock Slaughter 2001 Summary. March 2002.

The research I've done connected to dairy cow births suggests that the actual number of veal calves is probably higher, and definitely not lower, than one million calves.

First, I had to find the total number of dairy cows. In 2001, this number stood at 9.11 million. Agricultural Statistics Database. USDA, NASS. Annual Milk Production, Milk Cows and Milk per Cow. 2001 total, all states. (This number also appears in Dairy 2002; see previous footnote.)

Next, I found that 88.8 percent of cows and heifers in the United States produced live calves in 2001.

USDA. *Part I: Reference of Dairy Health and Management in the United States, 2002.* USDA: APHIS: VS: CEAH, National Animal Health Monitoring System, Fort Collins, CO. 2002.

That amounts to 8.08 million calves born to dairy cows each year. So we've got a total of slightly more than four million male calves born to dairy cows. That makes the USDA's total of 1.01 million calves slaughtered in the United States surprisingly low. The actual number of veal calves is likely somewhat higher for two reasons: the 1.01 million figure does not reflect veal calves who die prematurely while crated or in transport. Second, it's probable that not all veal calves are recorded, particularly those slaughtered upon birth for "bob" veal.

[73]Bureau of Land Management. Instruction Memorandum No. 2002-092. (Document issued to all BLM Field Offices.) 2002.

[74]Steers weigh an average of 627 pounds upon being sent to the feedlot, while females weigh 598 pounds.

2001-2002 Indiana Beef Evaluation and Economic Feeding Program. p. 4.

<www.ansc.purdue.edu/ibeef/2001-2002/2001-2002.pdf>

Accessed December 5, 2003.

[75]Monthly grazing fees on private lands typically amount to about $11.50 per animal.

USDA, NASS, Agricultural Statistics Board. *Statistical Highlights of US Agriculture 2001 and 2002.* p. 34.

[76]Many cattle are castrated at about two months of age. For others, castration doesn't happen until they are sent to the feedlot.

[77]Rhodes, Richard. *Farm : a year in the life of an American farmer.* Simon & Schuster, c1989. Excerpted from p. 88 – Approved by Mr. Rhodes, author.

[78]Rhodes, Richard.

[79]I emailed a DVM, who wishes to remain anonymous, who responded that a 10 ml. dose of lidocaine is appropriate for castrating two-month old calves. The best price he's seen for purchasing lidocaine at retail, in quantity, is 23 cents per dose.

[80]The 2002 calf crop was 38.2 million head, which indicates that about 19.1 million male calves were born.

USDA, NASS. *Cattle.* January 31, 2003. 31 pages. p. 1.

[81]Perdue University sponsors the Indiana Beef Evaluation and Economics Feeding Program, which recorded the weights of steers and heifers upon reaching the feedlot, and upon being sent to slaughter. The numbers here should be reasonably close to the national average. Upon arrival at the feedlot, steers averaged 627 pounds weight, while Heifers came in at 598 pounds. They remained at the feedlot for just under six months (181 days for steers and 166 for heifers.) At slaughter, the steers averaged 1209 pounds bodyweight, while heifers averaged 1109 pounds.

2001-2002 Indiana Beef Evaluation and Economics Feeding Program. Perdue University.

<www.ansc.purdue.edu/ibeef/2001-2002/2001-2002.pdf>

Accessed February 9, 2004.

[82] Henry W. Webster. "Growth Promotants in Cattle," Clemson Extension, Clemson University, Clemson, South Carolina. October 1989. Document LL45.

[83]Pollan, "Power Steer." *New York Times,* March 31, 2002, Late Edition - Final , Section 6 (Magazine) , Page 44 , Column 1.

[84]83.2 percent of large feedlots (1000 cattle or more) add antibiotics to their feed or drinking water.

USDA. *99 Feedlot—Part III Health Management and Biosecurity in US Feedlots,* 1999. USDA: APHIS: VS, CEAH, National Health Monitoring System. Fort Collins, CO. #N336.1200. December 2000. p. 15.

[85]Swanson, JC and Morrow-Tesch, J. "Cattle Transport: Historical Research and Future Perspectives." *Journal of Animal Science* 79 (E. Suppl. 2001) E102

[86]Most of the figures on this table indicate roughly a four-to-one decline of slaughter-houses. I chose the one statistic showing a three-to-one decline.

USDA. *Packers and Stockyards Statistical Report—2000 Reporting Year.* USDA Grain Inspection, Packers and Stockyards Administration. GIPSA SR-09-2. October, 2002.

[87]There doesn't appear to be any research done on average transportation times for cattle, but industry scientists commonly study the effects of cattle transported between sixteen and twenty-four hours. It's reasonable to assume that such transportation times are common in the industry. A review of the literature, involving many studies looking at long transport times, can be found at:

Swanson, JC and Morrow-Tesch, J.

[88]Most cattle slaughterhouses use a captive bolt pistol to accomplish this stun. Rather than shooting a bullet, a captive bolt pistol shoots out a rod that rams through the steer's forehead, causing a massive brain injury. The rod then retracts back into the gun, prior to being fired into the next animal. When a captive bolt pistol is properly used, the animal collapses in convulsions, and would quickly succumb to brain injury even if his throat weren't cut. It's disturbing to watch animals die in this way, but there's no doubt that captive bolt pistols represent a relative kindness over previous methods of killing.

[89]Shackle-and-hoist slaughter involved clamping a manacle around a steer's back foot, then hoisting him aloft, with his head dangling about four feet above the kill floor. Cattle are enormous animals, typically weighing well over 1000 pounds. All that weight suspended from one leg commonly caused leg bones to snap and hips to dislocate, guaranteeing that these animals suffered tremendously as their throats were cut. The government never made any attempt to outlaw shackle-and-hoist. This practice was stamped out only because its gruesome nature invited public exposure by animal rights activists. In the 1980s and 1990s, the late activist Henry Spira sent out letters to the largest fast-food and processed meat companies. Spira was well-funded, and he threatened to run full-page advertisements in top newspapers, calling attention to shackle-and-hoist slaughter. He promised that these advertisements would expose any company that continued to sell meat produced in this way. Every company he contacted quickly fell into line, and Spira never had to run a single ad. It wasn't long before all of America's largest slaughterhouses had gotten rid of their shackle-and-hoist equipment.

[90]Warrick, Joby.

[91]Warrick, Joby.

[92]Warrick, Joby.

[93]Warrick, Joby.

[94]Warrick, Joby.

[95] Mieszkowski, Katharine. "Would You Like Spinal Cord with That?"

[96] Mieszkowski, Katharine. "Would You Like Spinal Cord with That?"

[97]British investigators looking into the BSE crisis cited a UK cattle slaughterhouse running at 60 animals an hour as an example of a fast-running plant.

The BSE Inquiry: The Report. Volume 2: Science. Crown copyright. 2000.

[98] If you paid a slaughterhouse worker $30 an hour, and expected him to stun sixty cattle per hour, your cost per stun would be just fifty cents an animal. A wage of $30 per hour is a fortune compared to what most slaughterhouse workers make.

Chapter Three

[1] I was unable to find lifetime feed consumption estimates in the poultry industry's literature. This is hardly surprising, since poultry growers never let chickens live out their natural life span. But Farm Sanctuary has taken in thousands of rescued chickens since 1986, so they have a basis to know how much grain the average chicken will eat over a lifetime. Their "Chicken Care Guide," provides good information for people who want to take in rescued chickens. The original publication, which has since been replaced with one lacking the following feed consumption totals, indicated that the average layer-strain chicken lives five to eight years, and eats 150 to 200 pounds of grain per year. So if we go by the averages, and say the typical layer-strain rooster lives 6.5 years, and eats 175 pounds of grain per year, that comes to 1137.5 pounds of grain.

[2] USDA Layers '99—Part II. p. 29.

[3] A hen who goes through two forced-moltings will produce only about 82 percent of the eggs that she produced during her first laying cycle. On top of this, about 5 percent of the hens in a given layer house would be expected to die by the end of the second molting, which would further reduce the total egg output of a layer house housing hens on their third laying cycle.

Bell, Don. Poultry Specialist (Emeritus), University of California, Riverside. Personal Communication. February and November 2003.

[4] This added expense takes into account that free-range eggs cost about 25 cents each, and that, between the layer hen and her unproductive male counterpart, you've got something like four years of eating and housing required for each year that the layer hen is producing eggs. Add in good care and, when needed, individualized veterinary attention, and the costs would likely exceed a dollar per egg.

[5] I wrote this book while living Ithaca, New York, where a dozen large eggs from the town's leading supermarket (Wegman's) cost $1.59. The supermarket does not carry free-range eggs by the dozen. However, GreenStar, the local natural foods co-op, does not sell battery cage eggs. Instead, GreenStar sells large, organically-fed, pasture raised, free-range eggs for $2.99 a dozen—an 88 percent cost increase. Free-range egg prices are undoubtedly higher in cities and regions that don't have good alternative agriculture. Still, by any measure, at about 95 calories per large egg, free-range eggs are a relatively inexpensive food choice.

Everyday retail prices were surveyed in October of 2003.

[6] The USDA requires that in order to use the free-range or free-roaming terms for poultry products, all that is necessary is that "Producers must demonstrate to the Agency that the poultry has been allowed access to the outside." That one sentence is the sum of the USDA's regulations regarding free-range poultry. Beak searing is permissible. There are no minimum space requirements. Nor is there any requirement for veterinary care.

"Meat and Poultry Labeling Terms." USDA Food Safety and Inspection Service. Consumer Education and Information. January 2001.

<www.fsis.usda.gov/OA/pubs/lablterm.htm>

Accessed February 9, 2004

[7] Holstein cows who receive good veterinary care can live about twenty years. Jersey cows can live 25 to 30 years. In July of 2004, Farm Sanctuary's oldest Jersey cow was 28, and still in reasonably good health.

[8] If the dairy industry wanted, they could probably quickly develop technology that prevented male calves from being conceived. But even if they did, it would do little to change

the overall resource use that slaughter-free dairies would demand. Under the slaughter-free dairy scenario I've described, there is little need for additional female calves, since cows are already restricted to no more than two births. Switching to conception methods that prevented the birth of male calves would therefore provide little benefit to the slaughter-free dairy industry. The extra females being born would occupy the same unprofitable role that the males had formerly occupied, eating grain and requiring care for twenty years without producing a drop of milk.

[9]Even if breeding procedures were initiated that kept male offspring from being conceived, a slaughter-free dairy industry would still be less than one-tenth as efficient as a dairy that allowed slaughter. You'd still have an overabundance of cattle to deal with, and the females born in place of male calves could not produce milk without giving birth to still more calves.

[10]In Ithaca New York, where I wrote this book, the leading supermarket (Wegman's) sells half-gallons of whole milk for $1.57. They also sell half-gallons of milk from organically fed cows for $2.99. Organic milk at Wegman's therefore costs 90 percent more than conventional milk. Across town, at GreenStar, the local co-op, a half gallon of whole milk sells for $2.09. A half gallon of organic milk costs $3.25. Organic milk at GreenStar therefore costs 55 percent more than conventional milk. I surveyed everyday retail prices in October of 2003.

[11]Hens lay an average of 29 dozen eggs before their first laying cycle ends, at which time they must go through molting in order to lay additional eggs. Free-range egg farmers nearly always avoid forced molting, so it's reasonable to assume that free-range hens produce about 29 dozen eggs before being sent to slaughter.

In response to the footnoted sentence, and the above entry, Don Bell writes: "Your [footnoted] sentence really has nothing to do with 'free-range' chickens as such. Yes, there is a cost of producing food for humans which involves the eventual death of an animal. There is also the death of humans involved in the production of vegetables and other produce, automobiles, and what have you."

Bell, Don. Poultry Specialist (Emeritus), University of California, Riverside. Personal Communication. February and November 2003.

My response to Prof. Bell: In this passage, I was only concerned with figuring out how many eggs a free-ranging hen would produce before being sent to slaughter. The best way to obtain that number is to find out how many eggs commercial hens lay before the egg farm must choose between slaughter and forced-molting. I do not argue with the fact that there is plenty of human suffering, and even some fatalities, linked to all aspects of food production—not just the meat industry. If animal agriculture had a lower rate of worker injury and fatality than other forms of food production, that would certainly be a good argument against vegetarianism. But this is not the case; in fact the reverse is true (OSHA records indicate that on-the-job injury and death rates of slaughterhouse workers exceeds that of farm workers, and by a wide margin at that.) So, once again, I am returning the main thrust of my argument to the fact that egg production of any kind results in substantial killing. Despite its gentle reputation, the amount of animals killed for free-range egg production is substantial.

[12]The stockyards are situated in Lancaster, Pennsylvania.

[13]Hansen, Don and Bridges, Victoria. A survey description of down-cows and cows with progressive or non-progressive neurological signs compatible with a TSE from veterinary-client herd in 38 states. *The Bovine Practitioner* 33.2(1999): 179-187.

[14]Wolfson has written about farmed animal welfare laws in:

Wolfson, David J. *Beyond the Law : Agribusiness and the Systemic Abuse of Animals Raised for Food or Food Production.* Watkins Glen, New York: Farm Sanctuary, 1999.

[15]Nev. Rev. Stat. Ann. s 574.200.6 (Michie 1994.)

[16]Wolfson, David J. Personal communication. November 5, 2003.

[17]Moore, David W. "Public Lukewarm on Animal Rights: Supports strict laws governing treatment of farm animals, but opposes bans on product testing and medical research." *Gallup News Service.* May 21, 2003.

Chapter Four

[1]Moore, David W. "Public Lukewarm on Animal Rights: Supports strict laws governing treatment of farm animals, but opposes bans on product testing and medical research." Gallup News Service. May 21, 2003.

[2]Moore, David W.

[3]The number of US mink farms dropped 73 percent between 1983 and 2003. There were 1098 mink farms in 1983, and only 318 left by 2002. The number of pelts these farms collectively produced fell from 4.14 million in 1983 to 2.6 million in 2002.

<http://usda.mannlib.cornell.edu/reports/nassr/other/zmi-bb/mink0703.txt>

Accessed February 10, 2004

[4]The case stemmed from a PETA investigation into Belcross Farm, in North Carolina. Three felony indictments were handed down in 1999. In 2000, two of the workers pleaded guilty to misdemeanor animal cruelty charges, and the third was convicted of misdemeanor animal cruelty. One of these workers, Raymond Sanchez, was forced to pay $2216 in fines and costs, and ended up serving 125 days in jail.

[5]"Three Men Plead Guilty to Animal Abuse in Beating Calf." The Associated Press, July 26, 2002

[6]The total assets of HSUS grew from $11 million in 1982 to $94 million in 2002. Over that same period, the ASPCA's assets have risen from $6 million to $61 million.

[7]In 1996, the natural food industry had $310 million in sales for vegetarian convenience foods. For 2002, were projected to reach $1.5 billion. And they are expected to nearly double again by 2006, reaching $2.8 billion.

Mintel. *The Vegetarian Food Market—US Report.* Chicago, IL: Mintel International Group Limited, 2001.

[8]As of 2004, there were 146 Whole Foods Markets in the US plus store in Canada. Additionally, more than 25 new stores were scheduled to be opened.

<www.wholefoodsmarket.com/stores/list_allstores.html>

<www.wholefoodsmarket.com/stores/newstores.html>

Accessed February 10, 2004.

[9]"2002 Brings Record Meat Consumption." *Newsfax.* North American Meat Processors Association 61.14. December 31, 2002.

[10] Numbers obtained from the following USDA/ NASS documents: "Poultry Slaughter 2002 Summary," February 2003. "Livestock Slaughter 2002 Summary," March 2003. "Chicken & Eggs," March 2003. "Turkey Hatchery," April 2003. "Meat Animals Production, Disposition, & Income 2002," April 2003. "Chicken & Eggs," August 2003. "Poultry Slaughter," August 2003. "Livestock Slaughter," August 2003.

USDA. Agricultural Statistics 1977. Tables 439, 441,454, 474, 564.

[11]Donna Maurer's book *Vegetarianism: Movement or Moment?* does a superb job of summarizing the polls and studies that have estimated the US vegetarian population.

Maurer, Donna. *Vegetarianism: Movement or Moment?* Philadelphia, PA: Temple University Press, 2002. p. 14-18.

Chapter Six

[1]My belief that animal agriculture *can* be eliminated is quite distinct from the contention that animal agriculture *ought to* be eliminated. Animal rights supporters, to their great credit, have loudly and repeatedly proclaimed that animal agriculture should be stopped. But nobody has seriously advanced the idea that a force can be amassed within our lifetimes that will put animal agriculture into an irreversible decline.

[2]I say "third party" here, with the idea that the first party was the slaves and slave owners, the second party the abolitionists, and the third party the federal government.

[3]Dismantlement's activities and its methods of action will be profoundly different than those utilized during abolition. Most importantly, it won't take a war to eliminate the animal agriculture industry; in fact, the whole task should occur nonviolently without human losses on either side.

[4]Racist beliefs were common, not just among Union soldiers, but even among the abolitionists. For instance, during the Lincoln-Douglas debates, on October 13, 1858, Lincoln suggested that blacks may not possess the "intellectual and moral endowments" held by whites.

[5]Taken together, the number of animals killed for animal research, hunting, fur, and by shelters due to dog and cat overpopulation likely amounts to less than 300 million per year. None of the numbers below are as reliable as they ought to be, and I've deliberately estimated on the high side for hunting (by taking the hunting of small animals into account.) Taken together, I've put the total number of non-farmed animals killed by people at 283.6 million, which is 2.8 percent of the amount who die annually in the US animal agriculture industry.

Animal Research: Nobody knows how many lab animals die in research each year, but figure it's about 20 million. The USDA keeps tabs on six types of animals, plus farmed animals, used for research, and in 2000, the total for these animals came to 1,416,643. However, the USDA does not record rats, mice, and several other species which together are thought to make up 85 to 95 percent of all testing. With this in mind, and given that the USDA's numbers probably under-report the actual number of lab animals, it's reasonable to suspect that the total number of animals used in US research may surpass 20 million.

USDA Animal and Plant Health Inspection Service. Animal Welfare Report, Fiscal Year 2000. Table 36, p. 39. July 2001.

Hunting: No records are kept on the total national kill, largely because hunters aren't required to file a report for each animal killed. Nor are there any reliable estimates. The USDA, does, however, say that Americans spent 153 million days hunting deer and other large animals in 2001. A reasonable guess might be that every four days spent hunting resulted in a kill. If this is the case, hunters killed about 38.25 million large animals in 2002.

Hunters also spent 108 million days in 2002 hunting smaller animals like squirrels, as well as birds. Doubtless, these hunters had far higher kill rates, many probably killing multiple animals per day. A reasonable guess might be the average small animal or bird hunter killed two animals per day hunting, which would total 216 million animals.

So under these estimates, the total number of animals killed by hunters would be 254.25 million

U.S. Department of the Interior, Fish and Wildlife Service and U.S. Department of Commerce, U.S. Census Bureau. 2001 National Survey of Fishing, Hunting, and Wildlife-Associated Recreation. P. 22.

Fur: According to the Humane Society of the United States, the number of fur animals either farmed or trapped in the US is, as of 2003, about 5.6 million per year.

Dog and Cat Overpopulation: The number of dogs and cats euthanized at US animal shelters due to lack of homes is estimated to be between three and four million per year. A more reliable estimate should be available after 2007, since national humane organizations are working to standardize data collection from shelters around the country.

<www.hsus.org/ace/11830>

Accessed December 5, 2003.

[6]One day, the stickier and more complex issues of vivisection, companion animals, and hunting will be contemplated by society. But as long as we're living in a society where something so needless and cruel as animal agriculture is permitted to exist, there will be no hope of the public debating these other topics in productive ways. In this respect, dismantlement is probably a laboratory animal's best friend, as it will hasten the day when society can rationally evaluate all forms of animal use.

Chapter Seven

[1]Tolstoy was fond enough of this observation to make it the opening sentence of *Anna Karenina.*

[2]I'd estimate that upwards of 80 percent of people involved in animal protection are politically to the left of center.

[3]The animal protection movement is clearly dominated by political progressives, and I'm not the first person to observe that progressives tend to be ineffective at organizing. In popular literature, Stephen King based one of his most acclaimed horror novels (*The Stand*) on the idea that good-hearted people are terrible at uniting and achieving progress. Ken Wilber has also written extensive analyses that seek to explain this phenomenon. He gave this subject lengthy treatment in his first novel: *Boomeritis.*

King, Stephen, *The Stand: The Complete & Uncut Edition.* New York : Gramercy Books, 2001.

Wilber, Ken. *Boomeritis : a Novel that Will Set You Free.* Boston : Shambhala ; [New York] : 2002.

[4]Total spending by Vegan Outreach in 2003 was $194,085.

Ball, Matt. Personal Communication. November 18, 2003.

[5]PETA's total spending for 2003 was $21,749,107

<www.peta.org/feat/annualreview2003/numbers.asp>

Accessed February 11, 2004

[6]"Tyson Foods Announces Unprecedented Multi-Protein Branding Initiative." Press Release: Tyson Foods, Springdale, AR. January 21, 2003.

[7]Kirk, Jim. "New Campaign at McDonald's has Lovin' Feeling." *Chicago Tribune* June 12, 2003, Business Section p. 1.

[8]It's important to keep in mind that HSUS is not affiliated with the hundreds of local humane societies operating in the United States, many of which do superb work and are chronically short of funds. 1998 was the last year before IRS-mandated salary caps for nonprofits took effect. After receiving this package, Paul Irwin remained as the group's CEO, and in 2001 his contract was extended through the end of 2004. In 2002, Irwin's annual compensation amounted to $306,607.

[9]Animal People. PO Box 960, Clinton, WA 98236. <www.animalpeoplenews.org>

[10]You can invest in a well-run company that nevertheless gets trounced by the competition. In activism, there is no competition. So long as the organization you support is doing meaningful and productive work for the animals, your money is making a difference.

Chapter Eight

[1]In her Cornell University Ph.D. thesis, which won two national awards, Antonia Demas studied how children responded to efforts to include healthy eating in the school curriculum. She found that with proper teaching, children would favor healthy lunches over fast-food style junk food.

Demas, Antonia. *Food education in the elementary classroom as a means of gaining acceptance of diverse, low-fat foods in the school lunch program.* Cornell University thesis. 1995.

According to Dr. Demas: "One of the strategies of my research is to take the nutritious commodity foods such as legumes, bulgur, brown rice, and build a curriculum around them By the time I have the kids cook these items with their peers in the classroom, they have learned a tremendous amount about them. I believe this problem has got to be addressed at the curricular level and we need to highlight the importance of food education."

[2]Moskowitz, Karyn and Romaniello, Chuck. *Assessing the Full Cost of the Federal Grazing Program.* Prepared for the Center for Biological Diversity Tucson, Arizona. October 2002.

[3]Moskowitz, Karyn and Romaniello, Chuck.

Chapter Nine

[1]Harper Josh. Presentation: "Militant Animal Activists: Underground Heroes or Domestic Terrorists?" Cornell University, Rockefeller 132. November 6, 2003.

[2]Between August and November of 2002, Compassion Over Killing carried out a number of visits to the Red Bird Egg Farms, in Millington, MD. Over the course of these visits, they conducted an open rescue involving ten hens. In December of 2002, the *New York Times* ran a lengthy and favorable piece about the rescue. This article was followed by coverage by the Associated Press, which was in turn printed in more than a hundred newspapers.

Becker, Elizabeth. "Advocates for Animals Turn Attention to Chickens." *New York Times,* December 4, 2002, Late Edition - Final , Section A : Page 20 , Column 1

Biemer, John. "Animal Right Group Alleges Egg Farms Cruel" Associated Press. December 4, 2002.

[3]Becker, Elizabeth.

Biemer, John.

Chapter Ten

[1]To research most of the animal welfare and environmental claims about vegetarianism, not any library will do. It's best to have access to a university agriculture library, and those libraries are few and far between.

[2]This bill (H.B. 433) would have also mandated that Texas set up a website used to identify animal protection activists. This site would have stigmatized activists as terrorists, and have been run similarly to government websites that identify sex offenders.

[3]Sandler, Robert. "House Rejects Law Against Photographing Farm Animals." Associated Press, May 13, 2003.

[4]Under this law, a first offender gets a $100 fine, while a second offense can result in a $1000 fine and up to six months in jail.

Stern, Eric. "State Toughens Farm Trespass Laws." *Modesto Bee.* January 2, 2004.

[5]This comment was made by Loni Hancock (D-Berkeley), of California's State Assembly.

Stern, Eric.

[1]LaMattina, Diana. "Genoa Man Arrested for Alleged Mistreatment of Spencer cows: White Facing 59 Years in Jail." *Ithaca Journal,* 8 January 2004, Page 1.

[2]Gene Bauston of Farm Sanctuary became involved in this case early on. He told me that several egg farms in the Southeast offered to take in some of Biggers' hens. Biggers rejected these offers, as he was determined to try to sell these birds with his farm.

[3]Squires, Chase. "State Considering Charges in Starvation of Chicken." *St Petersburg Times.* June 25, 2003. Pasco Times Section: p. 3.

[4]Squires, Chase.

[5]Squires, Chase.

[6]Hoffman, Ian. "War on Terror May Save Fowl." Alameda Times-Star. March 14, 2003.

[7]Associated Press. "San Diego DA Says Chicken Ranchers Won't Face Cruelty Charges." *San Jose Mercury News.* May 14, 2003.

[8]Fitzsimons, Elizabeth "Live Hens were Put into Wood Chippers." San Diego Union-Tribune. April 11, 2003.

[9] Gillick, Kathryn. "DA Asks for More Information in Chicken Chipping Case." *North County Times* (San Diego and Riverside, CA). April 19, 2003.

[10] Associated Press. "San Diego DA Says Chicken Ranchers Won't Face Cruelty Charges."

Appendix A

[1] Key T, Davey G. "Prevalence of Obesity is Low in People Who Do Not Eat Meat" (letter). British Medical Journal 313 (1996): 816-817.

Fraser GE. "Associations Between Diet and Cancer, Ischemic Heart Disease, and All-Cause Mortality in Non-Hispanic White California Seventh-Day Adventists." *American Journal of Clinical Nutrition* 70 (1999): 532S-538S.

[2] Key T, Davey G.

Fraser GE.

[3] CJ and Colditz, GA. "Modifiable Risk Factors for Cancer." *British Journal of Cancer* 90 (2004) 299-303.

[4] The Centers for Disease Control estimates that there are 5200 deaths each year in the US from foodborne pathogens. 62 percent of these deaths are due to Salmonella (31 percent), Listeria (28 percent), and E. Coli (3 percent).

Mead, Paul S. et al. "Synopsis: Food-Related Illness and Death in the United States." Emerging Infectious Diseases. 5.5 (September-October 1999): 607-623.

In 2002, there were 42,815 vehicle-related fatalities in the United States.

Tyson, Rae. "2002 Highway Fatalities Highest Since 1990; Injuries Hit an All-Time Low," NTSA Now. 9.6 (August 11, 2003.) U.S. Department of Transportation. National Highway Traffic Safety Administration.

[5] Key TJ, et al. "Mortality in Vegetarians and Nonvegetarians: Detailed Findings from a Collaborative Analysis of 5 Prospective Studies." American Journal of Clinical Nutrition. 70.3-Suppl (Sept. 1999): 516S-524S.

[6] Key TJ, et al.

[7] Flegal KM, et al. "Prevalence and Trends in Obesity Among US Adults: 1999-2000." *JAMA* 288 (2002): 1723-1727.

[8] Centers for Disease Control. National Health and Nutrition Examination Survey. "Healthy Weight, Overweight, and Obesity Among U.S. Adults." (2-page data brief). Document 03-0260. July 2003.

Appendix B

[1] Feed conversion ratios for cattle were once far worse than they are today. As recently as 1995, a ten-to-one conversion of feed to live weight gain was considered realistic:

Baker, Michael. "For Livestock Farmers." *American Agriculturalist* Aug.1995: 15

But industry experts indicate that cattle have become far more efficient at converting grain to beef. Lately, the industry claims a conversion ratio of about 6.5 pounds grain for each pound weight gain.

Herring, WO and Bertrand, JK. "Multi-Trait Prediction of Feed Conversion in Feedlot Cattle." *Proceedings from the 34th Annual Beef Improvement Federation Annual Meeting.* Omaha, NE. July 10-13, 2002.

<www.bifconference.com/bif2002/BIFsymposium_pdfs/Herring_02BIF.pdf>

Accessed October 21, 2003

Since cattle yield only about 50 percent of their body weight as boneless beef, this means that the feed-to-beef conversion ratio is about 13:1.

[2] Chickens raised by Tyson Foods gain one pound of body weight for every 1.95 pounds of grain they are fed. Tyson expects efficiency to slightly improve in the future, with a chicken in 2005 gaining a pound for each 1.90 pounds of grain. Upon slaughter, Fukomoto and Replogle found about 68 percent of weight is retained after loss of blood, feathers, and internal organs. This means that every 2.867 pounds of grain fed to chicken yields a pound of chicken meat and bone (estimate calculated using Tyson's 2000 conversion

ratio of 1.95 pounds feed for each pound of weight gain.) Another estimate, by Ricard, says that deboning, evisceration, plucking, and blood loss leaves 61.7 percent of the bird's initial weight as meat. This estimate yields a conversion ratio of 3.16 pounds feed for each pound of boneless chicken meat.

Tyson Foods. Investor Fact Book 2003-2004. Springdale AR. p. 5.
<www.tysonfoodsinc.com/IR/publications/factbook/default.asp>
Accessed January 20, 2004.

Fukomoto, Glen K. and Replogle John R. *Livestock Management.* Cooperative Extension Service. College of Tropical Agriculture and Human Resources. University of Hawaii at Manoa. April 1999.

Ricard, FH. 1980. "Carcass Conformation of Poultry and Game Birds." *Proc. 15th World's Poultry Science Association Symposium on Meat Quality in Poultry and Game Birds,* Norwich UK 1979. P. 31-50.

[3]Pigs require 3.6 to 3.8 pounds of grain per pound of weight gain. Upon slaughter, about 57 percent of their body weight produces meat for retail sale. Pork Facts 2001/2002. Des Moines, Iowa. The National Pork Board. p. 3, 20.

[4]This 5200-gallon figure was published until about 1996 in EarthSave's *Realities* booklet. It was then published once again in 2001, in John Robbins' *The Food Revolution.* Numerous fliers, websites, and other vegetarian advocacy literature have reprinted this 5200-gallon claim. To see how this far and wide this claim has spread, type the words '5200 gallons pound beef' into an Internet search engine and look through the results.

[5]Herb Schulbach and Tom Aldrich. "Water Requirements for Food Production." *Soil and Water.* University of California, Cooperative Extension. No. 38 (Fall 1978): p. 13-17.

[6]Kreith, Marcia. *Water Inputs in California Food Production.* Sacramento, CA: Water Education Foundation, 1991.

[7]California ranches are unusually inefficient in water use, primarily because the state's rangeland tends to be more arid than rangeland in most other states.

[8]About 75 percent of the water in Kreith's non-irrigated scenario comes from rainwater which is absorbed by rangeland plants. Beckett and Oltjen don't count this rainwater in making their 441 gallon estimate, for good reasons that I cover in the main text. If this rainwater is removed from consideration, the Kreith estimate is not terribly different than the estimate put forward by Beckett and Oltjen. It's primarily because Kreith counts the rainwater absorbed by rangeland plants that her estimate exceeds Beckett and Oltjen's by such a huge margin.

[9]Oltjen, JW. personal communication. November 11, 2003.

[10]Oltjen, JW. personal communication. November 11, 2003.

[11]Beckett, JL and Oltjen, JW. "Estimate of the Water Requirement for Beef Production in the United States." *Journal of Animal Science.* 71.4 (1993):818-26.

The article concluded that 3,682 liters of water are needed per kilogram of beef. This converts to 441 gallons of water cited by Robbins.

[12]John Robbins. "2,500 Gallons All Wet?" *EarthSave: Healthy People Healthy Planet* 11.2 (Spring 2000): 3, 6.
<www.earthsave.org/newsletters/water.htm>
Accessed November 1, 2003.

[13]I was unable to find gallons of water per pound of beef anywhere but in Water Inputs in California Food Production. I'm not thrilled to be relying on these statistics, since the book's water usage analysis for beef was, in my opinion, done poorly. However, analyzing water needs for crops is a much simpler and more straightforward than it is for beef. Such analysis is therefore much more likely to be correct. According to Kreith, a pound of tomatoes requires 28.55 gallons of water, and a pound of broccoli requires 42.4 gallons.

Kreith, Marcia. p. 6.

[14]Meat contains far more calories per pound than do fruits or vegetables. When you compare meat to produce, in terms of food weight yields from a given quantity of water, produce comes out way ahead. But when you compare total calories yielded from this water, the differences between meat and produce are far less significant.

[15]A 3.5 ounce (100 g) serving of regular ground beef, medium broiled, contains 289 calories. By contrast, a 123 gram tomato has just 26 calories. Jean A.T. Pennington. *Bowes & Church's Food Values of Portions Commonly Used.* Sixteenth Edition. Philadelphia/New York: JB Lippincott Company. 1994. p. 203, 317.

At 441 gallons per pound of beef, 100 gallons will get you 0.226 pounds beef. That converts to 102.6 grams of beef. At 2.89 calories per gram, 102.6 grams beef contains 296.5 calories.

At 28.55 gallons of water for a pound of tomatoes, 100 gallons of water yields 3.5 pounds tomatoes. That converts to 1587 grams of tomatoes. 1587 grams, divided by 123 grams per tomato, then multiplied by 26 calories per tomato, equals 335.46 calories.

[16]Professor James Oltjen, the co-author of the UC Davis study mentioned above, had his preliminary estimates of the amount of water necessary for beef, chicken, and pork published in 1991. Professor Oltjen says his final models, cited above and published in 1993, were more accurate. But his preliminary data indicated that a pound of pork required 430 gallons water, a pound of beef required 390 gallons, and a pound of chicken required 375 gallons. I'm including this preliminary data here because Professor Oltjen did not publish final results for chicken or pork.

Oltjen, JW. 1991. "Water needs for meat production." *Journal of Animal Science* 69 (Suppl. 1) 1991:227

Oltjen, JW. personal communication, October 13, 2003.

[17]United States Senate Committee on Agriculture, Nutrition, & Forestry. 1997. "Environmental Risks of Livestock & Poultry Production." Animal Waste Pollution in America: An Emerging National Problem. (This report was written by senate staff at the request of Senator Tom Harkin.)

John Sweeten, a professor of agricultural engineering at Texas A&M, considers the "wet" figure the USDA uses for manure to be, "sensational but marginally meaningless and misleading." I disagree with Professor Sweeten, since manure is produced "wet," and this water cannot be quickly and cheaply extracted. This moisture makes manure heavy and expensive to transport, and therefore contributes to water pollution problems, since manure cannot be cheaply dispersed to locales far from where it is produced.

Nevertheless, Professor Sweeten prefers an analysis that indicates the weight of manure if all its water was removed. He authored a 1992 study that found the dry weight of manure in the United States amounted to 57.5 million tons produced by confinement facilities, plus another 101 million tons dropped by animals grazing rangeland and dairy pasture. Professor Sweeten did not offer a guess at how the dry weight totals of US manure production have changed since 1992.

Sweeten, JM. Personal Communication, October 2003.

Sweeten, JM. "Livestock and poultry waste management: A national overview." In J. Blake, J. Donald, Magette W. (eds.). National Livestock, Poultry and Aquaculture Waste Management: Proceedings of the National Workshop. (1992) American Society of Agricultural Engineers, St. Joseph, Missouri.

[18]Midwest Plan Service (MWPS). Livestock Waste Facilities Handbook. Publication MWPS-8. Davidson Hall. Ames, Ia. 1993.

Appendix C

[1]Notice that I wrote steak rather than beef, since a large portion of beef is produced from culled dairy cows. Since this beef is of inferior quality, it's generally ground up for

hamburger. Whole cuts of beef, by contrast, nearly always comes from cattle that are raised specifically for meat.

[2]USDA Natural Resources Conservation Service. Summary Report: 1997 National Resources Inventory, Washington, DC: Natural Resources Conservation Service and Ames, Iowa: Iowa State University, Statistical Laboratory. Revised Dec. 2000.

[3]I've rounded up from 43.933

There are 1,893,792,000 (nearly 1.9 billion) acres in the continental United States. Acreage is calculated by getting the total land area of the United States, in square miles, and subtracting the land areas of Alaska and Hawaii. Multiplying this number by 640 gives total acres.

U.S. Census Bureau, Statistical Abstract of the United States: 2002 (122nd Edition). Table 335. Land and Water Area of States and Other Entities: 2000. P. 210.

[4]Conservationists estimate there were about five billion black-tailed prairie dogs inhabiting the United States in the late 1800s. Since then, the population has fallen by 98 percent, and the animals inhabit just 0.5 percent of their original habitat.

Mac, M.J. *Status and Trends of the Nation's Biological Resources.* (2 volumes.) US Department of the Interior, US Geological Survey. Reston, VA. 1998.

"Black-Tailed Prairie Dogs: 12-Month Administrative Finding." US Fish and Wildlife Service. Mountain-Prairie Region, South Dakota Ecological Services Field Office. 2000.

[5]Many of these animals were trapped or poisoned, and suffered lingering deaths. Exact numbers killed and species involved are 86,360 coyotes, more than 5000 foxes (red, gray, kit, and arctic), 382 black bear, and 194 gray/timber wolves.

APHIS/Wildlife Services. Number of Animals Killed and Methods Used by the WS Program, FY 2002. PDR 10.

[6]Jacobs, Lynn. *Waste of the West: Public Lands Ranching.* Tuscon, AZ: Lynn Jacobs. 1992. p. 203.

[7]Wuerthner, George and Matteson, Mollie, ed. *Welfare Ranching: The Subsidized Destruction of the American West.* Washington, D.C.: Island Press, 2002.

Appendix D

[1]Food and Agriculture Organization of the United Nations. *The State of the World's Fisheries and Aquaculture.* Rome: FAO. 2002.

[2]Food and Agriculture Organization of the United Nations.

[3]The Pew Oceans Commission included, among the eighteen people on its panel: Leon Panetta, a former White House Chief of Staff; John Hamilton Adams, President of the Natural Resources Defense Council; Mike Hayden, former Governor of Kansas; Geoffrey Heal, Professor of Public Policy and Economics at Columbia University; Charles F. Kennel, President of Scripps Institution for Oceanography; Tony Knowles, Governor of Alaska; Jane Lubchenko, past President of the American Association of the Advancement of Science; George Pataki, Governor of New York.

[4]Pew Oceans Commission. *America's Living Oceans. A Report to the Nation: Recommendations for a New Ocean Policy.* Arlington, VA: Pew Oceans Commission. May 2003. P. 2.

[5]Pew Oceans Commission. P. 2.

[6]"To the Last Fish: The Codless Sea." CBC. 2003.
<http://stjohns.cbc.ca/features/CodFisheries/history2.html>
Accessed October 24, 2003.

[7]Guterl, Fred et al. "Troubled Seas." *Newsweek International.* July 14, 2003.

[8]Hayden, Thomas. "Fished out: It's not too late to rescue the oceans—and keep seafood on our plates." *US News & World Report* June 9, 2003: 38-45

[9]Pew Oceans Commission. p. 5.

[10]Buck, Eugene H. "Shrimp Fishery and Sea Turtle Concerns." In: Oceans & Coastal Resources: A Briefing Book. Congressional Research Service Report 97-588 ENR. Washington DC: National Council for Science and the Environment. 1997.

<www.ncseonline.org/nle/crsreports/briefingbooks/oceans/d.cfm>
Accessed December 6, 2003.

[11]Hayden, Thomas.

[12]Pew Oceans Commission. P. 5.

[13]Hayden, Thomas.

[14]I haven't been able to find a reliable number of sea turtle deaths caused by shrimp nets, but this too is an acknowledged and heavily studied problem. Longline figures come from Part I of:

Alverson, D.L. et al. *A Global Assessment of Fisheries Bycatch and Discards.* FAO Fisheries Technical Paper. No. 339. Rome: FAO. 1994.

[15]Kirby, Alex. "Nets 'Kill 800 Cetaceans a Day'." BBC News. June 13, 2003.

http://news.bbc.co.uk/1/hi/sci/tech/2985630.stm Accessed October 24, 2003.

[16]Kirby, Alex.

[17]I rounded the percentages to the nearest integer. The FAO's percentages are 3.9 percent and 27.3 percent.

Food and Agriculture Organization of the United Nations.

[18]"The Promise of a Blue Revolution: How Aquaculture Might Meet Most of the World's Demand for Fish without Ruining the Environment." *The Economist.* August 7, 2003.

[19]Cramb, Auslan. "Fish farms 'may spell the end of wild salmon.'" Daily Telegraph (web edition) Filed: April 6, 2003.

<www.dailytelegraph.co.uk/news/main.jhtml?xml=/news/2003/06/04/
nsfish04.xml&sSheet=/news/2003/06/04/ixhome.html>
Accessed October 24, 2003.

[20]Pew Oceans Commission. p. vi.

[21]Cramb, Auslan.

[22]Cramb, Auslan.

[23]Food and Agriculture Organization of the United Nations.

[24]Sneddon, L.U., Braithwaite, V.A., and M.J. Gentle. "Do fishes have nociceptors? Evidence for the evolution of a vertebrate sensory system." *Proceedings of the Royal Society of London. Series B-Biological Sciences.* 270.1520 (June, 2003): 1115-1121.

[25]Rosen, Stacey. "Most—But Not All—Regions See Food Gains." *Food Review.* Volume 22, Issue 3. September-December 1999. Table 1.

Appendix E

[1]Deer-Vehicle Crash Information Clearinghouse. University of Wisconsin - Madison.

The states surveyed are Michigan, Wisconsin, Minnesota, Illinois, and Iowa. Of these Minnesota and Iowa supplied data for year 2000 only. The remaining three states supplied data for 2000-2001. The numbers I cited would, of course, be higher if Minnesota and Iowa supplied 2001 crash statistics.

<www.deercrash.com/data.htm>
Accessed on October 1, 2003.

[2]Deer-Vehicle Crash Information Clearinghouse.

Human injuries recorded totaled 4870. This number would certainly be over 5000 if Minnesota and Iowa contributed data for 2001, as they combined for 1,050 injuries in 2000.

[3]No federal agency has compiled hunting accidents and fatalities, but the International Hunter Education Association has taken on this task. Unfortunately, the numbers they provide have some huge gaps in reporting. For instance, Alaska, which has long lead the nation in accidents per hunter, did not contribute its statistics to the report. Actual

numbers of US fatalities and accidents are therefore almost certainly significantly higher than stated.

Hunter Incident Clearinghouse. "2001 North American Incident Summary." International Hunter Education Association, Wellington, CO.

<ihea.com/idb2001>

Accessed October 1, 2003.

[4]According to the US Fish and Wildlife Service, 13 million Americans went hunting in 2001. Given the US population of 292 million in 2003, the number of people who go hunting in a given year totals less than 4.5 percent of the population.

US Fish and Wildlife Service. "Quick Facts from the 2001 Survey of Hunting, Fishing, and Wildlife-Associated Recreation." (Flyer, 1 sheet, front and back.)

US Census Bureau population clock:

<www.census.gov/main/www/popclock.html>

Accessed October 1, 2003.

[5]US Fish and Wildlife Service.

[6]There were 15,980 cases of murder or manslaughter recorded in the United States in 2001. Rifles were the weapon used in 2.8 percent of these cases. Fewer than 3 percent of rifle-related crimes are done by people armed with assault rifles, so I obtained my figure by multiplying 15,980 by 0.028 and then by 0.97.

Sourcebook of Criminal Justice Statistics Online. Table 3.114, Number and rate (per 100,000 population) of violent crime and murder and nonnegligent manslaughter, and number of firearm-related violent crime and weapon-related murder and nonnegligent manslaughter. By type of weapon and State, 2001.

<www.albany.edu/sourcebook/1995/pdf/t3114.pdf>

Accessed October 1, 2003

[7]There were 15,980 cases of murder or manslaughter recorded in the United States in 2001. Rifles caused 3.6 percent of these deaths.

Sourcebook of Criminal Justice Statistics Online

[8]This percentage was obtained by adding the figures in the two previous footnotes (434 murders/manslaughters with a hunting rifle and 575 cases with a shotgun), and dividing the total (1009) by 15,980 (the number of murder and manslaughter cases in the US in 2001.

Appendix F

[1]A cow's pregnancy lasts about nine months, compared to just under four months for a pig.

Appendix G

[1]Heloisa Sabin, "Animal Research Saves Human Lives," *Wall Street Journal,* October 18, 1995. p. A21.

Appendix H

[1]In response to the public's reaction over The Jungle, Sinclair famously said something to the effect of: I aimed for America's heart, and hit its stomach, instead. (I've found at least three different supposed quotes, using slightly different phrasing.)

[2]The technologies underlying modern refrigeration had been under development since the mid-1800s. But it was during the first decade the twentieth century that inexpensive industrial refrigeration became possible. In the decade that followed The Jungle's publication, nearly every large meat plant installed compressor-based refrigeration systems, using ammonia as the cooling agent.

[3]Stull, Donald D. and Broadway, Michael J. *Slaughterhouse Blues: The Meat and Poultry Industry in North America.* Belmont, CA: Thomson-Wadsworth, 2003, p. 73.

[4]In fact, it was the first large-scale slaughterhouses, which relied on "disassembly lines," that inspired Henry Ford to utilize assembly lines in building cars.

Slaughterhouse Blues, p. 67.

[5]"Color it Green." *Newsweek.* March 8, 1965: 76-77.

[6]*Slaughterhouse Blues,* p. 73.

[7]Green, Hardy. *On Strike at Hormel: The Struggle for a Democratic Labor Movement.* Philadelphia: Temple University Press, 1990. Hage, David and Klauda, Paul. *No Retreat, No Surrender: Labor's War at Hormel,* New York: William Morrow, 1989.

[8]U.S. Department of Labor, Bureau of Labor Statistics.. Occupational Injuries and Illnesses: Industry Data, 2003.

<www.bls.gov/iif/oshwc/osh/os/ostb1109.txt>

Accessed December 6, 2003

[9]In 2001, the annual rate of injury in US manufacturing was 8.1 workers per hundred.

U.S. Department of Labor, Bureau of Labor Statistics, 2003. "Occupational Injuries and Illnesses: Industry Data." February 23, 2003.

<www.bls.gov/iif/oshwc/osh/os/osnr0016.txt>

Accessed December 6, 2003.

[10]Injury rates, which totaled 42.4 percent, are taken from *Slaughterhouse Blues,* p. 76.

Nearly every month, at least one or two slaughterhouse workers succumb to horrific accidents. The most common of these seem to involve workers who get caught in machinery and pulled into grinding units, or who are overcome by toxic fumes while cleaning waste tanks. The most recent detailed figures available, from 1998, showed 72 people dying in food manufacturing industry during that year, and of these deaths, 46 came in the meat and poultry industry.

<www.bls.gov/iif/oshwc/cfoi/cftb0114.txt>

Accessed December 6, 2003.

[11]Osborn, M. "Repetitive Stress Injuries Up During Downturn." *USA Today,* January 20, 1992.

[12] Stull, Donald D. and Broadway, Michael J. "Killing Them Softly," in: Stull, Donald D., Broadway, Michael J., and Griffith, David, ed. *Any Way You Cut it: Meat Processing and Small-Town America.* Lawrence, KS: University Press of Kansas, 1995.

[13]*Slaughterhouse Blues,* p. 85.

Index

Vegan.com

Erik Marcus publishes Vegan.com, a leading source of discussion, information, and recipes for the animal protection community.